Easy to Love
but Hard to Raise:
Real Parents, Challenging Kids, True Stories

Edited by
Kay Marner
&
Adrienne Ehlert Bashista

Foreword by Edward Hallowell, M.D.

drt press
books for families

Published by DRT Press, P.O. Box 427, Pittsboro, NC 27312, www.drtpress.com. Compilation copyright (c) 2012 by Kay Marner and Adrienne Ehlert Bashista. Copyrights to individual works belong to the authors.

Books are available at quantity discount for fundraising purposes. For information please contact DRT Press at the address above, or e-mail us at editorial@drtpress.com.

Publisher's Cataloging-in-Publication data

Marner, Kay.
    Easy to love but hard to raise : real parents , challenging kids , true stories /edited by Kay Marner and Adrienne Ehlert Bashista ; foreword by Edward Hallowell, M.D.

    p. cm.
    ISBN 978-1-933084-15-2 (pbk.)
    ISBN 978-1-933084-14-5 (Hardcover)
    ISBN 978-1-933084-16-9 (e-book)
    ISBN 978-1-933084-17-6 (audiobook)
    Series : Easy to love

    Includes bibliographical references and index.

1. Parents of children with disabilities. 2. Children with disabilities. 3. Children with disabilities --Family relationships. 4. Parent and child. 5. Parenting. 6. Attention-deficit hyperactivity disorder. 7. Attention Deficit and Disruptive Behavior Disorders. 8. Mentally ill children. 9. Developmental disabilities. 10. Autism. 11. Asperger's syndrome. 12. Sensory integration dysfunction in children. I. Bashista, Adrienne Ehlert. II. Hallowell, Edward M. III. Series IV. Title.

HQ759.913. M37 2012
649/.152 --dc22   2011929800

CONTENTS

Foreword

by Edward Hallowell, M.D.

This is a unique book. I have never seen one like it.

That is altogether fitting, because the subjects of the book are unique as well. I say plural, subjects, because this book is about the experiences of a variety of people, parents of children who are, to use the umbrella term, "different."

Of course, every child differs from every other child, so in that sense all children are different. But this book is about the parents of children whose ways of being different pose more than the ordinary problems and lead to more than the ordinary pratfalls of childhood. This book is about parents whose children live in the world of alphabet soup: the world of ADHD, OCD, BPD, MD, RAD, AS, DD, LD, PDD NOS, TS, GAD, AN, and other undefined combinations. The entire alphabet might as well be draped around these children's necks, as they walk into doctors' offices, schools, birthday parties, shopping malls, restaurants, ballparks, restrooms, carnivals, airports, churches, synagogues, or playgrounds.

There are many books about these children. But, to my knowledge, there hasn't been a book about the parents of these children. I am so glad that there is one now. And I am proud to be able to write its foreword. You see, these parents are heroes in my estimation. They would never lay claim to such an honor, because they are too busy loving their children and doing the endless work these children require in the messy trenches of life. But they are heroes nonetheless. They keep loving, *no matter what.* They keep doing what needs to be done. They may need a few martinis along the way, they may need a hefty dose of laughter, they may need a private place to scream, and they may need a lawyer and a doctor or two, but they basically do it on their own, sometimes with the help of a spouse, often with the help of a teacher or another parent or a grandpa or grandma or a dog. (Especially a dog.)

I want to tell these parents, and any person who might read this celebration-of-life of a book, the most important lesson I've learned in my 30 years of practicing child and adult psychiatry. The lesson is this: love rules. Nothing, and I mean *nothing*, comes close to the power of love in the shaping of a child. Of course, more goes into creating a great childhood than love, but without love there is no good outcome, and with love, no situation is ever lost.

Some kids are easy to love. Some kids just sail through childhood getting love wherever and whenever they need it. But then there are the kids who live in alphabet soup. They are not so easy to love. They can be difficult, distant, disobedient, defiant, dangerous, even delusional. They can leave a parent crying herself to sleep every night, they can leave a parent feeling guilty for having negative feelings, they can leave a parent despairing that the child will ever find a way in the world, they can deplete the store of love every parent starts off with.

But they can't deplete it for long. That's what's so amazing about these parents. They keep on keeping on. They never give up. They give their all, and then they find more all to give. They are paragons of the best of the human spirit. And they earn this praise in the hot and dusty arena of the struggle to raise a child who can seem, at times, impossible to raise.

And what do they do, these parents? They laugh. They pray. They tell whoever will listen what a great kid they have, how if only you look closely you too will see how great this kid is, or could be. They go from door to door, from teacher to teacher, from parent to parent, talking up their kid. They keep showing the world the great kid the world seems determined not to see.

Until…one day…the world sees. What a day that is! What a glorious, glorious day. That day all the hard work, all those tears and prayers get rewarded. That day the kid takes off and flies. That day the kid feels proud and keeps feeling proud.

I want to say to all these parents, *thank you.* Thank you on behalf of children everywhere, but even more, thank you on behalf of all humanity. Thank you for proving there is a best in the human spirit, there is an indestructible goodness, there is a power that can never die. It is the power of love. Thank you for showing it to us all.

Introduction

I've been writing an ADHD parenting blog, *My Picture-Perfect Family*, for *ADDitude* magazine's website since May of 2008. At first, although I was thrilled to be offered the opportunity, I wasn't sure why the editors hired me to write the blog. I am *not*—by any stretch of the imagination—a parenting expert. My only credentials for blogging about parenting kids with ADHD are: a) I'm raising a child with ADHD, and b) I feel inclined to write about that experience. But what in the world could I write that might interest other parents who are facing a similar challenge?

No, I'm not a parenting expert, but I am an expert on my child and the complex and contradictory emotions that come with raising her. In time I've learned that there's value in sharing these emotions. Expert advice is not the only thing struggling parents need. We also need to know we're not alone; to know that other parents are going through similar experiences, making similar mistakes, and searching for similar answers. We need something experts can't give us: we need each other.

Easy to Love but Hard to Raise started out as a simple anthology; a collection of essays written by parents of kids with ADHD and other conditions (sensory processing disorder, pediatric bipolar disorder, obsessive-compulsive disorder, pervasive developmental disorder, and an alphabet soup of others) that take the already difficult job of parenting and add to the challenge. My co-editor (Adrienne Ehlert Bashista, Publisher, DRT Press) and I envisioned the stories' emphases—on what it's like to parent challenging children, rather than on the disorders, or the children themselves—would set this book apart. We'd create a whole book to bring parents of challenging kids together: to show our parent-peers that they are not alone.

The honest, painful, and occasionally funny stories in this book clearly accomplish that goal. In fact, they illustrate commonalities that I never dreamed existed. When the essays are read collectively certain patterns emerge; of feelings this brand of parent tends to experience throughout the various stages of parenting; from when we first imagine ourselves as parents, to when our children become adults. Together, these commonalities paint a fascinating portrait; an archetype, really, of Everyparent of an *Easy to Love, but...* child. If the essays from our amazing parent-authors are the heart of this book, then Everyparent is its soul. It goes beyond telling parents that we're not alone. It assures us that our feelings—even the dark ones we rarely dare to express—are normal; even expected. It's what makes this simple anthology into something more.

Allow me to introduce you to Everyparent. Since the majority of the parents she represents are mothers, I'm assigning her the female gender. I'll dare to call her Eve, for short (not to be confused with the other archetypal woman who shares her name). Then, to be fair to the men, I'll make the *Easy to love, but...*child male. I'll call him Eli. And, because it's often the case that one parent takes the lead in a child's diagnosis and treatment, Eli's dad will be mentioned, but won't play a large role in this story. This is all said with the understanding that in real life, genders and roles vary from those in this portrayal.

I predict that parent-readers will find many elements of this example quite familiar. We've heard and read these sentiments being echoed again and again, by special needs parenting bloggers, and other parents, some of whom are quoted in this book. Still, I don't expect any one reader to identify with everything. While the Eve and Eli composites are fascinating, in reality every child and every parent is different.

Our hope for other readers, those who are not parenting neurologically diverse children, is that you will come away with newfound compassion and understanding for those of us who are, and for our children.

Meet Everyparent of an *Easy to Love, but...* Child

Like so many girls and young women, Eve has a fantasy of parenthood, formed during childhood play, and reinforced through years of romantic musings. Finally, it's her turn to live the fantasy. Her son, Eli, is born (or adopted). Eve's a mother!

Before long Eve is confused. Although she loves him, the experience of parenting this child is nothing like she thought it would be. Eli's differences begin at birth. He's colicky, impossible to console, overly sensitive to light and sound, and even to his parents' touch. It seems as if he never sleeps. Eve thinks she must be doing something wrong, or her baby wouldn't be so unhappy. She is always physically and emotionally exhausted. She privately mourns the loss of her long-held fantasy-motherhood.

> **The experience of parenting this child is nothing like she thought it would be.**

Eli's differences continue into early childhood. He won't follow directions and has violent tantrums, sometimes for little or no apparent reason. He never wants to slow down long enough to eat. He doesn't share or take turns at playgroup. Eve would love to connect with the other mothers there, but she is unable to relax and talk with them, because she's constantly chasing, correcting, and redirecting Eli. Neither of them is getting anything positive out of it. They quit going.

Eve had expected standard discipline tactics to work with Eli, but they just don't. She's frustrated and angry, with Eli and with herself. She reads parenting book after parenting book, and tries strategy after strategy. Nothing works. And when they don't, Eve blames herself. Eve starts to question her ability to parent.

The idea that Eve is at fault is reinforced by others. Family members, friends, the parents of her child's peers, his teachers—even strangers in the grocery store—are critical of her parenting abilities. Eve is far from a lazy parent; in fact, she has no choice but to work harder than most, but her efforts aren't reflected in her child's behavior for others to see. Some people express their criticism of Eve outright. Others show their disapproval through their expressions, their reactions.

Eve often feels shame in situations where other adults can observe her with Eli, and she starts to withdraw from her former supports. She begins to feel isolated. Being judged by her family hurts the most. They believe Eve's leniency created her child's behavior problems. It's an age- old story—when children have problems, mothers, in particular, are believed to be entirely at fault.

Those fingers that point at her, coupled with her own self-doubts, cause Eve to stop trusting her parenting instincts. She's humiliated to know that she's not the calm, firm but loving parent she thought she would be. She yells too much, but how could she not be angry and frustrated with this child? And, she knows she's not always consistent, but she's overwhelmed and exhausted and is at a loss as to how to do any better. She gives this child her all. She has no energy left for herself, her other child/children, or her husband. She no longer recognizes herself when she looks in the mirror. She feels like a failure as a mother, and that's tough to swallow, because at this point in her life, being a mother is her defining role.

But despite all this, Eve's parental instincts keep cropping up. She has an inkling that there's more to this situation than her poor showing as a parent. Something about this child is different. Something is wrong.

That first inkling cements into valid concern around the time Eli starts preschool, and then kindergarten, when he is expected to conform to more rules. According to his teachers, Eli can't sit still on his carpet square, keep his hands and feet to himself, or color inside the lines. Eve realizes (or the teachers convince her) that she must act.

Eve begins the search for someone to diagnose Eli's problems, unaware that this is just the beginning, that her quest will continue for years. She believes that if professionals assign the right name to her son's problems, then they'll be able to solve them. He's diagnosed with ADHD (or sensory processing disorder, or Asperger's syndrome) and even though Eve was more or less expecting this, hearing the diagnosis hits her hard. This is not what she wanted for her child. She alternates between grief and anger. She's been ripped off! This is not what she signed up for! But she's also relieved. Now that she knows what's wrong, she can start to fix it.

She immerses herself in researching her son's disorder. She reads books, searches the Internet, and joins some online forums. Knowing Eli's diagnosis does help—it explains many things about him—but it doesn't solve all of his problems. Eve doesn't find "the" answer. In fact, she learns that there isn't a magic bullet; one right answer doesn't exist.

> **Eve's parental instincts keep cropping up. She has an inkling that there's more to this situation than her poor showing as a parent. Something about this child is different. Something is wrong.**

Like so many other parents in her situation, Eve is initially opposed to giving her son medication. She's afraid he will lose his personality, and worries how the drugs will affect his developing body and brain. Besides, she's always heard that medication is just a poor substitute for good parenting, and to some extent, she believes this. So, she tries other interventions first: sticker charts and schedules, changes in diet. They don't make a discernable difference.

In the meantime, in elementary school, Eli continues to fail socially and academically and has discipline problems at home and school. Eve dreads hearing the phone ring, afraid that the call is from school. Eve questions, educates, advocates, pleads and harangues Eli's teachers and school officials to find positive, productive approaches to managing Eli's behavior, instead of losing recess or having in-school suspension, as well as for the academic supports he needs.

Eli's peers seem to mature more quickly. They stop inviting him to birthday parties. He joins Scouts, but quits because he feels excluded. No one plays with him at recess. Sometimes he's teased or bullied. Eve aches for him. Her pain is as palpable as Eli's own.

Eve's isolation grows in tandem with her child's. Since Eli isn't invited to sleepovers, doesn't excel at team sports, and isn't part of various other groups, Eve's not part of the mom cliques that surround these activities. In addition, because of her aggressive advocacy for Eli at school, she worries about where she stands with school administrators, counselors, or teachers.

Finally, Eli's problems reach crisis proportions. He sees himself as reflected by those around him—bad, unlikable, stupid. Eve can no longer sit back and watch this happen. She gives in to a trial of medication.

Meds—when they help—help significantly, but finding what works requires ongoing trial and error, and what works for a while often doesn't keep working. Eve feels guilty about putting him through so many med trials, especially when he experiences negative side-effects. Eve never completely accepts that her decision to give her son medicine was the right one. Eli is easier to manage, easier to love, when his meds are working. Guilt nags her. Is she giving him meds for the wrong reasons?

Medication isn't the whole answer. Eli continues to have problems, such as not turning in work at school, and with controlling his temper. Things worsen as he approaches puberty. Eve's instincts kick in again, telling her that something more than ADHD is affecting her child. By this time she's educated herself about ADHD and other conditions. She's interacted enough with therapists and doctors to know that they aren't gods and goddesses, they don't know everything, and they aren't always right. In fact, because of her singular focus on her child and his condition, she often finds herself educating the experts. She's regained some confidence in herself as a parent, if only by learning that her child's problems are brain-based, they are not all her fault. So this time, even though no one else believes her, she pushes, prods, insists, and squeaks wheels until someone listens. She was right to do so. In addition to ADHD, Eli has a mood disorder (or OCD, Tourette's syndrome, autism, an eating disorder, fetal alcohol syndrome). This discovery opens the door to more effective (though still imperfect) treatments.

Eventually, in person and online, Eve meets a few other moms of kids with ADHD or similar issues. These women get it. They know how it feels to have their parenting skills judged, so they aren't about to judge others. Eve and these friends support each other and share ideas and resources. By now, Eve is no longer trying to "fix" Eli's problems, to "cure" his condition. Instead, she focuses on finding coping skills and tools to help him. She's learned that each small accomplishment deserves a celebration. Eve also opens up to a few others about some of Eli's symptoms, and how he deals with them. When there's no shame, there's no secret. When there's no secret, there's no shame.

Eve and Eli muddle through his middle school and high school years. Eve has always had to parent more vigilantly than parents of neurotypical kids, and years of maintaining this vigilance has made it an ingrained habit. Eve tries to micromanage Eli to get him to do his homework, and the two often clash. Eli wants to stop taking medicine, and for a time, they argue about that. They compromise by lowering his dosage. Eve stays on Eli's back, urging him not to experiment with drugs and alcohol, reminding him of his increased risk of addictions.

Eve worries constantly about Eli's future. Will he graduate from high school on time? Will he be able to go to college? How will he handle the transition to adulthood? Outside forces start to challenge Eve's hyper-vigilant style of parenting. Eli must negotiate his part-time job without her smoothing the way for him, as she is used to doing. Eve is awake all night the first time Eli goes camping with a friend, but the police don't call! Eli comes home safely.

Before she knows it, the time is here. Eli begins community college. He lives in an apartment with a roommate. He hits a few roadblocks—he learns the hard way that he isn't good at managing money, and after a dismal first semester he gives in to using the resources the college offers to students with learning differences. But overall, Eve is surprised to find, he's succeeding.

Looking back, Eve realizes that Eli was coming into his own, finding his niche, long before she saw it. He turned his "bad" habit of doodling into a weekly comic strip for the local paper. He found a few friends that accepted him, quirks and all—and vice versa. His growing self-confidence pulled him through, even while she still doubted him.

> He's going to be okay, after all.

Who would have thought that the boy who spent so much time in in-school suspension would turn into this handsome, caring, creative young man? Eve's right to be proud of him. He still has symptoms to manage, but he is managing. His differences are a part of him, part of a wonderful whole. Eve releases a sigh. He's going to be okay, after all.

(May we all be so lucky!)

Contributors

As I stated above, the essays written by parents of *Easy to Love, but...* children are the heart of this book. These contributors include parents of young children, teens, and adult children. Some are immersed in parenting now, while others reflect back on their parenting experiences. Some stories will elicit tears; many are laugh-out-loud funny. Some contributors are professional writers, others hobby writers, as you'll read in the biographies in the Resources section. Regardless, in these essays they're parents first; parents who open up and offer their self-doubts and imperfections—as well as their hope and determination—to the special needs parenting world.

Additional special needs parents lent their voices to the book through brief quotes, which appear under the heading "Eve Speaks." They echo themes evocative of our archetype, Eve, and in doing so, they contribute to bringing her to life for our readers.

By now, you've read the book's Foreword, written by the esteemed ADHD expert Dr. Edward Hallowell. We are honored that he believed in this humble project enough to support it with his wise words. And, we are flattered and grateful that so many other prominent experts gave generously of their time, knowledge, and experience to further illuminate prominent trains of thought that weave in and out of the essays. You'll find their contributions, in Q & A format, under the heading "Tell Us More."

My co-editor, Adrienne Ehlert Bashista, and I are indebted to each of these people for making this book possible. We thank them all from the bottoms of our hearts.

Many of the essayists are continuing to contribute beyond the book itself. You'll find them on our blog, at http://www.easytolovebut.com/, where they support, share stories, commiserate, give tips, and provide safe haven to fellow parents. You'll also find us on Facebook, under the same name. We would be delighted to welcome you to this community. So if you find yourself in communion with these moms and dads, don't despair when you reach the end of the last essay. The book is only the beginning of the story.

~Kay Marner

From the editors

Finding no perfect word or phrase to describe *Easy to Love but Hard to Raise* children, we chose to refer to these kids in a variety of ways. We use "challenging," "special needs," "neurologically diverse," and other terms interchangeably, with no negative connotations intended, and with much love and respect for those children.

Similarly, you'll find mental health disorders named in a variety of ways. In many cases, in order to maintain the authors' voices, we chose language that is used colloquially rather than formal diagnostic terms. Terminology that some may deem inaccurate or outdated is used intentionally, and in this context, we believe, appropriately.

As the title states, the essays in this book are true stories, from real parents. However, some authors chose to use pseudonyms for any or all of the following: themselves, their child, and various other individuals and institutions mentioned, in order to protect their own and their child's privacy.

The topics highlighted with additional information from experts were not chosen in order to further any particular treatment, theory, or viewpoint. Rather, they answer questions that emerged organically from the text. They expand on ideas we believed the reader would want to know more about. Likewise, the fictional character Eve's feelings and beliefs are not meant to be interpreted as reflecting the opinion of the editors or of other individuals involved in this book, nor as fact. The same is true of information and opinions stated by our parent-authors. (Even our experts would disagree with each other on some points!)

~Kay Marner and Adrienne Ehlert Bashista

Part 1: Glimpses of Things to Come

A Lightbulb Moment
by Cyn Kitchen

Will, age six, had been playing outside and had come in for a bathroom break. He was in the bathroom, doing what little boys do in bathrooms: taking a leak, washing his hands (theoretically), getting distracted by the way he could fill the sink to the overflow, soaking the front of his shirt, taking off his soaked shirt, wadding it up and using it to wipe, er, move around, the water now cascading down the front of the vanity, pooling on the floor.

He walked out of the bathroom, shirtless, fly gaping open.

"Your barn door's open, and I didn't hear you flush. You left the light on, too," I said.

He looked at me in a way that fooled me into thinking he was processing the information I'd just handed him, when in reality, in *his* reality, he was probably thinking about an imaginary army of Zobots taking over the world and his need to save it from certain destruction, and the spaceship he was building in the backyard out of two-by-fours and leftover PVC pipes.

Instead of going back into the bathroom, as per my suggestion, he wandered into the living room, sniffed back his runny nose and hiked up the jeans that were too big for his skinny waist.

"Hey, Kingfish," I said. "I'm talking to you."

"Huh?" He turned around.

"Go turn off the light and flush the toilet."

"Oh." He walked back toward the bathroom.

I don't know what he did while he was in there, maybe turn around twice, rub his head and pat his stomach, but there was no flushing sound, and when he walked out again the light was still on.

"Hey," I said. "I just told you to go into the bathroom, flush the toilet and turn off the light. Did you do any of that?"

He was looking at me as I spoke. I swore he was listening.

He returned to the bathroom, shut off the light and walked out making shooting sounds, his finger cocked like a gun, one eye squinting down an imaginary barrel.

"Bud. Stop." This time I put my hands on his boney, little-boy shoulders. I made eye contact. I wasn't angry, but I wanted him to get it, you know? "You turned off the light, but you still forgot to flush."

> I was beginning to see, though, that he was wired differently. His thought processes took the path of that little kid in the "Family Circus" cartoon. There wasn't a straight line to anywhere.

He acted like it was the first time he'd heard me speak, but I was encouraged by the way his eyes ignited with understanding.

He went into the bathroom, turned the light back on and walked out.

"Okay, stop," I said. "Listen to me." By then I was in awe. This was basically a normal kid I had here: healthy, average birth weight, smooth delivery, potty-trained at two and a half, non-spectacular childhood save a few stitches here and there. I was beginning to see, though, that he was wired differently. His thought processes took the path of that little kid in the "Family Circus" cartoon. There wasn't a straight line to anywhere. "Go into the bathroom, turn off the light, flush the toilet."

"Okay," he said, and ran into the bathroom, flushed the toilet and walked out. As soon as he saw me he stopped, thought for a beat, then ran back through the door and hit the light switch. Finally!

"Can I go back outside?" he asked, as I helped him put on a dry shirt.

"Do you have a lot on your mind today?"

"Huh?" he said.

"Never mind, get out of here." He took off out the back door. "Zip your pants!" I yelled.

"I love you too!" he yelled back.

The author says:

When I walked into my very first parent-teacher conference, my oldest son's third grade teacher greeted me saying, "What the hell's wrong with that kid of yours?" He was only half-joking. Now that kid is a 23-year-old Marine and Iraq war veteran with plans for a college degree. This essay is dedicated to the two sons I call my "book-ends" for without their fascinating and frustrating minds I would never have known the joys of raising children with ADD.

"Joe couldn't sit still even in the womb. He wanted out way too early. At 20 weeks I was in pre-term labor and had rescue surgery to save the pregnancy. On complete bed rest with a device that pumped anti-labor meds into my body around the clock, I got Joe to 35 weeks. He was born with only minor complications and came home on schedule. But after only a few days, Joe realized his error. He didn't want to be out after all. The world was an overwhelming place, and he wanted back in.

For the first six months of his life, Joe cried. His bottom lip was forever pouted out and his brow was always deeply furrowed. The only way to console him was to carry him close to my body; so that's what I did. I carried him in a baby sling for hours at a time, some days from morning till night. My back ached, but Joe was comforted and quiet. I feel like I've been carrying his extra weight ever since."

Tammy Murphy, mother of Joe (ADHD)

Butterflies

by Rachel Penn Hannah

Butterflies are migrating through our neighborhood. I watch as hundreds of painted ladies fly through my yard, and between the trees and houses that line my street. This year's painted lady population is huge. They are lovely; lacy, black and orange. Flying north for the summer, they are quick, flying over obstacles rather than around them.

My nine-year-old daughter, Sarah, and her best friend, Noah, are trying to catch one. Sarah stands in her green Crocs, wet bathing suit under a sweatshirt. Her hair—half wet, half dry—is matted to the side of her head. She is determined to catch just one painted lady. "Persistence" is Sarah's middle name.

Sarah's dad, Robert, gave Sarah a professional butterfly net when she was just five years old. Already a seasoned bug enthusiast, she had been searching for bugs since she was about 20 months old.

"Mama look!" Sarah toddled in from the back yard, fist clenched, palm facing up, and came to a wobbly stop right in front of me. I bent down to see why she was so excited, and she slowly, awkwardly opened her chubby fingers to reveal a tan and black potato bug, about two inches long, its legs wriggling.

"Look Mama big bug!" There she stood in her sagging diaper, shirtless, big belly begging for kisses. She galloped in place with glee.

"How wonderful, Sarah. Look at that bug!"

"A bug! A bug! Look Daddy look!" She ran off to show her dad. That was just the beginning.

During the summers that followed Sarah spent hours every day following butterflies and looking under rocks for insects. During this one pursuit Sarah's intense, quiet focus revealed itself, contrasting sharply with her usual loud, unsettled, and chaotic self.

Sarah was a colicky baby, a fussy toddler. She never slept for very long and was always moving. Clumsy, emotionally intense, she'd go from zero to 100 in seconds. Wherever she went she created a big mess, and then moved on to the next thing. The floor in Sarah's room was cluttered with toys, game pieces, rocks, leaves and branches, bug containers with a variety of live and dead critters inside, clean clothes that she had pulled from her drawers, stuffed animals, and Legos. Playing, to Sarah, meant taking things out, examining them, fiddling with them briefly, and then moving on to create more mess.

Sarah was frustrated easily; too hot, too cold, irritable, melting down during any transition. Driving with her in the car was always a challenge. She screamed with intensity whenever she was in her car seat. Conflict was unavoidable when her siblings were in the car with her. Getting her to sleep took hours and she never stayed asleep for long. I remember the looks people gave me when they saw how hard I patted Sarah to get her to sleep. Sarah needed a firm pat—it calmed her—but it must have looked as if I was hurting her. To get Sarah to fall asleep I walked the floors of our house for hours, bouncing and patting, feeling like I might fall asleep myself mid-stride. Both Robert and I were always exhausted.

We have two older children so we knew that parenting Sarah was radically different. A bedtime routine that involved lowering the lights, reading a book, nursing, and singing worked well to get our older kids to sleep when they were babies, but nothing seemed to help Sarah. My older two children only had to be told once that they couldn't buy something special at the grocery store, but with Sarah saying "No" to practically anything led to a major tantrum. Time outs were an effective way of getting my older son and daughter to calm down. Not so with Sarah, who reacted with rage. Why had our parenting seemed so natural and effective with our two older children and yet felt so inadequate with Sarah?

I sought out advice in books and on the Internet. I looked to William Sears for advice on the "High-Need" baby, and then, when Sarah was a preschooler, I read *Raising Your Spirited Child*. To this day my bookshelves are filled with the parenting books that I bought hoping to find answers that might help us to help Sarah.

Sarah was in kindergarten when my husband and I decided to consult a neuropsychologist. She warned that the behaviors we saw in Sarah could be early signs of a mental health problem. She recommended we take Sarah to an occupational therapist for help with sensory integration and mood regulation.

> **Why had our parenting seemed so natural and effective with our two older children and yet felt so inadequate with Sarah?**

During the summer after Sarah's kindergarten year she was diagnosed with attention deficit hyperactivity disorder (ADHD) by her pediatrician, and referred to a child psychiatrist. Despite our fears about medication, we started her on a stimulant right before first grade.

I felt isolated, alone. No one seemed to understand how difficult it was to parent Sarah. I felt judged. I tried to participate in "Mommy and Me" classes and get-togethers with friends, but instead of connecting with other moms I spent my time chasing Sarah, trying to soothe her many upsets, and feeling detached from the group.

"Have you read any parenting books?" the school psychologist asked at our first of many meetings.

"In our day a good spanking would have taken care of that," some older relatives said, and laughed.

Popular parenting techniques simply did not work with Sarah, yet without having the experience of parenting a complicated child, how could anyone *not* feel that Sarah just needed consistent, clear limits—that we were letting her run the show?

When Robert gave Sarah the professional butterfly net I was worried that she would not be strong enough to lift the thick, four foot wooden dowel. Sarah had gone through at least five plastic toy nets; the handles snapped and the nets were prone to holes. Now, at age nine, Sarah has command of the net. She looks hardy holding the heavy, worn, weathered gray pole; some old duct tape for grip, the net a dirty off-white, yet still free of holes. Sarah slowly tiptoes around the yard trying to catch just one of the traveling butterflies. But these butterflies are on a mission, flying as a determined group. The term "social butterfly" comes to mind.

Out of the hundreds of painted ladies we are watching, one occasionally stops for a rest on a blossom on our cherry tree, or for some other reason falls away from the group. Those butterflies, the outliers, seem lost and out of sync with the others. Sarah has always been one of those butterflies. She's had one best friend since kindergarten—Noah. Thank God for Noah. Sarah and Noah found each other early in elementary school and their friendship is a blessing for both of them. Neither fits in with any of the groups of kids migrating through the social world of the school playground.

"We're weird and we want to be weird!" Sarah and Noah declared in second grade. They spent all recesses and lunches together, talking, losing themselves in the fantasy-based play they both loved.

My husband and I don't really fit in with the parents of other children Sarah's age either. We don't often get together with other families, because we can never be sure that Sarah will have the emotional reserves for us to follow through with plans. While other parents use basic parenting interventions with reasonable success, such as time outs and 1-2-3 Magic, we have found that these techniques actually escalate Sarah's misbehavior.

I remember a time when our extended family met at a fancy restaurant to celebrate a grandmother's birthday. Sarah wanted—and expected—to sit next to me at the table. The other grown-ups had a different seating arrangement in mind. My brother-in-law sat next to me. I knew that I had a choice. I could either tell Sarah that she had to sit across from me instead of next to me, as she expected, and risk a meltdown, or I could ask my brother-in-law to move. I chose the latter. I could tell from the looks I received from the other adults that they thought I was a wimp, and Sarah a brat. My feelings of being misunderstood and embarrassed were all too familiar.

My husband and I have spent a lot of time thinking, talking, and worrying about Sarah and the social challenges that stem from having ADHD. Reading social cues is hard for kids with ADHD, and this is true for Sarah. We've done everything we could think of to help with that: putting her into a friendship group, having lots of play dates, and giving her horse riding lessons to teach her nonverbal communication. We have also identified and nurtured her strengths; her love of animals and the natural world, a passion for many children with ADHD.

> **I felt isolated, alone. No one seemed to understand how difficult it was to parent Sarah. I felt judged.**

At age nine, Sarah tried to make the best of being "quirky" and found other "quirkies" to hang out with. Sarah's third grade teacher told us that he liked to read books to the class about kids who are different, and that Sarah often spoke up to say she related to the story. Her teacher commented about how disarming this approach was. It's as if Sarah was saying, "I'm different too, and that's just the way I like it!" and the other kids in the class responded with a no big deal attitude.

Despite this coping skill, feeling different has been quite painful for Sarah. Her awareness of her differences started in kindergarten. Unlike preschool, kindergarten was all about conformity, which goes against Sarah's grain. She was expected to sit on her carpet square, keeping her body contained to a small space, but her limbs kept moving and touching other people. This bothered other children and led to negative feedback from the teacher.

"Sarah had to sit out today because she kept touching Nicki on the rug," the teacher told me on a regular basis.

Art projects meant replicating the teacher's sample exactly, and letters were to be formed precisely, neither of which Sarah could do. When I volunteered in the classroom Sarah's frustration was visible. As the students moved from one activity to another at a pace that was clearly too fast for Sarah, she became more and more irritable and agitated, and was rude to the other kids and teachers. After a full day of trying to hold it together she often melted down in the car on the way home. It took years for me to understand why and even longer for Sarah to be able to say why she was so aggravated.

Then there was the social chaos. Take the age-old game of the boys chasing the girls, for example. From her perspective, in this game the girls were the prey and the boys the predators, and Sarah was not about to be prey. Her solution was to join the boys' team and opt out of the girls' group altogether, which was how she met Noah.

Our suburban neighborhood's elementary school is densely populated, with almost 800 kids. I was amazed to see how quickly cliques formed during kindergarten and first grade. There are groups based on sports, Girl Scouts, swim team, soccer, and dance. And of course there are the mom cliques; clusters of two to four women laughing, talking, and planning play dates for their kids. It felt impossible to join since I was preoccupied with worry for Sarah.

Given that kids with ADHD are generally delayed socially, they are often unable to keep up with the social migration like other children. This difference is not as apparent in preschool, but as ADHD kids get older the gap widens. We found this to be especially true for Sarah because she's a girl. People seem more accepting of ADHD behaviors such as hyperactivity and inattention in boys, while being less tolerant of the same behaviors in girls.

"Oh, he's just a boy!" people say when a young boy is plays rough or is forgetful. A girl with ADHD really stands out.

During the second half of third grade Sarah started to develop an interest in playing with girls. We invited various girls over to play and most of them accepted, but no one ever asked Sarah over in return.

I signed Sarah up for Girl Scouts during third grade. She wasn't actively excluded by the troop members, but she was definitely on the margins. During a Girl Scout field trip, I got a glimpse of the social culture of girls.

Sarah, Jessica, Katie, and I were walking together from the school office to the car. We were off to a candy making class. Jessica and Katie walked arm and arm. I reached out to hold Sarah's hand, but she pulled her hand back.

"I just love you, Jessica! I just love you!" Katie said.

"Thanks," Jessica said, smiling, as they gave each other a sideways hug.

"It feels good to be loved, doesn't it?" I chimed in.

"You mean to be popular," Jessica corrected me.

"Oh. Are being loved and popular the same thing?" I asked.

"Yes," Jessica and Katie said in unison.

"Hmm...I'm not so sure about that," was the only response I could muster. Sarah looked away. A knot formed in my stomach. Sarah and I both knew that "popular" was not a game she could play.

A couple of months later Sarah was invited to a boy's birthday party, along with all of the other kids in their class. Sarah was thrilled. Before the party she was anxious about her hair and clothes, and being on time, things she had never worried about before. When we arrived I walked her into the house and out to the pool where the kids were congregating. Sarah ran up to a group of four or five girls who were standing in a semi-circle.

"Hi," Sarah said.

The girls looked at Sarah for a nanosecond, looked at each other, and then ran off, having said nothing in return.

That's it! I thought to myself. By third grade the cliques were set and there was no way Sarah was getting in. But she had changed! She was no longer the little girl who melted down at school, crying, and yelling for others to stay away. Her interests had expanded from insects and animals to some things more girly. But she was in a box and wasn't getting out. I started to think Sarah needed a fresh start; to go from an ocean of social sharks to a small pond, where she could perhaps shine. I also thought she might get more help for her learning issues at a small school.

We found that small school not far from where we live; a private school with a small community feel. This was Sarah's chance to have a new beginning. She, too, was eager to try something different. We enrolled Sarah in the new school for fourth grade.

The first three months were hard. The girls in her class had been together since kindergarten and had formed deep friendships. And, with only 10 kids in the class, they worked really, really hard on academics. Exhausted and frustrated, Sarah's learning issues seemed magnified. She started to melt down again. When Sarah was frustrated by work that was too hard, when plans were changed, or when some expectation of hers was not met she would hide in a bathroom stall, cry, and try to calm herself down. But the staff could not tolerate her being alone in a bathroom stall and pursued her.

"Leave me alone! Get away from me!" Sarah would scream.

The school office would call and tell me to come to the school immediately. No matter how many times this happened I reacted with dread and anxiety, and had to will myself not to cry.

Sarah struggled to connect with her classmates and felt the girls in the class were mean to her.

"It's like kindergarten all over again!" she screamed at me one day as we drove home from school.

We had Sarah's neuropsychological testing updated and adjusted her medications, and Sarah started to calm down a little at school. The girls in her class played a game based on a series of books about a boarding school with a focus on horseback riding. Sarah read the first book—a 200 page chapter book without pictures—the first age appropriate book Sarah had ever read independently. Once Sarah knew the books' plot she could speak the girls' social language, and the girls started to let her play with them at recess and during lunch. Sarah was thrilled and her mood brightened. No more meltdowns. We were ecstatic.

> **We have learned to look at Sarah and be proud of her perseverance, of her strong yet sensitive soul.**

One day in the car on the way home from school I commented to Sarah that she seemed to be getting along better with the girls in her class.

"Yes I am. It finally worked Mom!"

The girls in Sarah's class are no longer "mean" to her. They let her play, but her descriptions of the play reveal to me that she is still clearly the new girl. Sarah still hasn't been invited to play dates, but she is invited to birthday parties, because of a school rule that everyone in the class should be invited. (Shouldn't that be a rule everywhere?) For now this is good enough for Sarah, and therefore, it's good enough for us.

Sarah is traveling the social milieu in a group. While not yet a social butterfly, she is finding her way on the migration. These developments in Sarah have eased, though not erased, our anxiety about her stability and future. As she progresses, we have more time to give to ourselves and each other. I have taken up yoga and take more time for writing, pursuits that were unheard of in years past. Robert and I can also see that the amount of attention we give our other children is a bit more balanced, which is really important to us.

As I sit on the porch watching Sarah's determination in action I am grateful that she's experiencing longer periods of stability and growth. We have learned to look at Sarah and be proud of her perseverance, of her strong yet sensitive soul. I don't know what next year's migration will bring, but I am at peace for now. No matter what Sarah's future holds, I'll be here, watching.

The author says:

Sarah is now in the fifth grade and has returned to her old elementary school. It turned out that the small private school did not differentiate instruction and was unskilled with intense temperaments. Sarah can be lonely at school, but has a warm, brilliant teacher who understands her. Sarah continues to be friends with Noah and has found a spunky girl-friend through horseback riding. While Sarah's friend lives 30 minutes away, this is the close friendship with a girl that Sarah has been wanting. And truly, there is no limit to how far we would drive to bring Sarah together with a good friend.

Tell Us More: Expert Q & A with Cathi Cohen, LCSW, CGP

Author of *Raise Your Child's Social IQ* and *Stepping Stones to Building Friendships*

Q. It's very common for children who have ADHD to have problems making and keeping friends. Why is that?

A. The child with ADHD frequently exhibits a constellation of characteristics that may interfere with successful social development. The child with ADHD is often impulsive. When a child lacks the adequate pause between impulse and action, social blunders inevitably occur. Poor listening skills are a common byproduct of impulsivity.

The child with ADHD may be insensitive to subtle interpersonal cues. Being able to recognize and understand other people's body language and facial expressions requires kids to constantly scan their environments for clues that will guide their social actions. Because kids with ADHD often struggle to stay tuned in to their environments, they frequently misread social signals. Misinterpretations may lead to under-reacting. The kids who don't see these signals may be insensitive to the feedback cues others are giving them, leading to anger from peers who feel that their "social hints" are being ignored.

A child affected by ADHD can't control what captures his or her attention. Any internal or external stimulation can be distracting to a child with ADHD.

Children with ADHD have a hard time learning from experience, whether the experience is positive or negative. When a child who does not have ADHD makes a social mistake and receives a hostile reaction from a peer, chances are high that the same mistake won't happen again. The child with ADHD, on the other hand, may make a mistake repeatedly before learning not to do it again. The child with ADHD has trouble applying past experiences to future problems and is unable to predict the consequences of his or her actions.

Children with ADHD may have a difficult time predicting audience response. A child who does not have ADHD is able to see himself or herself through another child's eyes. This self-reflection informs his or her behavior. Children with ADHD get themselves into social binds without being aware of their predicament or of how they got there because they lack awareness of the consequences of their social behavior

Q. What can parents do to help their ADHD children have an easier time making friends?

A. Some children can't learn social skills on their own—they need help. Your involvement as a parent is essential to help your child learn new skills and use them in a variety of settings. You already help your child to develop social skills by modeling good social skills yourself and by creating situations in which your child can practice. For example, when you invite children over to play or get your child involved in extracurricular activities, you are helping him or her build social skills.

As a parent of a child affected by ADHD, you may need to be your child's "social coach" in order to address the social challenges highlighted above. Raise your child's social IQ by using the following techniques and strategies:

- Talk to your child about the need for social skills. During a quiet time of the day, discuss with your child the importance of making friends and getting along with others. An ideal time is when your child is complaining to you about a social incident with another child. Tell your child you are going to try to help him or her learn the skills needed to be "an even better friend than [he or she] already [is]."

- Set a social goal with your child. It's important to be as specific as possible when setting a goal, and to set only one goal at a time. The goal must be one that your child sees as important. For example, you may want your child to stop interrupting others during conversations, but if he doesn't agree or doesn't feel able to meet the goal, he will not succeed. If your child agrees with you, his goal might read: "You will interrupt in conversation 50% less this week than last week." (Note: Before you can set an attainable goal, you need to know your child's current level of functioning. You'll need at least a week to observe your child at the same time each day before you can set a realistic goal for improvement.)

- Carefully arrange a supervised, time-limited date for your child to spend with other children to practice newly learned social skills. Many children with ADHD may be unable to spend hours playing with another child. It's too much time to negotiate the complicated interactions of play. Instead, set up a play date that is limited in length. Make sure the date ends on a positive note whenever possible. Children tend to remember more vividly the last 15 minutes of an interaction.

- Review social goals with your child prior to social outings. For instance, "What are you going to do when you first get to the birthday party?" "Well, Dad, I'm going to walk over to where the other kids are playing and try to go with their flow." "That's right, you've got it!"

- Choose play activities that are intrinsically simple and enticing. Keep activities easy in terms of attention span and stimulation. Ask a friend to a highly attractive event like ice skating or a trip to the movies. These occasions minimize the need for intense social interaction, and thus increase the likelihood of social success for your child with ADHD.

- Involve your child's teachers and guidance counselors in helping to reinforce social goals. For example, your child's teacher could use check-off sheets to give his parents daily feedback on his progress on his goal of decreasing his interruptions in class. This encourages accountability and consistency for your child.

- Videotape or audiotape your child at home. Sometimes children affected by ADHD have trouble seeing themselves through others' eyes. Review these tapes with your child to increase self-observation and awareness.

- Prompt your child to think about the feelings, reactions, and needs of others. Help your child understand the motivations and feelings of others by observing out loud what others' faces and bodies are telling us. For instance, you might say, "How do you think the other girls feel when you only want to play what you want to play?"

- And finally, consider a social skills group. Some children do need more individualized attention. If you are frustrated with your child's progress, there are other options you can pursue. First, consult with your school's guidance counselor. Many schools conduct social skills groups to help children develop positive social behaviors. Although these groups are generally time-limited (meeting for less than eight weeks) and brief (usually a half hour long), they can be effective in reinforcing the skills you are teaching your child at home. In addition, a school group can work nicely in combination with an outside therapy group.

Treasure in the Sand
by Erica Wells

My husband, Brian, and I walked with our son, Ken, down the pier, taking in the scene that is Cape Cod—boats, the breeze blowing salty air, and the gulls screaming as they looked for tidbits of food dropped by tourists. We were walking hand in hand, swinging our arms and enjoying the sunny day, when Ken saw something shining on the small shore below.

"Look!"

Without warning Ken let go of my hand, pointed, ran, and jumped. He flew off the pier, his little feet air-running; no ground beneath them. He fell about 20 feet, landed in sand, and began to dig. A large, hooked scaling knife appeared. Brian and I stood dumbfounded, as our five-year-old brandished a large knife and smiled like a pirate.

"Look! Look what I found!" he yelled.

Should we jump the 20 feet to reach him, or walk all the way around the pier to the sandy shore by the docks? The water near him was deep, and the knife was sharp—and very dirty.

My feet moved as if they had a mind of their own. I ran around the pier. Other tourists stared, or tried to get out of the way as I pushed by them, yelling to my son, "Don't move!"

The few seconds it took to run to Ken felt like an eternity. I stood before him panting, sides heaving. I held out my hand and snapped, "Give me that!"

"But look how cool it is! There're fish scales on it!" My son smiled, and flicked a scale to show me it was true.

Brian reached us a couple minutes later and found me holding Ken by the shoulders, listing all the things that could have happened to him with his latest escapade. The lecture already forgotten, Ken turned to his father.

"Look what I found! Isn't it cool?"

I shook my head. Another of my safety lectures was going in one ear and out the other. The discovery of a "treasure" was far more interesting than another of mom's talks.

We returned to the hotel and spent the rest of the day on the shore in front of our room, where there was no danger of Ken leaping off a pier, and where if he needed a time out he could have it without turning tourists' heads. There had been enough excitement for one day.

Unfortunately, this scene was all too typical for our family. Ken has attention problems (along with a few other diagnoses) and his impulsivity has gotten him into some serious predicaments. Upon witnessing Ken's escapades, friends, family and passers-by would shake their heads at Brian and me, wondering what we were doing. The truth is we really didn't know. My husband and I were doing our best with Ken. We just wanted to have fun together like a "normal" family.

> **Upon witnessing Ken's escapades, friends, family and passers-by would shake their heads at Brian and me, wondering what we were doing. The truth is we really didn't know.**

Even on the home front Ken's safety was a concern. One afternoon when he was in sixth grade, he was playing lacrosse in the road with a friend. After an hour or so, they came in for drinks. As Ken reached into the cupboard for glasses, his shirt rode up revealing a large, swollen bite mark.

"My God. What happened to your stomach?"

I lifted his shirt up again. The wound showed individual teeth marks in the shape of a large circle. The punctures were bloody and already turning purple.

Ken shrugged. "The lacrosse ball rolled in the neighbor's yard. Their pit bull was tied up out front. I didn't see him."

"We need to clean that," I said, as I randomly opened drawers and cupboards looking for peroxide, antibiotic cream, bandages—and my heart, which had fallen through my stomach and dropped somewhere on the kitchen floor.

Through the years, my husband and I lost our hearts many times. We learned that nothing could surprise us; the unexpected became the expected. After each near-disaster we rededicated ourselves to mastering Ken's behavior. We visited doctors and therapists. We set up detailed schedules, rules, and reward systems. I won't say that none of the strategies worked, but nothing changed the fact of our son's diagnoses. He is who he is, and 23 years later that remains to be true.

Of course, there were lessons my husband and I learned about parenting, but we also learned there is beauty in people for who they are as human beings. Some individuals "beat to their own drum" as Thoreau once said. Children, with or without disabilities, can't be put into categories and slots.

If I could go back and do it over, I would put less emphasis on trying to make Ken's behavior fit into the world, and instead would help him see how the world blossomed with him in it.

He's the boy who could see the treasure in the sand.

The author says:

Heartfelt blessings to Ken, who always sheds light on the interesting and unique possibilities in the world. Always look for the diamonds.

Finding My Way

by Lorraine Wilde

Sending my twin 5-year-old boys off to kindergarten last fall was harder for me than for them. They don't yet know about or understand the social baggage that can come with qualifying for special education. They're still too young to realize that they're different than a lot of the other kids in their class.

Unlike other developmental disorders that affect speech, reading, or writing, Tristan's and Will's issues are primarily behavioral. They have trouble controlling their emotions. They get upset very easily, and take a long time to calm down.

Tristan taught himself to read at age four. Will is a master of all things Transformer and Lego, and wields logic and reason like

> **Every eye in six checkout lanes probed us. *Can't you control your kids?***

a pirate wields his sword. Both test well above average on standard intelligence measures. But if the little things aren't going their way, or if they can't make something work *perfectly*, they get lost in a 20 minute meltdown, as if the world is literally about to end.

Since they were around 18 months old, I have spent an astonishing amount of time just trying to figure out what is upsetting them. One unforgettable day it took me 40 minutes to figure out that I'd inadvertently caused a crisis by cutting their PB & J sandwiches in triangles instead of squares. A trip to the grocery store ended badly when checkout took more than the usual three minutes. The boys felt stuck in the checkout line, trapped like cattle in a shoot, and cried with lung power Michael Phelps would envy. Every eye in six checkout lanes probed us. *Can't you control your kids?* But with two weeks' worth of groceries already unloaded on the conveyor belt, I couldn't escape their scrutiny. I tried not to cry as I wiped the sweat off my upper lip, entered my PIN on the card reader, and resisted snapping at the cashier's benign questions. A kind woman in line behind us said with sincere pity, "God only gives us what we can handle."

My feelings vary from moment to moment about this life I've chosen. I wouldn't say I'm embarrassed by my children's behavior, at least not anymore. But I mourn the lost picture of motherhood I've carried since I was a young girl. My life is not the syrupy TV show I'd once imagined it could be. We have our share of June Cleaver tender moments, but they are far outnumbered by something much closer to the "before" part of "Super Nanny." I'm ashamed to admit I could use the guidance of a stern British headmistress.

Not-so-fond memories from my own ancient school days have predisposed me to worry. Will the other kids like my boys? Will they get invited to birthday parties and sleepovers? And the number one fear of every perfectionist PTA mom: Will their limitations affect their self-esteem—and their happiness—in the long run?

Some days hiding away at home is the only way I make it through the day. On those days denial is a comfort I cannot refuse.

* * * * *

We're no strangers to labels. At first, the teachers of the parenting classes I attended politely suggested the term "spirited" (*Raising Your Spirited Child* by Mary Sheedy Kurcinka) to describe my boys, but that was just the gateway label, a precursor to the diagnoses to come. Fellow parents of "atypical" children then led me to the term "sensitive" (*The Highly Sensitive Child* by Elaine Aron) and eventually a diagnosis of sensory processing disorder emerged. I hate that unfortunate word—disorder—and what it represents: a collection of symptoms, of unknown cause, with no known cure. We must learn to live with all that the label represents. We sign up for therapies like they're intramural sports.

I thought an official diagnosis would guide us to wellness, and to some degree it has, but I wasn't really ready for the finality of the verdict when it came. It felt like a life sentence. Somewhere around my twentieth self-help book, I found the six words I'd been unconsciously seeking: "the disorder can lessen with age." A ray of sunlight pierced my otherwise shadowy sky.

A school psychologist suggested we investigate Asperger's disorder. Back to the library I went. The A-word made me uncomfortable because some "Aspies" aren't able to live as independent adults. If I had blinked at the wrong moment, I might have missed the sentence that changed our lives: "5-10% of children misdiagnosed with Asperger's actually have the metabolic disorder pyroluria, involving an abnormality in hemoglobin synthesis." (*Asperger's Syndrome: Natural Steps Toward a Better Life* by Suzanne Lawton) The disorder causes vitamin B6 and zinc deficiencies which result in Asperger's-like symptoms. BINGO! A couple of urine tests later, lab tests confirmed that my boys inherited this metabolic disorder from me. (Is "guilt" actually in the dictionary definition of "mother?") Soon, I was back at the library becoming an expert on yet another obscure ailment.

> **We sign up for therapies like they're intramural sports.**

I'm ashamed to acknowledge the exhaustion Tristan and Will's behavior causes me. A mother's well of patience is supposed to be bottomless, and mine isn't. When I look back at my own childhood, I realize that I was also a moody, paranoid, and irrational child. But my parents and teachers controlled my behavior without therapy. They relied on the standbys of their generation: corporal punishment, intimidation, and humiliation. These are tools that I make a daily, conscious effort to avoid.

* * * * *

Tristan's and Will's transition from preschool to kindergarten has been psychologically draining for me. The hardest part was letting go of control over the situation. Before kindergarten I was leading the way, pushing for assessments and treatments, being the squeaky wheel that moved things forward. Now that the boys are in public school I'm still very involved, but more like a high level executive who gets monthly reports of the bottom line. I am not there every day to monitor Will's and Tristan's progress, or to micromanage everyone involved.

When I pictured becoming a mother I never imagined the exhausted, frumpy mom that I have become, laughing off our social awkwardness and our inability to arrive *anywhere* on time. I'm trying not to care that we don't sign up for soccer (tactile sensitivity) or attend the library fair (noise and visual sensitivity). The label that I'm embracing these days is "twice-exceptional" or "2e" for children that are both gifted and learning disabled (*The Mislabeled Child* by Brock Eide). It has a nice ring to it. But my lost fantasies of mommyhood perfection are like mosquitoes buzzing annoyingly around my ears, just out of swatting reach.

> **My lost fantasies of mommyhood perfection are like mosquitoes buzzing annoyingly around my ears, just out of swatting reach.**

Since correcting the boys' vitamin deficiencies, getting an aid in the classroom, and immersing them in a host of occupational, language, and behavior modification therapies, our lives have settled down to a more typical level of chaos. Last week the school's special ed supervisor uttered the phrase I'd been dying to hear, "We're very excited because both the boys are doing so much better." Maybe I'm in the running for Supermom after all.

My airy spring days were filled with planning for summer activities to sustain the great strides the boys have made this year. And this week, my time will be spent deciding if there is a *right* first grade teacher for the fall. I guess a mother's work—with 2e twins—is never done.

The author says:

With the help of their therapists, teachers, school employees, family, and friends, Tristan and Will have successfully integrated into their classrooms and continue to improve.

A Land that I Heard of

by Rachel Zients Schinderman

When I was a little girl, it was Dorothy who got to me the most. She sang of "somewhere over the rainbow," of a land that she heard of where dreams come true. I'd watch *The Wizard of Oz* over and over again in the little den off our kitchen, and dream about this land; this other place. I began to believe in it, to long for it.

In this land, I would be a mother.

Even as a little girl I knew I wanted to be a mother. My own mother taught me that girls are born with all of the eggs that become our children. Each evening, on channel five, the announcer would say, "It's 7:00 p.m. Have you hugged your child today?" and I would hug my belly.

It was just the two of us, my mother and me, since my father died when I was four. I slept in her bed, next to her, until I was about 10 years old. We were lonely, though never with each other. I would not have been able to express it then, but as I slept in her bed I dreamt about how it would all be different when I became a mother. There'd be a daddy. Problems would be solved, sadness thwarted.

When I did grow up I married a lovely man. I even walked down the aisle to "Over the Rainbow." Motherhood—this land that I heard of— was now just around the corner.

* * * * *

I was standing with a group of friends at a barbeque, when the host, a mother of three, began:

"In the great green room…."

Everyone laughed. And someone answered, "…there was a telephone…."

The women recited these words with such ease. They clearly knew them by heart. And everyone else, everyone but me, knew where these words came from. They all seemed so comfortable in their motherhood skin.

I tried to play along, smiling, as if in recognition. I was pretty sure they were quoting a book. *Goodnight Moon*, perhaps? I didn't know *Goodnight Moon* was that famous. It seemed it was a big deal. And it seemed they knew something I did not.

I know I was read to as a child. My mother was a journalist, after all. But the soothing comfort of books as a regular bedtime routine did not register on my childhood memory meter. I watched movies, like *Funny Girl*, *My Fair Lady*, and *The Wizard of Oz*. *Goodnight Moon* was not part of my childhood.

Hearing these mothers recite this bedtime story, these words; hearing their knowing laughs, I wondered about this club I had not yet joined. Would I be allowed in if I didn't know the words? If I didn't know their language?

* * * * *

On July 27, 2006, I became a mother.

It didn't go exactly as planned.

There had never been much movement in my belly during my pregnancy, but that day there was none. There was a problem with my placenta. My child, Benjamin, still in my womb, began to bleed through the umbilical cord, to have a fetal/maternal transfusion. After an emergency c-section he was whisked away from me and rushed to the neo-natal intensive care unit (NICU).

I was praised by family, friends, and doctors for knowing my body, for mentioning the lack of movement, but I felt like a failure. My body turned on my child at the time it was meant to nurture him the most.

I was sent home from the hospital without him. I felt as if a piece of my life was on hold, living elsewhere, outside of me, leaving me leaking.

I visited Benjamin in the NICU daily, and soon we got into a routine, a rhythm. I learned to nurse hidden from other families by a curtain. I learned that when Benjamin's monitor alarm went off it was only because he moved his foot, not because he was crashing. I learned to take a deep breath and prepare for what I may find each and every time I entered the hospital.

But on the morning of the thirteenth day, the doctor said, "How do you feel about taking him home today?" I hadn't allowed myself to think that day would come. And now here was my baby, ready for me. Me, his mother. Me. It was breathtaking.

My husband and I placed Benjamin in his red stroller. We hurried through the streets of our neighborhood, almost floating to our apartment, eager to welcome him into our home, our world. My mother trailed behind us snapping picture after picture. I couldn't believe our great fortune.

* * * * *

Once we were home, gifts started arriving in the mail. Books, toys, clothes. *Goodnight Moon*. It *was Goodnight Moon* those other mothers were reciting! I was right.

Another *Goodnight Moon*. Then another. Until there were six. Six *Goodnight Moons*. Were people trying to tell me something?

A beautiful hard-bound copy rests high up on a shelf. This one we do not read. It is too nice to touch. But the others are small cardboard books, made for rereading, begging to be worn. These we read. Often. These are always within an arm's reach.

At first Benjamin would just listen as we sat in our yellow rocker reading. Then his eyes found the pages and he could follow along.

This was our routine. Every night. We cuddled and read this book.

I devoured it, became obsessed.

"Did you know they never say goodnight to the telephone?" I asked my husband.

"Who has an open flame in a toddler's room anyway?" I continued.

"Do you think we could find those pajamas somewhere? They're very cute."

I considered a preschool based solely on the fact that they had a tree house painted like the bunny's room. And I spent so much time comparing it with *Runaway Bunny* that I could have written a dissertation on the similarities and differences.

> As I rocked my son and read to him each night, it felt like I was getting it— motherhood—right.

I was now one of those mothers who knew it, breathed it. I was a part of it. A speaker of the words. When I read, all points clicked. I did not have to try or think. My voice took over, as if I were an actress, and every sound was the right amount of quiet, the perfect inflection.

I have a favorite part. "Goodnight nobody." The pure white of the page is so lonely and yet so strong.

As I rocked my son and read to him each night, it felt like I was getting it—motherhood—right.

* * * * *

When Benjamin was around 18 months old, a friend mentioned casually that his daughter's first word was "moon." I was crushed. I realized that Benjamin wasn't really talking.

I knew his body was delayed. We were getting therapy for that. His birth trauma had affected his muscle tone, but we'd been told by several neurologists that he didn't have cerebral palsy, that he was okay. But still milestones came and went unmet. Was there something more?

We sat in a developmental pediatrician's office. I retold the story of Benjamin's birth, of his NICU stay. The possible lack of oxygen to his brain. I cried a little. This motherhood thing was a little different than I imagined. The doctor gave me a tissue.

She asked us questions. She observed him. She pulled out blocks to test his skills. And then, she brought out *Goodnight Moon.*

"Where's the red balloon?" she asked.

He knows this, I thought. *We won't have to see this doctor ever again. We do this every night, Sweetie. It's right there. Right there. Right, right there.*

It was all I could do not to lift his hand up, not to direct his finger.

But Benjamin didn't move. He just looked at the pictures, ready for a story. The doctor put the book away and moved on. And we made another appointment.

* * * * *

I don't read *Goodnight Moon* every night anymore.

"No *Moon,*" Benjamin says while pushing it away. He's his own individual now. I try not to force it. But every now and then I pull it out.

"Where's the red balloon?" I try to ask casually, not wanting to set myself up for disappointment, but often doing just that. But I need something, some glimmer between therapy sessions, something to replace the tale we are becoming.

* * * * *

One day, with great ease, Benjamin pointed to the red balloon. He didn't need my hand to guide his finger. It was better than any bedtime story. Soon, he could point to the clock and the mouse too. And the telephone.

Recently Benjamin pointed out the car window to the actual moon.

"Moon!" he said. "Cow over moon."

My husband and I, who cherish each new word he throws at us, began reciting the book by heart. And our son answered us from the backseat, also by heart. He made it almost half way through.

That night I took the big nice book off the shelf and read it to him. He did not push it away. He let me read it as he followed along.

[He has taught me that I know what I am doing.]

From that night on, *Goodnight Moon* was just a book. The words did not dance and sing. The images did not intimidate me. When I stumbled over a line it did not crush me, because I know that I am a member of the club now.

But I also know that there is no secret code, no actual language of motherhood, only the language between mother and child. And my son and I have developed our own language, as my mother and I did when faced with our own challenges. He has taught me that I know what I am doing.

And though he is fickle with books, specifically with *Goodnight Moon*, there is one constant in his world.

"*Rainbow?*" He asks each night before he goes to sleep.

Each and every night in the dark I hear, "*Rainbow?*" And I know he is my son.

As I sing to him I realize that I no longer dream of some other place. I now know that the rainbow led Dorothy right back home. I no longer hear longing in the lyrics. Now I hear of surviving the tornado.

Life is not a fairy tale, a bedtime story, or a lullaby. Parents die. Children are challenged. Still, in this land lions do find their courage. Little girls outsmart witches.

In this land we do not "wake up where the clouds are far behind us," instead we take stock of the landscape before us and know that we can embark on new, unplanned adventures.

On this adventure, I have learned through my son that there is beauty in saying goodnight to the simplest little things, like nobody, and valuing those of us who are a little different or forgotten, like the telephone.

The author says:

I'm the subject of the children's book Rachel and the Upside Down Heart *(Dancing Magic Heart Books, 2006) written by my mother, Eileen Douglas, so I understand the challenges of writing about your children. I hope Benjamin and Eli will be flattered that I write about them. I am quite proud of both of my children. Benjamin has made great strides and can't wait for Eli to "be a kid so [he] can play with him." Benjamin now insists that I sing "Rainbow" to Eli at night. So I do—happily.*

Part 2: Square Pegs, Round Holes

Holding On
by Lisa Randazzo

Monday mornings were the best. While most people dreaded the start of another work week, I looked forward to finally catching my breath. Ryan was still asleep, but in less than an hour the school bell would ring and my first grader would bound into his classroom, leaving me with an empty house and an opportunity to recover from another high energy weekend. Not an out of control, or insane, or demoralizing weekend. No. Even then, one year before Ryan would be labeled with attention deficit hyperactivity disorder (ADHD), I tried to view his challenging behavior in positive terms. Our boy had a joie de vivre, I thought, an energetic spirit and a fierce determination that would serve him well through a lifetime of challenges. Nevertheless, I was looking forward to just folding laundry in complete silence that morning. Parenting Ryan was a wild ride, and sometimes the most mundane tasks were a welcomed respite.

I sat at the kitchen table and unzipped Ryan's book bag. Chewed up pencils, wads of notebook paper, the library book he kept forgetting to return, and stapled worksheets spilled out onto the table. I took a bite of my toast and sifted through the stack of papers. Crumbs sprinkled a blue card at the corner of my placemat. I brushed them away and read: *Horton Council of PTAs cordially invites you to the Reflections Recognition Ceremony, Achievements in the Arts.* I smiled. We had been looking forward to going to the ceremony that evening.

My seven-year-old, the boy I worried would not be able to contain himself in a regular classroom setting, had won first place in his school for the essay he'd entered in the literature category of the Reflections program, in the primary division. The inspiration for his winning essay, "I Can Make a Difference by Teaching People to Read," came from his weekly visits to a favorite kindergarten teacher's room. As a reward for good classroom behavior Ryan would spend a few minutes at the end of the day reading stories to the kindergartners and helping them with their spelling and letter writing. The younger kids looked forward to his visits and he took great pride in his tutoring responsibilities.

I leaned back in my chair. The house was quiet, and I enjoyed the stillness of the morning, a rarity in our home unless you were up before "the son." I sipped my tea and gathered the papers that could be trashed.

"AAAAAAARGH." A low guttural roar shook the house, followed by the thump, thump, thump of footsteps from Ryan's bedroom, through the hall, and into the bathroom. He was up.

Slam. Flush. Then, singing. No particular song or tune. Just sing-songy nonsense words and sounds. Ryan was the only person I knew who literally jumped out of bed each morning and took off running.

Squeak. Bang. Squeak. Bang. Squeak. Bang. The springs of the bed. The headboard against the wall. Ryan was jumping, probably naked or close to it, in the process of changing from his pajamas to school clothes. I put my cup in the sink and headed for the stairs.

BAM. He'd launched off the bed. He weighed only 50 pounds, but by the sound of the thud, I feared he might crash through the floor one day.

Thump, thump, thump, thump. Footsteps down the stairs.

Ryan appeared fully dressed in clothes I had laid out the night before. His shirt was on backward and his pants were unfastened, but I was impressed nevertheless. He'd made record time, with no parental reminders.

He was beaming. I was beaming. We were off to a good start. We sat down for breakfast.

"I can't wait until tonight, Mom," he mumbled between waffle bites.

"Neither can I. I'm very proud of you."

"I'm gonna be really good in school today."

"Better than last week, you think?"

Ryan swiveled left and right in the chair and nodded like a bobble head doll on speed. "Yes. I'm gonna try really hard."

Ryan must have liked Mondays too. They offered new beginnings, and my son could use as many of those as he could get.

After I said goodbye to Ryan in the school lobby I proceeded to the cafeteria to deposit more money into his lunch account.

"Mrs. Randazzo."

I turned around to find the principal walking toward me. I paused. She probably wanted to congratulate me on Ryan's award or thank me for my recent volunteer work.

"Did Mrs. Lowden speak with you?" she asked.

I shook my head. "No."

"Well, I just wanted to make sure you were aware of Horton Public School's policy. After three behavior notices a student is to receive a day of in-school suspension. I believe Ryan had his third behavior notice last week, so he's really supposed to spend today in I.S.S."

Whoosh. There went all the joy, the happiness, the positive energy from the morning. In only a matter of seconds she sucked it from my core. Minutes ago I was on top of the mountain. Now I was plummeting downhill on what felt like a runaway bicycle, wheels spinning, handlebars vibrating under my clenched palms.

That's what it feels like some days when you're the parent of a child with ADHD, an extreme mountain bike ride. There's just this one little problem. I didn't sign up for this bike tour. I don't like speed. I don't like heights. And when did I have time to train? I should be peddling alongside all the other parents and neighborhood kids out for a leisurely ride around the block. Instead, I'm faced with another challenging incline that I know will kick my butt.

"Do you understand the school policy about I.S.S.?" the principal asked.

No. I didn't understand. In-school suspension? For a first grader? I.S.S. was for bad kids, those who carried weapons or smoked in the bathroom. Students who skipped class or destroyed property. Not for my son, who merely "repeatedly used a tissue to blow his nose and threw it on a student's desk," as documented by his teacher. She called the offense "a health issue concern." Then why not write up every snot-nosed, booger-eating, non-hand-washing student in the germ-infested room?

> That's what it feels like some days when you're the parent of a child with ADHD, an extreme mountain bike ride. There's just this one little problem. I didn't sign up for this bike tour.

I had no idea the school had a "three strikes and you're out" policy, but I did remember that Ryan received two previous behavior notices, one the week before, and another two months prior to that one. But would Ryan remember that? He struggled to recall what he had for dinner the night before. A day in seclusion, restricted to a desk, with limited stimulation, was not a cure for impulsivity, but rather a set up for failure. It would only create more stress for Ryan, who desperately wanted to be "a good boy." I felt the heat rise in my face, and I clenched my jaw.

Ryan had left home that morning with such hope for the day. This latest development would crush his spirit.

Time to shift gears and strap on my helmet.

"It sounds like you haven't made a decision yet," I said. "Should you decide that I.S.S. is the appropriate place for Ryan today, call me before you put him there and I will take him out of school."

I've been on this trail for a while now and I've learned to navigate the course, but still there are times when the constant peddling of being Ryan's mother wears me down. I take a tumble. I ache. I gasp for breath.

> I've been on this trail for a while now and I've learned to navigate the course, but still there are times when the constant peddling of being Ryan's mother wears me down. I take a tumble. I ache. I gasp for breath.

I exited the school and walked briskly through the parking lot. It wasn't until I closed my car door that I allowed the tears to flow. I drove home. I did my household chores with a knot in my stomach. I froze every time the phone rang. Damn them for ruining our special day.

The principal never called. There was never any other mention of I.S.S. We went to the awards ceremony that evening. Ryan accepted his first place medal and also received an award for excellence at the district-level in the Reflections competition. The principal was there, pleased no doubt that Ryan had achieved such an honor for her school. A winner who almost spent the day in I.S.S.

In the years to follow Ryan won several more awards in the PTA Reflections program. He performed in the school talent show two years in a row. He appeared as a guest meteorologist on the local news. He won the third grade spelling bee and took home first prize in the city-wide science fair. And in between all these accomplishments, he scaled a bathroom stall, ran around his classroom when he was supposed to remain seated, shoved his peers, laughed too loud, sang too much, spoke out of turn, and disrupted instruction on numerous occasions with his silly antics.

Ups and downs. Twists and turns. Highs and lows.

I fall, recover, and get back on the bike.

Ryan is 10 years old now and in the fourth grade. I still love my Mondays and Ryan still loves jumping on the bed. Despite his additional seven inches and 24 pounds our ceiling hasn't caved in. Years of experience have made the ride easier. With the support of my family and an amazing boy by my side I continue to hold on tight, bracing myself for whatever's around the next bend.

The author says:

I dedicate this essay to the incredible boy who has taught me so much in our 10 years together and continues to prove that anything is possible.

Tell Us More: Expert Q & A with Peter Gray, Ph.D.

Research Professor of Psychology, Boston College; author of the *Freedom to Play* blog, *Psychology Today*

Q. In "Holding On," seven year old Ryan can't stay seated, laughs too loudly, sings too much, and speaks out of turn. Several of our parent-writers claim that their spirited children's differences weren't identified as problematic until kindergarten or first grade, when they were expected to sit on a square of carpet, keep their hands and feet to themselves, color inside the lines, and so on. Could you comment on their observations?

A. There is indication that diagnoses are being made earlier and earlier as time goes on. In fact, increasingly, diagnoses are being made during the preschool years, for kids who are in academically oriented preschools. I've heard of children as young as three years old, in some cases even two, being put on Ritalin or other stimulants. This is the result of our pushing of "academic" work to ever earlier ages and our increasing intolerance of normal childhood play.

Q. Are the structure and expectations of public school too one-size-fits-all, in other words, does school actually create the problem? Are there kids who take meds in order to succeed at school who wouldn't need meds if schools could adapt to their learning styles?

A. The diagnostic criteria for ADHD make it clear that this is very much a school problem. Many of the official diagnostic symptoms have to do specifically with school behavior: e.g. "Makes careless mistakes in schoolwork;" "Often does not follow instructions and fails to finish schoolwork;" "Often gets up from seat when remaining in seat is expected;" "Often blurts out answers before questions have been finished." Most diagnoses are initiated by teachers, who suggest to parents that their child has ADHD.

In a survey I conducted of people homeschooling or "unschooling" a child diagnosed with ADHD, only six of the 28 families who responded reported that their ADHD-diagnosed child was still on any sort of medication for this condition. Of the remaining 22 individuals, 13 were never medicated and nine had been medicated previously, when they were students in a traditional school, but were successfully removed from medication after they were removed from the traditional school. The majority of those responding said that their children learned well without medication as long as they (the children) were in charge of their own learning. For the full report, see "Experiences of ADHD-Labeled Kids Who Switch from Conventional Schooling to Homeschooling or Unschooling," (Peter Gray, *Freedom to Learn*, Psychology Today Blogs, Sept. 19, 2010; http://www.psychologytoday.com/blog/freedom-learn/201009/experiences-adhd-labeled-kids-who-switch-conventional-schooling-homeschool).

It appears that in situations where students can take charge of their own learning, most of those currently diagnosed with ADHD can learn very well—in some cases exceedingly well—without medication. However, this requires a radical change from current school policies, not just minor adjustments.

Q. On the other side of that hypothesis: don't children need to follow those rules in order to get along in society?

A. The evidence I have seen suggests that most kids diagnosed with ADHD are quite capable of following the rules of society in general. In no other normal setting in our society are rules as restrictive and unreasonable as they are in standard schools, where students are confined to their seats for inordinate periods and are asked to do many hours of busywork that serves no constructive purpose. Most people with ADHD are very good at responding to realistic demands on their time in the workplace, as long as it serves some purpose that makes sense to them. Most have no particular difficulty following the general laws and customs of society, though they may be, on average, more inclined to push the edges than are others.

The Great Third Grade AIDS Scare
by Michael Shay

In August 1993, when we moved from Wyoming to Maryland, our son, Kevin, attended his third school in four years. It's no picnic to move cross-country. And changing schools can be traumatic. But my wife, Chris, and I looked forward to sending our son to third grade at a new school, in a new town, in a new state.

Kevin had already cut a swath through schools in two states. His ADHD-inspired hyperactivity and impulsiveness got in the way of learning and friendships and almost everything else. Children were scared of "The Tornado Known as Kevin." A Denver daycare kicked him out for biting other kids. At kindergarten in Fort Collins, Colorado, Kevin had pushed fellow students off of the slide and jungle gym. During soccer games he had a tendency to kick the players instead of the ball. The teacher had no choice but to keep him inside during recess. He sat at a desk coloring. He needed exercise, as do all "hyper kids." He craved movement. But there he was, sitting at a desk coloring.

His first grade teacher in Cheyenne, Wyoming had been an angel. His second grade teacher at the same school, well, she was the opposite of an angel. She would not abide by the terms of Kevin's Individualized Education Plan (I.E.P.). She would sit in the team meetings and nod approvingly during the I.E.P. discussion. Back in the classroom, she belched fire at Kevin. Chris and I finally had to get the principal to intervene. Looking back, we should have changed teachers.

When you have a child with ADHD, you spend a lot of time looking back.

We liked the new school in Montgomery County, Maryland; a nifty little schoolhouse on a tree-lined street in Smartville, a town with its own quaint train station. We didn't live in Smartville. We lived nearby in the slightly less picturesque town of Rockville. The bus picked up and dropped off Kevin at the end of our street.

Things were going pretty well at Smartville Elementary until The Great Third Grade AIDS Scare.

It began when Kevin's teacher asked for volunteers for "Student of the Week." Kevin was the first to raise his hand. He didn't just *raise* his hand, of course. He waved it as if he'd been shipwrecked and was trying to signal the rescue ship. *Over here! Me me me! Over here!*

The teacher, a kindly woman nearing retirement, knew that Kevin had ADHD and took Ritalin, the number one drug for hyper kids back in the 1990s. He took 15 milligrams (one white pill, one yellow) in the morning and 15 milligrams after lunch. She'd been briefed on Kevin's medication and impulsiveness and hyperactivity.

> **When you have a child with ADHD, you spend a lot of time looking back.**

According to Kevin his teacher assigned his classmates to conduct an interview. They asked Kevin about his origins, his likes and dislikes, his hobbies and his family. The class scribe wrote it all down and gave it to the teacher. Since the teacher's hobby was calligraphy she dutifully transferred Kevin's answers onto a "Student of the Week" poster. She must have been stumped by the last item on the list: "I have AIDS and I take Ritalin for it."

The teacher might have chuckled about the student scribe's silly mistake. On the poster she left off any mention of ADHD and Ritalin.

But the word was out. The scribe told her parents about her new classmate with AIDS. Her parents told others. The next day the school principal fielded calls from concerned third grade mothers and fathers. The principal told them all the same thing: "The boy in question does not have AIDS, but ADHD." Then she had to describe ADHD. The parents apparently had a much better grasp on sexually transmitted diseases than neurobiological malfunctions.

It was not so easy to defuse a rumor based on mistaken initials, especially back in 1993 when those initials carried such weight.

That didn't faze Nikki, a girl from the Philippines in Kevin's class. She asked Kevin to come to her birthday party. Kevin was excited about the party.

"I'm the only boy!" he told Chris when he came home from school. "We're going swimming!" He always spoke with plenty of exclamation marks (and still does).

Kevin loved swimming. It was a medium for movement and a friend in all its forms. He loved to swim, dive, body surf, skate, sled, ski. He could jump into water and glide through it like a dolphin. When it froze, he could reach dizzying speeds on the sharpened edges of skates. And skiing! The first time he strapped on a pair of skis he aimed himself down the beginner's hill and only the hay bales at the bottom stopped him. He had never asked about stopping, thinking all the time about going, just going.

Kevin didn't care that the upcoming party was all girls. He was just glad to be part of the group, even if they all thought he had an incurable blood-borne virus. He was glad that the party was at a pool.

A few days later Nikki's mom called Chris. Nikki's mom asked about Kevin's AIDS. Chris was surprised that this issue had not been resolved. She told Nikki's mom that Kevin had ADHD and not AIDS. She explained his history. It was a long conversation.

Chris filled me in when I came home from work. I wondered how all these brainiacs could be so dense. The students at Smartville Elementary School were the sons and daughters of researchers working nearby at the National Institutes of Health campus, or doctors at Walter Reed Army Hospital, or bureaucrats (like me) working on projects for various federal agencies. They came from all over the world. The school boasted that its students represented more than 50 cultures. Instead of holding a fall carnival, Smartville Elementary held an International Day. Students wore native dress and brought in native foods. Chris and I attended with our baby daughter, Annie. I marveled at this mini-United Nations, reveled in the food and costumes. A real diversity stew. Kevin's classmates came from El Salvador and Kenya and India and even Maryland. Kevin did his best to represent Wyoming's exotic cowboy culture.

As it turned out, Kevin did not go to the swimming party. He brought home no official invitation from Nikki. Nothing arrived in our mailbox. The date for the birthday arrived. We asked him about it. He said that Nikki didn't like him anymore and told him not to come to the party.

We were sad for him. That night we found a babysitter for Annie and took Kevin out to dinner and then swimming at the local rec center. Kevin spent most of his time leaping from the high dive. I kicked myself for not bringing the video camera to film his jumps. Chris and I liked to watch him on the VCR in slow motion. It was the only time we could linger on his expressions. Movement lent an unmistakable aura to that face.

When he was moving, he had the face of an angel.

The author says:

Our loveable, hyperactive, and now-grown-up son Kevin is a student and works in the technical theatre department at Pima Community College in Tucson. His most recent stage role was as Willie, a "marble game maniac" in William Saroyan's 1939 play, The Time of Your Life.

More Cory Stories

by Jeanne Kraus

My son, Cory, now 29, was diagnosed with attention deficit hyperactivity disorder (ADHD) when he was six years old. Nicknamed "Taz" because his whirling dervish energy level reminded us of the cartoon character the Tasmanian Devil, Cory had the classic symptoms of ADHD; hyperactivity, inattention, and impulsivity. His early life events inspired me to write *Cory Stories: A Kid's Book About Living With ADHD,* published by Magination Press in 2005. Throughout his childhood Cory provided me with many more "Cory Stories."

Impulsivity causes kids with ADHD to act and speak before they think. This spontaneous style makes life rather trying for their parents. By the age of three Cory had earned a reputation for acting impulsively at the school where I taught. After school one day Cory visited my fourth grade classroom. The next thing I knew the fire alarm was going off. Somehow Cory had left the room without me noticing and had pulled a fire alarm in the hallway. My son singlehandedly evacuated an entire elementary school staff.

So it was no surprise that I was a nervous wreck when we attended the faculty picnic with the kids later that same year. Of course, I kept my super-mom eyes trained on Cory. Relaxing at social events was for other moms. I couldn't relax; I never knew what Cory would do next. Somehow, on that day my eagle eyes failed me.

My boss, the principal, called out, "Mrs. Kraus, where are you?"

Within full view of the entire faculty and staff, Cory, pants around his ankles, was letting loose a stream of urine, watering a patch of grass. It's now 25 years later and friends and colleagues still like to remind me of that incident.

Impulsivity keeps a seven-day-a-week schedule; it doesn't rest on Sundays. When Cory was four years old he sang in the church junior choir. Blonde and tiny, he resembled an angel when singing. One morning the children's choir marched up the aisle and assembled at the altar. Cory stood dead center in the front row. I'm not sure why, but for one song the children praised God by playing kazoos. As the kazoo interlude ended Cory stored his kazoo between his legs. There he stood, singing with all his angelic heart into the microphone with a kazoo sticking out between his legs. I slumped down into my pew as a ripple of chuckles ran through the congregation.

Kids with ADHD often seem to be afflicted with verbal diarrhea. Serene, thoughtful moments didn't exist for our family. From early in the morning till blessed bedtime "Cory Chatter" filled any quiet time that might have been. His older brother, Jeff, trying to get a word in edgewise, pointed out to him,

[**Relaxing at social events was for other moms. I couldn't relax; I never knew what Cory would do next.**]

"Not everything that enters your brain has to exit your mouth. Save some of your less important thoughts for yourself." But we remained Cory's captive audience for every thought, every emotion.

Like many kids with ADHD Cory had an active imagination and often embellished his stories for entertainment purposes. For months when Cory was about five years old we worried about his tales of having lived many lives before this one. At bedtime I was tucking him in.

"My other mother used to do that, too." Cory grinned up at me, his tooth gaps evident.

I sat down on the edge of the bed. "What other mother?"

"You know, in my other life. Well, in one of them anyway."

"How many other lives have you lived?"

"Oh, 89 or so. No, maybe 68. I can't remember. There were too many."

This prompted a panicked conference with my husband. We determined it was just "Cory Talk." Previous lives were not something Cory had heard anyone talk about in our home; we were just trying to muddle through this life.

Cory didn't mention his previous lives again until we drove to Naples, Florida for a weekend a few weeks later. He pointed to a condominium.

"I used to live there."

"No, Honey," I replied. "We never lived here. It probably just reminds you of somewhere."

He was adamant. "I lived there with my other family in my other life." My husband almost ran the car off the road.

This time we consulted a psychologist. *What was wrong with our child?* He told us to give Cory more one-on-one attention. It worked. His previous life discussions ended.

Some of Cory's uncensored public pronouncements were tragically true, like when he left the pediatrician's office and detoured over to a woman in the waiting room. He lifted up his shirt, stuck out his stomach, and said, "I have scabies!" I wanted to die.

Another time Cory and I picked out a beautiful necklace for his second grade teacher. (Cory's teachers scored big-time on holidays and Teacher Appreciation Day; combat pay for their extraordinary patience.)

Mrs. Clayton loved the necklace, and said, "Cory, you shouldn't have!"

"Oh, don't worry," he told her. "Mom got it for half price." I couldn't face Gail Clayton for several days.

Cory's most famous faux pas happened in sixth grade. My husband and I attended an open house to meet his teachers. His science teacher was sniffing and pressing his nostril shut as he spoke. Unfortunately, Cory overheard our comments at home. The next day Mr. B asked the kids how their parents liked Open House. Cory shared with the whole class that his parents suspected that Mr. B was a cocaine user.

By middle school I thought I had Cory dead center figured out. Cory wanted to take his hockey stick to school. He said his PE teacher asked students who had a hockey stick at home to bring it to school for practice. I wasn't born yesterday.

"Absolutely not!" I said. I could just see Cory bopping some kid in the head, causing massive head trauma. And I was going to put the weapon in his hands? I didn't think so.

Cory begged. "Come on, Mom. Please!"

> Cory's teachers scored big-time on holidays and Teacher Appreciation Day; combat pay for their extraordinary patience.

I was a rock. "No! You know what could happen. Forget it."

Then Cory zoomed in for the kill. "Mom, you need to give me chances to be more responsible. How am I ever going to learn if you don't let me try? I promise no one will get hurt."

Well, he had hit the "Mom Button," the one that says you have to believe in your kids sometimes, even if they pee at picnics and set off fire alarms. I didn't like it, but the writing was on the wall. So Cory set off for school with his hockey stick and 101 warnings about what not to do with it. He came home, slouching, clutching the dreaded yet familiar referral form.

"Oh, no!" I grabbed the referral. My biggest fear had materialized. The coach had written: *for hitting another student with a hockey stick.* My heart was broken. I could have prevented this catastrophe. I began to grill Cory, preparing to call the school and ask about the condition of the other student.

Then Cory laughed and said, "April Fool, Mom!"

Well, it *was* April first, but my brain could not wrap itself around the possibility that this was just a prank. Finally, with a little corroboration from the coach, who had been in on it the whole time, Cory convinced me that it was a joke.

Kids with ADHD often have trouble with social skills. For years we practiced appropriate responses with Cory. We attempted to become models of perfect social etiquette. Now Cory, all grown up at age 29, works for Apple and is very involved with customer service. He is amazing at working with people. Who would have predicted that?

As an adult Cory still has impulsive moments. Impulsive spending became a problem when Cory first moved away from home, but with the help of an ADD life coach he learned to manage his money. He is a responsible driver, employee, and a wonderful son.

Cory and I have reversed roles now that we are both older. I have reached the age where it is my turn to say whatever's on my mind, socially appropriate or otherwise. As a matter of fact, Cory is frequently embarrassed by my comments and behavior. There you have it – we've come full circle. It's all good.

The author says:

This essay is dedicated to Cory, for letting me tell so many "Cory Stories," which provide inspiration and stress relief to parents and other kids dealing with ADHD issues. Cory is now 30 years old, works for Apple computers and is happily married.

Eve Speaks:

"Javi's teachers don't have extra time or patience. They aren't interested in finding a way to press his reset button. They aren't going to sit him down after his many daily crashes to help him sort through the wreckage, attempt to understand what key actions or behaviors pushed him down that course to start with, and come up with some solutions to keep it from happening again. What they will do is call out his name with furrowed brows and angry voices. They will skip warnings, because their nerves are worn raw and he just won't stop singing, interrupting their lessons, talking out of turn, touching the students around him, tossing paper balls into the air, and talking back."

Kelly Quiñones Miller, mom of Javier (ADHD)

Insights by Moonlight
by Elizabeth Moore

My daughter, Kate, has Asperger's syndrome, and at times her anxiety winds around her like a tangling vine. It seems like just as I disentangle one snarl, the world puts an extra twist on another.

One day, when Kate was in third grade, I attended a meeting at her school. Afterwards, I climbed in my car and was about to leave when I spotted her. The students were outside for recess, and Kate stood alone at the edge of the playground with a handful of leaves, watching as the other kids played hopscotch and jump rope and circled the schoolyard like flocks of birds.

Do what you've learned, I urged her silently. Most children know instinctively how to approach other kids and join in a group, but kids with Asperger's often don't. Social deficits are a key component of the disorder. For years I'd been trying to teach Kate to use phrases like, "Can I play?" and "Look what I found!" as ways to initiate interactions with others, but role playing is different from real life, and I was anxious to see if she could apply what we'd practiced.

I was happy when she finally approached a group of girls, put her hand out, and showed them the burning reds and oranges she held there. She kept her eyes on the pile of color, clearly pleased. The girls looked around at one another, and for a moment they were still. Then suddenly, hilarity burst forth. They laughed and fled, one big jumble of locked arms and skipping legs, hurrying off as fast as they could, leaving Kate with her clutch of leaves. She stood there for a moment watching them go, and then crouched down to resume her search.

Kate had been attending social skills groups since she was four, when we realized how difficult it was for her to interact with other kids. A psychologist had observed her at preschool and advised us to get specialized help. After an evaluation Kate began working with a speech therapist on receptive and expressive language difficulties, as well as an occupational therapist on sensory integration and social skills. Yet after all of this help, when she played with other kids she'd pull their hair and snatch toys from their hands. I had agonized over her behavior, but finally I began to see improvement. And now, after she'd worked so hard learning to share and be pleasant, the other kids wanted nothing to do with her. There was a time when she wouldn't have minded, when she was content to play by herself, but that wasn't the case anymore. Now, she longed for friends.

I wanted to run to her, admire her leaves, and show her how each one—with its special swirls of pattern and color—was a treasure. Or to tell her to get her books and come with me, to steal her away from school, on the pretext that I'd planned a surprise adventure for the two of us.

And then, as always, I remembered what I'd been taught.

"Give her room," the specialists we'd worked with had told me. "You can't protect her from the world."

Of course, I knew that. But what was she learning? That she wasn't good enough to attract one friend, or to get a compliment from her teacher? How were these life lessons helping? All I saw was her anxiety, like a big pile of rotting leaves, getting higher after each raking.

I started the car and drove away, leaving my heart in Kate's seven-year-old fist, in the collection of leaves that I knew she would try to sneak into her desk after recess. I hoped she would succeed, that the teacher wouldn't spot them and make her throw them out. I hoped she'd be able to run her fingers over the smooth, veiny surfaces of the leaves as she sat in class, struggling to stay in her seat and keep to herself, and then bring them home after school to show me.

It was a long day, as many days had been since we'd moved from California to Toronto the year before. Adding to the difficulty of adjusting to a new city, my husband, Greg, had taken a job out of town and commuted back and forth on weekends, leaving Kate and me alone during the week. I felt vulnerable that day, a feeling that was becoming more and more familiar. I kept my eye on the clock all afternoon, and when it was finally time, I went to pick Kate up from school. She raced to the car looking excited.

"Can Isabelle come over?" she begged, head poked through the open car window, her white hair bow slipping down from its place on top of her head.

"You're about to lose your bow," Isabelle's mom said.

"Can Isabelle come over, please?" Kate repeated, feeling for the bow on top of her head. The bow slipped from her fingers and fell to the ground. The mom picked it up and handed it to Kate. Then she raised her eyebrows as she looked at her daughter, who clearly didn't want to come over.

"We can't today," Isabelle's mother said, pushing her sunglasses up with the tip of a red nail. "Thanks, anyway. Say 'thank you,' Isabelle." As they walked away, the mom tilted her head towards us and said, "Maybe another day."

There was a tinge of discomfort in the words, a hint at the apology she'd never make. I knew there would be no other day with Isabelle, or with Megan, or any other girl in the class, but Kate didn't. She kept hoping, and I knew she would ask someone else the next day. The mother would say "no" in the same polite way as a waitress would say, "Sorry, there's no cherry pie left today, but we'll have some tomorrow." But the waitress would have given you the pie if she could have. It wasn't personal. She was telling the truth: there really would be cherry pie the next day.

Kate was gradually withering. Eventually, she stopped asking kids over, and it wasn't long after that when she stopped going to school regularly.

"School is not a choice," I'd say. But her childhood was becoming a series of headaches and stomachaches and sore throats, and she was getting too big for me to pick her up and put her in the car. When she stayed home she clung to me, wanting my attention. I had a hard time focusing on much of anything.

As Kate withered, I became exhausted. We found our way to a child psychiatrist, whom we both liked. She gave Kate an antidepressant for her anxiety, which helped some, but not enough to get her to school every day.

"Develop a passion and stick to it! Find friendships with other moms!" the psychiatrist advised me. Yet that was harder than it sounded. Since we'd moved I hadn't had the time to get to know many people. I didn't even have time to fold my laundry. How could I make friends? Develop a passion? The fact that I'd done neither made me feel as if I was failing yet again.

The psychiatrist said, "Have some fun!" But what did she know? She didn't have children tethered to her legs, holding on for dear life. Her kids weren't kicking and raging because they were unable to process their emotions. It's not that I blamed her. She was doing her job and was terrific, but she didn't really understand. I needed to figure out some things on my own.

Like my little girl, I felt a strong connection to the natural world and was drawn to participate in it. Bereft of energy and ideas to help Kate or myself, I started slipping outside, wanting only to sit, after Kate went to bed.

One night, when the rain that had fallen earlier had stopped, I sat down outside. I watched a glowing half-moon sail across the sky under windblown clouds like a rock skipping across water. The drops that hung from the leaves of the cherry tree winked as the light of the moon came and went. A rabbit made a beeline for the neighbor's hedge, and disappeared with a white glint of tail. What a night! I breathed it in, smiling as the wind lifted my hair. I sat outside for a long time, breathing in, breathing out, and felt the rain-washed air start to heal me.

I told Greg about that beautiful evening. I knew the sadness he often heard in my voice during our daily phone calls weighed him down, so that night I eagerly shared the details of those lovely moonlit moments.

Soon after, we had another wonderful phone conversation, this one about a fresh start for Kate. I'd thought that I didn't know how else to help her, but one night when I was outside watching the fall leaves skitter down and drift through the yard, and my mind grew quiet, I had a revelation: *I've got to get her out of that school.*

> I'd thought that I didn't know how else to help her, but one night I had a revelation: *I've got to get her out of that school.*

The school Kate attended was private, but it wasn't designed for children with special needs, and she wasn't getting the extra attention I had thought she might get there. The people at the school didn't appreciate her: not the teachers, not the students, not the parents, and she was beginning to follow suit and not like herself.

It took a while, but with Greg's approval, I moved Kate to a public school. Because she was afraid of this new place, we made a plan to diminish her anxiety. On her first day the special education teacher came out to the parking lot to take her in, and she stayed for just 15 minutes. At the end of the 15 minutes we celebrated her success.

After three months of spending longer and longer stretches of time at the new school, she is finally able to go full time. She has even made a friend—a girl who is like her, and who also loves collecting natural specimens. Together they search for grasshoppers, special rocks, and fall leaves. They are sometimes the brunt of jokes, but they notice less because they have each other.

Life at home has become a bit easier, although when Kate is too overwhelmed to do homework, too wound up to fall asleep, or yelling because she doesn't like my rules, I still have days when I barely make it, and she still has days when she's too anxious to go to school. Yet having some quiet to look forward to at the end of the day keeps me going, and being outdoors helps me make better decisions. The night air helps me grab a fresh perspective. You might say I've found a passion.

Greg is now home from his two year assignment. After work he shoots baskets with Kate or helps her with her homework. The time they spend together gives me some time to catch up, and to restore my energy—the energy I need to give Kate the extra support she requires. After she goes to bed, I still go outside, on my own, or sometimes with Greg, to watch a raccoon lumber across the street or to breathe in the scent of sand cherry blossoms. Refreshed, we catch up with each other and talk about how Kate is doing, often coming up with new ideas.

Someday I might just sign up for French cooking or fly off to a Swiss hillside with Greg to pick wild raspberries and listen to church bells chime. But for now, I'm happy taking in the night. It's amazing what some moonlight and a rustle of wind can do.

The author says:

I dedicate this essay to Michelle Benson. Her tremendous insight, support and professional competence have made a huge difference in our lives. As she's worked to help strengthen our family dynamics, she's done so with great respect and kindness. We will always be grateful to her.

Tell Us More: Expert Q & A with Kirk Martin

Behavioral therapist, author, and founder of CelebrateCalm.com

Q. Why might teachers see a different side of a child than the parents see at home?

A. The school environment often exploits our kids' weaknesses—they struggle with sitting still, recalling information, auditory processing, social skills and anxiety. It takes extraordinary emotional energy to hold it together. Parents' first question after school is, "How was school? Ready to do homework?" Cue the meltdown! After school, ask your children about their passions and interests. Get them engaged using their talents, exercise with them, and provide an emotional release.

Here's another way to look at this behavior: If you think about it, it is no surprise that children behave differently at school. After all, don't we behave differently at work? We sometimes yell and scream—in essence, throw our own tantrums—at home, but we would never be caught acting the same way when facing frustration at work. It's normal for all of us to behave differently in different environments.

Q. Not all parents have the option of moving their child to a different school. How would you change schools so that our kids would fit in and succeed?

A. Here's the tragic part. With even two hours of training, we have shown thousands of teachers how to help kids who struggle with anxiety, ODD, sensory issues, ADHD, and Asperger's be very successful in the classroom. Without insight into why our kids process information more slowly, are distracted by sensory input, or shut down with anxiety, teachers may assume our kids are being lazy, undisciplined, unmotivated, or purposefully difficult.

We don't need new schools or more money. Teachers just need simple, practical tools—using rhythm to improve processing, doing chair push-ups to relieve aggression, or giving specific, concrete jobs to overcome anxiety—to transform challenging children into classroom leaders. Students equipped with this understanding can take ownership of their academic and behavioral choices.

ADHD Supergirl
by Frank South

"I can't do this! I can't! I'm too *stupid!* My teacher will hate me!"

My daughter, Coco, loves her seventh grade social studies teacher, which makes this particular looming homework disaster feel even worse.

"She'll hate me and give me an F!" she yells, tears welling.

When my wife, Margaret, tries to help her, Coco lashes out, throwing her planner down, and running out of the room.

"Leave me alone. You don't know *anything.* I can't do this. It's *impossible!*"

Coco has attention deficit hyperactivity disorder (ADHD). So do I, and so does my 21-year-old son. My wife is the only "normal" one in the family, except the dog, and we're not too sure about him. But Coco and I are almost symptom twins. We also have very similar temperaments and mindsets, and consequently are pretty close as fathers and daughters go. During this crisis I'm away on business, and I try to help when Margaret puts Coco on the phone.

First I tell her, like Margaret had just told her as well, "You are not in any way stupid. You are very smart."

Behind the sniffles and ragged breathing I can hear that Coco wants to believe this, but it's not sticking. The evidence in front of her right now is too overwhelming. So I remind her of the miraculous progress she's pulled off in the last years.

And it was miraculous. Besides ADHD, Coco also has to deal with learning disabilities (LD), like pretty severe dyslexia, and some comorbid memory issues that are similar to mine. And, a hair-trigger temper that's very similar to mine.

For years it seemed as though she'd never be able to read or write. In second grade she still couldn't recognize letters. It was a daily frustrating and heartbreaking struggle for her as she worked at it at home with us, in school with her teachers, and after school with tutors. There were days where she'd seem to get it—recognize letters and words and how sentences worked—and then the next day it'd be gone again.

"I can't do this! I can't! I'm too *stupid*," she'd cry, imprisoned by constant defeat. Each time we'd continue the patient encouragement, always reassuring her that she wasn't stupid at all. We told her that soon she'd be able to understand, though we too were beginning to lose faith that that day would ever come.

> When an "ADHD Perfect Storm" of missed assignments, overdue work, broken promises, and final deadlines hits [these kids] call themselves stupid and lazy—and worse—before anyone else can.

Then, when she was 11 years old, Coco somehow put it all together, and seemingly overnight made a startling breakthrough in reading and writing. Of course it wasn't overnight. Breaking through this barrier was the cumulative result of the years of her hard work combined with the mystery of the growing adolescent brain.

By the beginning of seventh grade she wrote for school assignments, and wrote stories about her life. She was able to read above grade level and read like crazy for enjoyment, going through books from the whole *Twilight* vampire series to the juvenile delinquent classic, *The Outsiders*, to the death and disaster-filled *The History of Shipwrecks*. She likes her reading with a little edge.

Coco had worked hard and had busted through a huge barrier not only in reading and writing, but also a barrier of defeat that had held her confidence and hope hostage to an unrelenting internal judge, constantly denigrating her self-image. She broke that pattern when she accomplished what had for so long seemed impossible, and she reawakened her natural curiosity and openness as well.

Then came the end of the spring semester of seventh grade.

Despite our help and her dedication to checking her planner during the semester, Coco had lost or not completed overdue homework in math, English, and science. But, I remind her over the phone, "You buckled down in the last couple of weeks, went to study hall and got it all turned in."

"So what?" Coco yells, interrupting my long distance pep talk. "All that's ancient history. Tonight is tonight and tomorrow I'm *dead!*"

Tomorrow is the last day of the school year. She's completely spaced the end of year social studies report and PowerPoint presentation on the history of Norfolk Island. She hasn't even started it. And she's told her teacher she knows how to make a PowerPoint presentation, when in fact she doesn't have the first clue. And it's six p.m. and the whole mess is due first thing the next morning.

Everybody, and certainly every junior high school kid, has faced a similar dismal landscape of looming disaster. But sometimes my daughter, and other kids with ADHD and learning disabilities, face that landscape knowing that no matter what they accomplish, there are so many landmines of demoralizing surprises ahead of them that failure seems preordained. They get worn down with the immense effort it takes to do what they expect of themselves. So when an "ADHD Perfect Storm" of missed assignments, overdue work, broken promises, and final deadlines hits them, they call themselves stupid and lazy—and worse—before anyone else can. And then they fall back behind the barriers they've worked so hard to break down, and are once again trapped, but protected, inside the walls of their low expectations.

These are the times that try kids' souls.

Coco is understandably in despair, lashing out in panic when her mom or I try to help or encourage her. She's trapped back in the barriers of constant expectations of failure that many ADHD and LD kids and adults know too well. I try to do what I can to help keep this from being a defeat that defines the end of this school year for her, but being a dad over the phone is not the same thing as being a dad who's there—not by a long shot. I have to hang up and wait to hear how it will turn out.

Three hours later I get a call from my wife and daughter. Facing a tidal wave of impossibility, Coco, unaware she was doing it, pulled out the ADHD secret weapon: hyperfocus.

> Facing a tidal wave of impossibility, Coco, unaware she was doing it, pulled out the ADHD secret weapon: hyperfocus.

After finally allowing her mom to show her how to make a basic PowerPoint page, Coco demanded to be left alone to figure the rest out, do her research, write her report, and make her presentation. Over the next couple of hours she typed and moused away, never leaving the computer, never taking her eyes off the screen, mumbling and musing to herself over interesting things she'd found, or new ideas she'd come up with as she worked. Never once did she get distracted or bored, or even notice anything in the world except her social studies project. And with self-doubt and second-guessing banished due to some kind of emergency decree in her head, she blazed through it.

Margaret said it was an amazing thing to witness. Coco didn't see what was so amazing, but she was proud and happy that her report was done and the PowerPoint was safely tucked onto a flash drive for school in the morning. The self-hatred and panic banished, she and her mom were now going to have some ice cream and then get some sleep.

We'll keep working on the organizational and other skills to deal with the procrastination problems, but this time Coco's ADHD hyperfocus saved the day, and by the way, she got an A on the project.

With all the sometimes overwhelming challenges that ADHD presents to children and adults, it seems only fair that it also can give us an awesome positive ability to pull out when we need to bust through the barriers, and realize we're not stupid, lazy, or crazy after all. We might even have superpowers.

A version of this essay first appeared on the blog: ADHD Dad: Better Late than Never *(http://www.add.itudemag.com/adhdblogs/6).*

Tell Us More: Expert Q & A with Patricia Quinn, M.D.

Developmental Pediatrician, Director, National Center for Girls and Women with ADHD, Washington, DC

Q. One of your areas of expertise is girls and women with ADHD. How is the experience of ADHD different for girls? How does puberty tend to effect girls with ADHD? Is this also true of boys?

A. Unfortunately, hormonal fluctuations only complicate the picture for girls with ADHD. When estrogen levels fall premenstrually, they precipitate a drop in the brain's monoamine chemical neurotransmitters, dopamine and serotonin. Lower levels of dopamine result in an increase in ADHD symptoms (premenstrual magnification), while a decrease in serotonin leads to PMS and depressed mood. In addition to the hormonal roller coaster, girls must also deal with a central nervous system that matures earlier than males and doesn't seem to have much room for positive organizational changes during puberty. Male brains tend to be larger than female brains (even after making allowances for smaller female size overall) with more cells that can then undergo excessive pruning and reorganizing during puberty. For males symptoms of ADHD tend to decrease during puberty while for females ADHD symptoms increase. In adolescent girls with ADHD, puberty may also be complicated by depression, anxiety, substance abuse, other risk-taking behaviors, and eating disorders, which emerge at that time.

Report Card Blues
By Frank South

My 14-year-old daughter, Coco, brought her report card home last night, and it's fine: an A, the rest B's and two C's. If I'd had a report card like that at her age I would have strutted home with banners flying in front of a brass band.

But Coco's not proud at all. She's miserable. She buries her head in a pillow crying hard, then hugs it to her chest, doing her best to hold her tears and sobs under control. Coco is embarrassed by her raging sorrow breaking out all over in front of people, especially her parents. Especially me, because she says I get too emotional. But tonight she's invited me into this intense mother-daughter talk. Coco's cross-legged on our bed next to her mom, with me planted at the foot, under strict instructions not to interrupt, or get all gooey—hug her and tell her how brilliant and talented she is. All she wants me to do is to listen to her. My wife, the only non-ADHD "normal" in the family, already knows how to listen, so she gets a pass on the instructions.

As Coco starts telling us what's going on, I'm not even tempted to interrupt or get gooey, because I discover, as I have repeatedly in the last year or so, that my daughter's not a kid anymore. I'm listening to a smart, perceptive young woman with a clear idea of what's making her so deeply unhappy. And what she wants—more than us trying to jump in and make it all better—is for her mom and dad to sit here, be patient, and hear her out completely.

No matter what we say, she knows her grades should be better.

"I'm trying hard, and then just as I start to get it, somebody says something, or something happens in the classroom, and everything gets nuts. And then I forget what the teacher was saying and I have to start all over, but then it's too late. A lot of the other kids in special ed, mostly the boys, just don't care about learning anything. They swear all the time, talk sex junk, call their moms bitches—the teacher can't really control them. I can't take it anymore."

It turns out that today one of the boys in study hall kept taunting and goading her and she hauled off and punched him in the arm. She accepts that she was wrong. She understands that you can't hit people no matter how aggravating they are—a lesson I finally got through my own thick skull sometime in my twenties. But the fact remains that she's desperately unhappy and frustrated in school, and she's come up with a solution.

"I want to be homeschooled for the rest of the semester," she says.

Now, this middle school has a bunch of dedicated teachers in special ed, and our meetings with them about strategies to help with Coco's ADHD and dyslexia, and starting to slowly mainstream Coco have been great. But Coco wants to be able to get away from all the social pressure and craziness at school, and study at home until she starts high school in the fall, after we've moved to Georgia.

> Crosby, Stills, and Nash had it wrong, I think. It's not: "Teach your children well." It's: "Shut up and listen."

I remember middle school being a nightmare when I was in eighth grade, but I don't remember thinking as clearly about solutions. I just brooded in my room, working out revenge scenarios where I was the wise-cracking TV gambler Maverick and the other kids were dimwit losers.

Coco looks at us from behind her hugged pillow, waiting to hear our response. She doesn't look too hopeful. I can imagine what she'd think we'd say to her idea. Something along the line of, "Are you out of your mind, sweetheart?"

But Margaret and I look at each other for a second, and then turn back to Coco.

"Okay."

"Okay?" Coco asks, a little stunned.

"Yep, if that's what you want, we'll call the school tomorrow."

Coco smiles.

"Thanks," she says "Thanks a lot, really." Then she looks down at the pillow in her arms. "I guess I better wash this. It's soaked."

Margaret and I scoot together and hold hands, watching Coco as she walks out of our bedroom.

Crosby, Stills, and Nash had it wrong, I think. It's not: "Teach your children well." It's: "Shut up and listen."

A version of this essay first appeared on the blog: ADHD Dad: Better Late than Never *(http://www.additudemag.com/adhdblogs/6).*

Walking Away
by Laura Weldon

I hesitated before opening the heavy glass doors and leaving my son Kirby's school. I'd cheerfully walked in and out through these doors many times. I volunteered here, served on the PTA board, joked with the principal and teachers, even helped start an annual tradition called Art Day. But now I fought the urge to grab Kirby from his first grade classroom and never return.

I'd come in that morning hoping to discuss the angry outbursts my son's first grade teacher had been directing at several students, including my little boy. But I entered no ordinary meeting. It was an ambush. Sides had clearly been chosen. The principal, guidance counselor, and Kirby's teacher sat in a clump

> **A conclusion had been reached without consulting me, my husband, or a mental health professional. My son required one vital ingredient in order to flourish in school: pharmaceuticals.**

along one side of the table. Feeling oddly hollow, as if my insides had been replaced by clouds of anxiety, I pulled out a chair across from them and sat down. Since I led conflict resolution workshops in my working life, I'd entered the room confident that we could talk over any issue and come to an understanding. I was wrong.

The counselor read aloud from a list of behavioral indicators of attention deficit hyperactivity disorder (ADHD) that Kirby's teacher had been tracking over the past few weeks. My little boy's major transgressions were messy work, lack of organization, and distractibility. The teacher nodded with satisfaction as the counselor finished reading, and crossed her arms over her chest.

No one had ever mentioned ADHD before.

I breathed deeply to calm myself. I gathered my thoughts, preparing to repeat what I was hearing in order to clarify, but the counselor barreled ahead, saying they had "a significant ADHD population" in the school system who showed excellent results with medication.

I gave the teacher kudos for dealing with a classroom full of children, and acknowledged the difficulty of meeting all their needs. Then, feeling like a mother bear defending her cub from nicely dressed predators, I tried to politely stand up for my child.

"Kirby's behavior," I said, "seems pretty normal for a six-year-old boy. Kids mature unevenly. He's very responsible in most ways, but reluctant to do worksheets."

The teacher shook her head and whispered to the principal.

The counselor spoke up. "First grade children have had ample time to adapt to classroom standards."

"Have any of Kirby's behaviors ever disrupted the class?" I asked.

The teacher didn't answer the question. Instead she sighed and said, looking more at the two men in the room than at me, "I've been teaching for 15 years. This doesn't get better on its own. I'm telling you this child can be helped by medication."

When I asked about alternatives, such as modifying Kirby's diet, the teacher actually rolled her eyes. "Plenty of parents believe there are all sorts of things they can do on their own. But students on restricted diets don't fit in too well in the lunchroom."

There was no real discussion. No chance to bring up her teaching style. A conclusion had been reached without consulting me, my husband, or a mental health professional. My son required one vital ingredient in order to flourish in school: pharmaceuticals.

As I stood at the door, my heart pounding in distress, I vowed to solve this problem rationally. I told myself such an approach would help my child and other misunderstood students. I made it all the way to the car without crying.

Over the next few weeks I took Kirby to several doctors. After only one appointment a psychologist diagnosed him with ADD. She tucked her written report in a stack of handouts from a national non-profit organization known for its ties to the pharmaceutical industry.

An allergist diagnosed Kirby with multiple food allergies, including almost every fruit and grain he liked to eat. And, a pediatric pulmonologist determined that Kirby's asthma was much worse than we'd known. In fact, the doctor said Kirby's oxygen intake was so poor that our little boy was likely to change position frequently, lift his arms to expand his lungs, and have trouble concentrating.

> **His third grade teacher deemed him an underachiever and pulled his desk next to hers, right in front of the whole class. That's where he spent the rest of the school year. His last school year.**

Kirby began intensive asthma treatment, and I started the process of eliminating allergens from his diet. I also researched. I began to see childhood learning in a wider way, as I read authors such as Joseph Chilton Pearce, David Elkind, and John Taylor Gatto. I talked to other parents who described managing ADHD using star charts, privilege restriction, immediate consequences for behavior, and maintaining close communication with teachers. Many parents told me their child's problems got worse during the teen years. Some described sons and daughters they'd "lost" to drug abuse, delinquency, chronic depression, and dangerous rage. One woman told me her 14-year-old son was caught dealing. The boy sold amphetamines so strong they were regulated by the Controlled Substance Act—his own prescription for a stimulant used to treat ADHD.

And I spent a lot of time observing my son's behavior. Yes, he was disorganized with his schoolwork. His room was often a mess too, but only because he had so many interests. I saw no lack of focus as he drew designs for imaginary vehicles, pored over diagrams in adult reference books, or created elaborate make-believe scenarios. I knew that he was easily frustrated by flash cards and timed math tests, methods that did little to advance his understanding. But I also knew that he easily applied math concepts to projects, such as designing his own models out of scrap wood. And, of course, he was distractible, and like most small children he resisted rote tasks. His mind and body naturally tuned in to more engaging stimulus.

But mostly I noticed how cooperative and cheerful he was. He didn't whine, easily waited for his turn, and loved to help with chores. As an admittedly biased observer, I found him to be a marvelous six-year-old.

Resolutely, I tried to make school workable. I let the teacher know how my son's allergies and asthma might impact his classroom abilities. I shared the psychologist's report. And I explained our home situation. In the past year our family had been victimized by crime, Kirby's father had been injured in a car accident and left unable to work, and several other loved ones had been hospitalized. I suggested that Kirby's untidy school work might be a reflection of a life that suddenly seemed messy and disorganized.

The teacher, however, only told me what my son did wrong. She was particularly incensed that he rushed through his work or left it incomplete, only to spend time cleaning up scraps from the floor. She did not find his efforts helpful. In clipped tones she said, "Each student is supposed to pick up only his or her scraps. *Nothing more.*"

My son's backpack sagged each day with 10 or more preprinted and vaguely educational papers, all with fussy instructions. *Cut out the flower on the dotted lines, cut two slits here, color the flower, cut and paste this face on the flower, insert the flower in the two slots, write three sentences about the flower using at least five words from the "st" list.* I'd have been looking for scraps on the floor to clean up too, anything to get away from a day filled with such assignments.

I spent another two years watching my child try to please his teachers and be himself in two different school systems that were, by necessity, not designed to handle individual differences. He put minimal effort into assignments, doing only as well as was needed to get by, except when the project at hand intrigued him. He appreciated the cheerful demeanor of his third grade teacher, who told me she didn't expect much from him, until his Iowa Test of Basic Skills

> Gradually I recognized that Kirby learned in a complex, deeply focused, and yes, apparently disorganized manner.

results came back with scores in the 98th and 99th percentiles. Then she deemed him an underachiever and pulled his desk next to hers, right in front of the whole class, to make sure he paid attention rather than look out the window or fiddle with odd and ends he'd found. That's where he spent the rest of the school year.

His last school year.

When Kirby was eight years old I took my children out of school forever.

Homeschooling didn't "fix" anything for Kirby, at least not right away. I made many of the mistakes I saw teachers make in school. I assigned projects that meant nothing to him. I used flashcards that did little to help him understand math. I cajoled him to sit still and get his work done. And I saw the same behaviors his teachers described. Every day, he sat at the kitchen table, a few pages left to finish before we headed off to the park or some other adventure. But then he'd drop his pencil so he could climb under the table after it, erase holes in his paper, or find a focal point out the window for his daydreams. He complained as if worksheets were mental thumbscrews. I would lie awake at night afraid that he'd never be able to do long division.

Yet every time I stepped back and allowed Kirby to pursue his own interests he picked up complicated concepts beautifully. I watched him design his own rockets; figure out what materials he needed, put them together carefully, and start over if he made mistakes. Gradually I realized his "problem" was my insistence he learn as I had done—from a static page.

The further I stepped back, the more I saw how much my son accomplished when fueled by his own curiosity. This little boy played chess, took apart broken appliances, helped on our farm, and checked out piles of books at the library each week. He memorized the names of historic aircraft and the scientific principles explaining flight, filled notebooks with cartoons and designs—and he was learning every moment.

Gradually I recognized that Kirby learned in a complex, deeply focused, and yes, apparently disorganized manner. It wasn't the way I'd learned in school, but it was the way he learned best. His whole life taught him—in ways magnificently and perfectly structured to suit him, and him alone. As I relaxed into our homeschooling life, Kirby flourished. Sometimes his intense interests fueled busy days. Other times it seemed he did very little. Those were times that richer wells of understanding developed.

But I sank back into worrying and nagging Kirby about the need to cover school-like topics more intensely during his last year at home before college. Although his homeschool years had been filled with rich learning experiences, I suddenly worried that he'd done too little writing, not enough math or formal science. I grew anxious about Kirby's success in college, but by then his confidence in himself couldn't be swayed.

His greatest surprise in college has been how disinterested his fellow students are in learning. He is as enthusiastic as they are bored. Now, in his sophomore year, my Renaissance man has knowledge and abilities spanning many fields. Of his own volition he wrote a scholarly article that a science journal accepted for publication. Self-taught in acoustic design, he created an electronic component for amplifiers that he now sells online. He also raises tarantulas, restores vintage cars, and plays the bagpipes. He's still the wonderfully cooperative and cheerful boy I once knew, now with a delightfully dry wit.

> Homeschooling showed me that children don't fare well as passive recipients of education.

Homeschooling showed me that children don't fare well as passive recipients of education. They want to take part in meaningful activities relevant to their own lives. They develop greater skills by building on their gifts, not focusing on abilities they lack.

Research is beginning to back up our experience. Psychologist Peter Gray studied ADHD children who are educated outside of conventional schools. He found that such children, when homeschooled, rarely require medication because their behavior improves as they learn in less restricted ways. He also noted that ADHD children typically have a high need for educational self-direction. Other studies note that a daily nature walk has the same beneficial impact as medication on an ADHD child's concentration and calmness. My son taught me that distractible, messy, and disorganized children are perfectly suited to learn in their own way, without medication. I only wish we'd walked away from those school doors sooner.

The author says:

"Walking Away" is dedicated to Kirby for being exactly who he is.

Tell Us More: Expert Q & A with Laura Weldon

Author, *Free Range Learning: How Homeschooling Changes Everything*

Q. How do our children benefit from spending time in nature?

A. Time spent in nature, even walking along a tree-lined path or playing in the backyard, can be remarkably restorative. Preliminary research findings now point to more specific benefits.

Children who spend time in natural settings:

- are less impulsive

- are less aggressive

- handle adversity better

- concentrate more effectively

The greater the exposure, the more beneficial the results. This includes:

- reduced stress

- improved resiliency

- increased concentration

In particular, children diagnosed with ADHD show significantly reduced symptoms after time spent in natural outdoor settings. The improvement noted is as good or better than that found with prescription medication for ADHD symptoms.

Q. What are some assumptions made in traditional schools that the concept of homeschooling challenges?

A. We assume that our children should:

- sit still and pay attention.

Of course, we all need to sit still and pay attention at times, but a heavy dose of this every day isn't conducive to learning. Unfortunately, the typical educational approach focuses on one hemisphere of the brain instead of the whole child. This actually limits deeper comprehension. Some experts contend that only a tiny fraction what we learn is acquired through instruction, and we're least likely to retain that information as compared to primary or acquired learning.

What works best? Children learn eagerly as they explore, discover, watch and imitate active behavior, collaborate, ask questions, and participate in meaningful ways. Research shows that these natural ways of learning sustain motivation and foster the highest levels of mastery. They also help our children mature into self-directed lifelong learners.

- meet age- and grade- appropriate learning goals.

Each child progresses at unique and personally appropriate timetables. Pushing them doesn't advance achievement. When a child is under pressure (including rewards and evaluations) studies indicate they have a weaker conceptual grasp of the material. Child development experts attest that when adults are highly directive and exert control over a child's activities (whether writing a poem or playing a game) the child's natural motivation is weakened.

- get good scores on tests.

Good scores only predict that they'll score well on later tests. Research tells us that education that's focused on raising test scores cultivates shallow thinking and compromises exactly the abilities needed for real success. Abilities such as independent, critical thinking are closely correlated with positive life choices. In fact, high test scores in school don't correlate with later accomplishments in adulthood. That includes career advancement or social leadership.

- participate eagerly in adult-led enrichment or recreation programs.

We humans are geared to learn, unless the learning situation is disconnected from the child's interests or designed specifically for evaluation purposes. Then we tend to resist. That's because we naturally avoid coercion and seek out what is meaningful, useful, and interesting.

Top down instruction and adult-run experiences have a place in a child's life, but they can't compare to the development gained when children have sufficient free time. There's tremendous value when children spend time in nature, in open-ended play, in family time, doing chores, and simply daydreaming.

Part 3: Searching for Solutions

My Dance with the Devil
by Laura Boss

Every morning my husband or I wake our eleven-year-old son with 24 milligrams of Concerta, an extended-release form of Ritalin.

If someone had told me 11 years ago that Nathan would start his day with a psychotropic medication I would have been outraged. Ritalin? *My* son? There was just no way. I wasn't going to use pharmaceuticals as a substitute for good parenting.

I was raised to be skeptical of traditional medicine. My family believed in good food, exercise, and listening to the wisdom of the body. My siblings and I ate whole-grain, natural, chemical-free food back when Wonder bread and Twinkies were standard fare for children. Consulting doctors or taking medicine were things my family did reluctantly, only as a last resort.

Both my mother and father were certified "Parent Effectiveness Training" (P.E.T.) teachers, passionate about the power of good parenting and determined to share their opinions and skills with the world. The P.E.T. approach was win-win, neither punitive nor permissive, but a way of resolving conflicts so that both parents' and children's needs are met. I'd watched my sisters raise their children using P.E.T. methods – Active Listening, I-Statements and No-Lose Conflict Resolution—with great results. When it was my turn for parenthood I was ready. I knew the formula and was committed to its implementation. I didn't expect it to be easy, but I did expect it to work.

During my pregnancy I lived by an iron discipline I'd never achieved before and haven't since. I practiced yoga regularly and renounced my decadent diet of French cheese, dark chocolate, and red wine to eat for maximum nutrition. I labored for 33 hours on my hands and knees, without drugs, in order to give my son a natural birth.

The long afternoons of Nathan's early infancy found me stretched out on the couch reading parenting books while Nathan slept on my chest. When he started walking, his dad, Al, and I signed him up for co-op preschool, and together we earnestly absorbed evening seminars like "Raising a Boy in Today's World," "Potty Training Your Toddler," and "Positive Discipline for Preschoolers." I thought I was ready for anything.

Before Nathan was born, when I thought about the kind of person he would be, I always assigned him our best traits. He would have Al's eyes, his intelligence, creativity, and sense of adventure. He'd have my teeth, strong bones, love of animals and books, and naturally low cholesterol. Of course, he would be outgoing and affable like Al. It never occurred to me that he might inherit my temperament. That was the last thing on earth I wanted to give him.

> I grew up feeling that I was fundamentally defective, but I didn't know what the defect was exactly, or how to fix it.

I remembered being a difficult child; sensitive and intense, easily overwhelmed with powerful emotions – sadness, embarrassment, anxiety, frustration. My anger, especially, frightened me. It felt too big, too awful, for my little body to contain. It felt like an enormous wave crashing over me, dragging me into its undertow disoriented and powerless, unable to breathe. I wanted to stop being angry, but once I'd reached a certain point I didn't know how to make it go away. I screamed and cried and raged, bewildered by my own behavior all the while. My poor parents were completely stymied.

Once, at five or six years old, I stormed off from an argument and locked myself in my bedroom, away from my family, choking with rage, trying not to explode with it. I hated feeling so overwhelmingly out of control. I wanted to turn off my anger, to back down, to make up and start over, but I was stuck. I just didn't know what to do. Then it came to me: *I'm going to break all my Christmas presents.* There was something strangely seductive about punishing both my parents and myself that way. I snatched up the nearest Christmas present I could see, a blue plastic hand mirror my mother had given to me. I loved that little mirror, but it didn't stop me from smashing it against the corner of my dresser. The glass shattered. The spell was broken. I ran to my mother shaking and sobbing in horror at what I'd done. I felt ashamed, embarrassed, and horrified, but I wasn't angry any more.

I was impulsive and distractible and couldn't seem to behave correctly no matter how hard I tried. I was spacey and unpredictable, oblivious to the chaos I always seemed to leave in my wake. I had no sense of time and was always late. I blurted things out without thinking and instantly regretted the damage my words caused. I grew up feeling that I was fundamentally defective, but I didn't know what the defect was exactly, or how to fix it.

As an adult I couldn't seem to get it together. I did reasonably well in school, but couldn't commit to a career path. I agonized about what I wanted to do with my life, what cause I wanted to devote myself to. While I endlessly weighed and reweighed my options I ignored opportunities, missed graduate school application deadlines, and ended up taking jobs that were completely wrong for me, jobs I actively hated, because they were available and I needed the income. It would only be for a little while, I told myself, just until I figured things out. I was stuck, unable to make decisions or to follow through on the decisions I tried to force. Ideas would pop into my head like popcorn, but I could never seem to implement them. There were novels and short stories I wanted to write, opera dresses I designed in my head, paintings I could see in my mind's eye, businesses I wanted to start, advanced degrees I wanted to pursue, schemes for traveling various parts of the world—joining the Peace Corps, teaching English in China, studying in France—but I never did any of it.

"You have so much potential," people would tell me. "Why don't you do something with it?"

In my early forties I was diagnosed with attention deficit hyperactivity disorder (ADHD). I sat in my doctor's office and cried with relief, grateful for at least an explanation. For the first time in my life it all started to make sense. The emotional disregulation, impulsivity, distractibility, and lack of follow through I'd always lived with had more to do with my brain chemistry than my character. I finally had something concrete to work with, to fight against.

Nathan was a sensitive baby. The normal sights and sounds of daily life – grocery store lights, background music, other people's conversations – were just too much for him. Overwhelmed, he'd cry and cry, tears running down his little cheeks. I couldn't take him to the store or to a friend's house or even to the park unless we walked there and could find a quiet corner to ourselves. He screamed as soon as I buckled him into his car seat, and the heart-wrenching sobbing only escalated as we drove. The more tired he became, the worse it got.

> *Why is he so unhappy?* I wondered. *What am I doing wrong?*

"If you leave him alone he'll cry himself to sleep," people told me, but he never did.

Why is he so unhappy? I wondered. *What am I doing wrong?*

When Nathan was three months old, Al and I signed up for an infant massage class, thinking it would be a lovely opportunity to bond as a family. At the first session Nathan screamed as soon as our oil-scented fingers touched his little body, and he continued to cry inconsolably for hours afterward. Nothing we did would calm him down.

At the start of the second session we all shared the week's experiences. One of the other mothers told us all how her baby *loved* being massaged, how she quieted so *easily*, and what a *good* baby she was.

"I always thought being a mother would be so hard," she said, looking, I was sure, pointedly at us. "I've been surprised at how easy it is."

I exchanged a murderous look with Al. I wanted to tear her throat out.

As a busy and curious toddler, Nathan grew to love preschool, but he was not exactly a model student. He had trouble sitting still at circle time, couldn't keep his hands to himself, and fought back physically when provoked. Transitions were a nightmare.

"Let's put away our rug pads, our rug pads, our rug pads!" Teacher Lorrie sang one day to signal that circle time was over. One by one the other kids obediently lined up and set their little squares of carpet in a neat stack. Nathan wasn't ready to stop clapping and singing, but Teacher Lorrie insisted it was time to move on. In what seemed like a slow motion scene from a horror film we all watched, paralyzed, as he raised his rug pad high over his head and smacked her over the head with it.

That kind of behavior marked Nathan as a problem child. Play date and birthday party invitations declined dramatically. I lost adult friendships as I became marked as an incompetent mother.

"If she would just set limits!" I overheard other mothers say.

Al and I altered Nathan's diet, practiced "Positive Discipline," followed the "Spirited Child," "Difficult Child," and "Strong-Willed Child" programs. We tried sticker charts and schedules and we set limits. We set limit after limit after limit after limit. We set up power struggle after power struggle after power struggle, which ultimately resulted in a lot of screaming and crying and frustration for all of us.

In preschool Nathan had enough freedom to pursue his passionate interest in the world around him, and his world became one giant science experiment. Kindergarten, on the other hand, was more about learning to follow rules and think *inside* the box. On the first day of kindergarten Nathan learned to stand in line and raise his hand when he wanted to talk. His teacher passed out sheets of lined newsprint and newly sharpened pencils.

"Write your name at the top of the page," she instructed.

He wrote "Nathan" phonetically in Egyptian hieroglyphics. He'd learned how at a museum exhibition of Egyptian art we'd attended that summer.

Nathan's kindergarten teacher was a kind and patient young woman who genuinely seemed to like our son and to appreciate his quirky personality.

> In preschool Nathan had enough freedom to pursue his passionate interest in the world around him, and his world became one giant science experiment. Kindergarten, on the other hand, was more about learning to follow rules and think *inside* the box.

Still, it seemed that every time I signed in at his school's office to volunteer in his class Nathan was sitting outside the principal's office in an adult-sized chair, swinging his legs, waiting to see her. He was often unable to contain his anger when a friend was teased on the playground, and he pushed or hit or kicked the teasers. In class he couldn't keep quiet, couldn't sit still, couldn't keep his hands to himself. Once he mooned the music teacher.

Nathan seemed to wind up in the principal's office when his teacher was tired of dealing with him, when she needed a break. I understood the feeling. She got the best of his behavior. After working hard to hold it together all day at school Nathan would fall completely apart as we drove home.

"I hate you!" he'd scream at me, hitting and kicking the back of my seat and throwing things at me. I tried every trick I'd learned in all of the parenting books I'd read, but nothing seemed to work. I felt lost and helpless and frustrated. I felt hopelessly incompetent as a mother.

In the meantime Al and I watched our bright, curious, passionate little boy; the boy who needed to know everything about all the things that interested him, whose enthusiasm for exploring the world around him burned like a white-hot flame, become frustrated with school and begin to doubt his abilities.

"I'm not good at school," he confessed to me one day. "I do everything wrong."

When Nathan was in first grade we took him to a psychologist who diagnosed ADHD. We didn't want to give Nathan medication so we tried every possible alternative. We tracked the minutiae of his day on a complicated spreadsheet with credits given and withheld according to behavior. We thought we could manage his symptoms through sheer force of will, but will alone wasn't enough. Nathan's brain chemistry interfered with his best intentions. The modest results we got from the mind-numbing tedium of logging his behavior and the countless hours of screaming and crying we endured each time we enforced compliance just weren't worth it.

In the second grade the stakes got higher. Nathan's teacher was male, six feet four with a big booming voice and high standards for behavior. The first two weeks of school I'd wait on the playground at the end of the day to take Nathan home, and every day he would emerge looking devastated; the last kid to leave his classroom, the teacher's hand on his shoulder, the teacher looking grim. My heart would sink.

No matter what Nathan's teacher asked him to do he couldn't seem to do it. One day, frustrated after receiving yet another consequence for bad behavior, Nathan jumped to his feet, put his fist in the air and shouted, "The revolution begins NOW!"

No matter how bad Nathan felt about what happened at school he couldn't seem to keep the same thing from happening the next day. He would tell me he was sorry, bring me his favorite stuffed animals to cuddle, and make little cards and drawings to cheer me up. He wanted to do the right thing; he just didn't seem able to do it.

I knew what that was like. In addition to undiagnosed ADHD I had lived with depression and anxiety most of my life. I knew I should exercise; knew I should be careful about what I ate, careful about what I thought and did, but when I was flattened by a depressive episode I just couldn't do it.

> No matter how bad Nathan felt about what happened at school he couldn't seem to keep the same thing from happening the next day. He wanted to do the right thing; he just didn't seem able to do it.

I went to a therapist for seven years; talked about my anger, talked about my unhappiness, my family, my relationships, my frustration, and still remained depressed. At times I was so depressed I couldn't function. I lost whole days, whole weeks to it. It was like being sucked into a black, ugly, bottomless whirlpool, and I used every bit of strength I had just to keep my chin above water. My therapist suggested trying antidepressants, but I adamantly refused. Depression was horrible, it seemed to me at the time, but at least it was real. I resisted the idea of being drugged, of the medicine making me a foreigner to myself.

"It's part of who I am," I insisted.

I read about Prozac and wondered wistfully what it would be like to take it. It was a little like wondering what I would look like with breast implants or a new nose; it seemed unnatural, way too easy, and ultimately irresponsible; a failure of will, a fundamental character flaw.

In a moment of weakness, during a particularly trying time and a particularly nasty episode of depression, I agreed to give medication a try.

"Okay, okay, okay," I said. "I'll do it."

I didn't care what happened. I just wanted to feel like a normal person for once in my life, even if that person was no longer me. I took the Zoloft my doctor prescribed with a self-destructive flourish, hoping to wipe myself out altogether.

I had been on Zoloft for a couple of weeks when I realized that I felt good, that I'd been feeling consistently good—not high, or drugged, or unnaturally happy—just good. There was no whirlpool sloshing around my waist, threatening to pull me under; no exhausting struggle to stay afloat. I was myself, finally, with no interference. Why hadn't I tried this 10 years earlier?

When I got my ADHD diagnosis several years later it was a much easier decision to try medication. The more I learned about ADHD the more obvious it became that my life could be a whole lot better if I could just get the symptoms under control. I imagined myself organized and competent, with a clean house, infinite patience with my husband and son, and the ability to follow an idea through to its completion. I couldn't imagine what that might be like, but it sounded awfully good. I took my first dose of Ritalin full of hope and ready for some fundamental changes.

"How will I know if it's working?" I asked my doctor.

"Oh, don't worry," he said, "You'll know."

After several days what I knew was that my mouth was uncomfortably dry and I felt shaky and irritable. We switched to Concerta and spent the next several months adjusting the dosage. I made some modest gains in focus and attention, but the side effects—the shakiness, irritability, heightened anxiety and painfully dry mouth—were nearly intolerable. We continued the med trials, eventually trying Adderall, Focalin, Strattera, Provigil and Wellbutrin.

When the experiment ended I had lost more than 30 pounds and was increasingly anxious and irritable. I knew it was time to stop when one of Nathan's playmates refused to come to our house.

"Their house is too messy and his mom yells too much," he told his mother.

Before the med trials I would never have raised my voice to Nathan in front of a friend. I had to face the fact that ADHD medication was not going to work for me; I was going to have to find other strategies to deal with life.

Given my background and my negative experience with ADHD medication it was an agonizingly difficult decision to try stimulant medication on Nathan, but what we were doing clearly wasn't working. I didn't want to put Nathan through a med trial as miserable as mine. But more than that I didn't want him to grow up like I did, feeling defective and frustrated, every day a painful reminder of the disparity between his amazing potential and what he could actually achieve. Al and I got a second opinion from a doctor whose judgment we trusted and read everything we could about ADHD medication, good and bad. We decided to take the risk. The doctor prescribed a small dose of Concerta.

"If it doesn't work we'll take him off of it," he told us. We held our breath.

When the bell rang at the end of Nathan's first day on medication I ran up the school stairs two at a time.

"How did things go today?" I asked his teacher.

"At first I thought Nathan was sick," the teacher said. "Then I remembered the medicine. He quietly took his chair off his desk, then helped the other kids with their chairs. And then," he paused for effect, "he sat down and cleaned out his desk."

My jaw dropped. *My* child? Cleaned out his desk? Ever since kindergarten I'd been able to pick out Nathan's desk from the others. It looked as if a hurricane had made landfall there, on that spot only. There were crumpled papers sticking out at odd angles, half-read library books crammed in sideways, stashes of forbidden snacks half-hidden in corners, and engineering experiments gone awry; all surrounded by a debris field of dried glue globs, capless markers, paper scraps, crayon stubs, and pencil shavings. That day it looked like any other desk.

> **Dealing with ADHD, we've learned, is a long, arduous, multi-pronged process, and medication is only a part of it.**

It turned out that Nathan had spent the day focused and cooperative. He participated in class discussions and kept control of his body. He was still lively and active, but in control. I asked him how it had gone.

"I had a good day," he said simply.

I wish all the days that followed had been as good; that the medication had been as consistently effective as it was that first day. Dealing with ADHD, we've learned, is a long, arduous, multi-pronged process, and medication is only a part of it.

There's no question that medication has made a significant and positive impact on Nathan's life and on ours. He's been able to keep his body under control in class and to focus and pay attention more easily. In fact, just months after he began his medication Nathan's newfound ability to focus was reflected in testing that allowed school personnel to see his substantial intellectual gifts. Those test scores got him into an advanced learning program. School has become much more challenging and engaging than it was before, and strangely enough, that makes it much easier for him to pay attention.

Now 11, Nathan has come a long way from being the squirrelly kindergartener who mooned the music teacher, but his journey's far from over. Keeping his desk semi-neat and organized, getting his assignments done and in on time, and catching the bus in the morning are all ongoing challenges. Medication can't do those things for him, but it can give him the focus and concentration to learn the skills to do them himself. It can clear away the interference that keeps Nathan from learning the strategies he needs to be successful. Mostly it helps Nathan to be himself; to turn off the physical, mental, and emotional static that keeps him from being the kid he'd like to be.

As for me, I wish I could say that I've become fabulously organized, tidy, calm, and punctual, but I'm afraid that's not the case. I still struggle with ADHD, but I've made progress. By being able to look my ADHD squarely in the eye—face it down and call it by its real name—I have opened an important door for myself. After a lifetime of rebelling against any kind of superimposed structure on my time I've begun to realize that the right kind of structure can be both liberating and productive. After dealing with the challenges of my life in isolation I now have a community of people who understand; people I can actually invite over to my messy house and speak frankly to about my difficulties as a parent. I've been able to let go of the perfectionism that tortured me in the early years of Nathan's life. I no longer take every one of his outbursts or difficulties as a sign of my own personal incompetence. I'm able to laugh at myself and my strange brain; we laugh together.

I'm still not completely comfortable with the idea of medicating my son. My orientation will always be toward a holistic and integrated approach to mental and physical health, but by challenging my own fears and prejudices I've been able to expand my definition of what that means. For me pharmaceuticals will never replace good parenting, but under the right circumstances, used carefully, they can be extremely useful tools. At this point I'll take as many tools as I can get. If medication can help him to be successful without losing himself in the process; if it can help him to get closer to becoming the person he was born to be, with all of that amazing and glorious potential, then I'm all for it. As long as he remains the sweet, smart, quirky kid I fell in love with 11 years ago then I'm willing to take a chance, to dance with a devil. And maybe—just maybe—in the middle of the dance I'll find an angel or two.

The author says:

Nathan is now in sixth grade, beginning his middle school career, which has sorely tested the whole family's executive function skills. As part of a recent science project on ADHD and creativity Nathan made an impassioned case for discontinuing his medication regime and reforming the school system. The first issue is on the table. The second remains securely locked in its own Pandora's Box, at least for now.

Tell Us More: Expert Q & A with Judith Warner

Author of *We've Got Issues: Children and Parents in the Age of Medication*

Q. As you researched and wrote *We've Got Issues*, what did you learn about how parents make the decision to use medication to treat ADHD or similar conditions? Do they make the decision lightly? Were you surprised by what you learned?

A. When I began *We've Got Issues*, I truly believed, as do most people, that parents were over-diagnosing and over-medicating their kids. I really believed that psychiatrists and therapists and teachers and schools were colluding in labeling and pathologizing kids. I believed that families were taking the easy way out of dealing with common behavioral problems, seeking "quick fix" solutions. I didn't think there really was anything wrong with most of the kids who were getting diagnosed with "flavor of the month" disorders like ADHD. I thought our culture—our competitive, frantic, often soul-crunching culture—was making kids sick.

But as I researched the book, hunting down numbers on over-diagnosis and over-medication, speaking with experts and, most importantly, speaking with parents, I found that my initial ideas were utterly wrong. Not only was there no "epidemic" of diagnosis or over-treatment; the real problem was that most kids with mental health issues weren't getting any treatment at all. (Only about 50% of children believed to have ADHD, for example, actually get treatment for it.) And parents weren't rushing to "drug" or "label" their kids. Most were highly resistant to hearing that there was anything wrong with their kids in the first place. Most put off seeing a specialist for as long as they could—they doubted teachers who reported that kids were having problems, they doubted their spouses; they doubted themselves. If they came around to agreeing to try medication, it was generally after trying whatever other alternatives were available to them, which largely came down to whatever alternatives they could afford. Sometimes these alternatives helped—things like fish oil, or dietary change, or martial arts practice, or biofeedback—and sometimes they didn't.

And often, oddly enough, if medication did help (as it did for many but not all kids), the parents felt somehow defeated. Because the success of the medication indicated to them that something truly was wrong with their kids. The problems were real. They weren't going away. And it wasn't within the parents' power alone to make everything better.

Reading Lia
by Ann M.

I begin stroking her, my fingers trailing the scratches on her forearm, as her body, taut with tension, begins to unclench. Tears stream down her beautiful eleven-year-old face. She is yelling for me to let her go, though not so loudly as before. Another tantrum, when she did not get her way about something, anything. There have been so many days, so many tantrums.

My strokes continue as Lia unfurls her arm for me. My fingers trace her skin from wrist to shoulder, inside and out, up and down, drawing invisible swirling lines. She stretches towards me.

What parenting book, what guide to mothering tells you this? That sometimes you will sit on the floor, your sobbing, heaving child beside you, and stroke her arm in a tantrum's aftermath, whispering soft sounds, setting off some reaction inside her that helps her to self-regulate? The strokes, the gentle, jumbled nonsense words bring her back to balance and harmony, if only for a short time. But it is enough. The storm is spent; this is a time of peace. I gather Lia into my arms and carry her to bed, a haven for her exhausted body, torn by the furies she cannot control.

I always wanted to be a mother. Single, approaching my fortieth birthday, I was galvanized to move forward with my plans for parenthood. I had majored in Russian language and literature in college, spent time in Russia, and adored the culture. So it was easy to decide to adopt a baby girl from Russia, the first of what I hoped would be two daughters. I had brothers, but had yearned for a sister. I could give my daughter a sister, at some point, and the girls would have each other for support when they were mature adults.

In September 1999 I brought home seven-month-old Lia from St. Petersburg. After a few weeks home, with good love, good food, and a good pediatrician Lia morphed from a skinny shadow of a baby into a shining vision of near-perfect health. Silky blonde strands now covered her formerly bald head. Her bewitching eyes—one blue, one green— sparkled. The sallowness of her skin fled, replaced by a soft peaches-and-cream complexion.

Lia was early to talk and walk. She smiled easily. The birds that scattered in her wake when she toddled after them made her laugh out loud. Playing peek-a-boo was good for many happy chortles. She beamed at people in the supermarket who stopped to admire her loveliness. She went to day care every morning and came home suitably messy each night. She seemed typical in every way.

> **What parenting book, what guide to mothering tells you this?**

Lia received early intervention services from the state almost as a matter of course. She had spent her first seven months of life in a Russian orphanage, so our state stepped in to provide her with whatever was needed to overcome this disadvantaged beginning. Physical and occupational therapists and educational specialists became part of her weekly routine.

When Lia turned two things started to change.

"She spins," her day care teacher tells me one day when I come to pick her up. I smile at the teacher blankly.

"She spins in circles," the woman continues, a slight note of urgency creeping into her voice. I look at her absentmindedly and then find my tiny daughter at the easel, covered in paint, wearing a long smock and holding a brush.

"Don't all two year olds like to spin around?" I ask the teacher.

"Not for as long as she does," the woman replies.

Lia's therapists from early intervention add their opinions.

"You really ought to have her examined by a neurologist," they tell me. I read over their reports. Lia is on target in most areas, somewhat behind in others, but overall seems to be doing well. So what if she can't fold a sheet of paper precisely into two even parts? Does she need to see a neurologist for that? She is "over the top," her therapists continue to report. I have no idea what this means.

I decide to take the therapists' advice and call a neurologist. I have to wait eight months for the appointment. He spends five minutes with us and laughs me out of his office, telling me that Lia falls well within the normal range for her age.

When Lia turns three I enroll her in preschool and her new teachers join the chorus of those voicing their concerns.

"Lia can't sit still at circle time."

She's too young, I rationalize.

"Aside from dramatic play, nothing holds her interest for even a short length of time."

She's a born diva, I figure.

"She distracts the other children with her wild antics, getting them to crawl around the floor barking like dogs, or leaping like frogs."

She is so social! I marvel.

Her teachers do not find any of this charming. They want me to have her evaluated by the public school system, and fast. So I do, and the consensus is that she has sensory and behavioral issues.

Lia starts therapy for sensory integration dysfunction (SID) with occupational therapists, whose work room filled with balls and swinging and hanging devices of all kinds is Lia's paradise. Strapped into a vibrating, rotating, moving contraption—going at full speed to nowhere—her eyes glaze over, her shoulders slump, her limbs relax and she enters her own nirvana. For a brief while after her session my daughter is calm.

It never lasts. Her voice is loud and constant. She runs when she should walk. She ricochets from one thing to the next, a pinball that no flipper can control. She rarely listens to me or follows directions. Inevitably and seemingly out of nowhere negative behaviors bubble up and burst out. She has tantrums constantly, yelling, whipping her head around, and flailing her limbs. This happens anywhere and everywhere: at home, on a play date, in the street, or in the supermarket. I visit therapists with her and get nothing but poorer.

I am exhausted. I need a break from Lia and her behaviors. I get one when I go to Russia solo to adopt the planned-for second baby girl. Now, I have another reason to adopt again. I believe that if I am busy with a second child Lia will be forced to mature and calm down. I leave Lia with my parents and stay in Russia much longer than I need to, resting my body and my mind while I get acquainted with Sarah, a quiet little baby who is content to lie in her crib and suck her thumb.

After returning to the U.S. and settling in as a mother of two I start going out socially. One night at a friend's house I meet Michael, the man who in August 2006 will become my husband and the children's father.

Meanwhile, with the demands of first grade upon her, Lia is squeezed between her impulses and classroom rules. It is hard for her to sit at a desk. She cannot listen to what the teacher is saying. She raises her hand

and calls out at inappropriate times. Physically she is present; mentally she follows her own muse. She begins receiving support services from her school and I follow up with a private tutor at home.

Lia's restlessness persists. At home we lurch from crisis to crisis. Her body is in a constant race with the many thoughts that whirl round and round her mind. She careens from activity to activity. "Drive-by playing" is her modus operandi. She talks non-stop. She is defiant. She must have her own way. She cannot compromise on anything. She has to control her environment and the people in it.

The demons do not quiet at night. Lia screams in her sleep, she flails in her bed, and she wakes up every single night to come to me. Sleep deprived and desperate, I ask her pediatrician to help me get a quick appointment with a local developmental pediatrician who is an expert on internationally adopted children. Most people wait about eight months to see this particular doctor; I have an appointment four weeks after I call.

> **Physically she is present; mentally she follows her own muse.**

The specialist tells me that Lia has attention deficit hyperactivity disorder (ADHD). She gives me pamphlets to read and I go home with a prescription and a list of books on the disorder. Michael and I mine Amazon for more ADHD literature. We get to know our pharmacist and the pharmacy techs very well.

I medicate Lia each day before school. We start with Ritalin (Grit and Grin), we move to Adderall (Atta girl!) and then to Metadate (Meditate). We switch to Concerta, which seems to calm and stabilize Lia well. Until it doesn't. Why do these drugs suddenly stop working their magic?

We land on Focalin Extended Release (Focalin XR). Success! Lia can now focus in school. But her metabolism is so quick that the morning dose's effects are short-lived, despite the extended release nature of Focalin XR. The long school day means that she needs more medication to get through her afternoon classes and be able to do homework. The short-acting form of Focalin is added to the mix. The timing of her medication becomes an art. How much medication do we give Lia and when do we give it? Does she have an after school activity? Does she have a lot of homework? Are there any group projects that she needs to work on after school? What if she needs to go to bed early; do we eliminate the afternoon pills?

There is a silver lining behind every cloud, and a cloud behind every silver lining. The silver lining is that Lia can pay attention in school. Thanks to Focalin she can learn, because she can sit still and be quiet long enough to absorb the lessons. She does not call out unexpectedly in class or talk to her friends while the teacher is talking. But the cloud is dark indeed; Focalin has its side effects. Lia becomes clingy and paranoid, afraid to be alone. Her personality, so bold and compelling, disappears. Her medicated doppelganger is shy and withdrawn, afraid to make eye contact. Already too thin, she now has no appetite. She is awake far into the night.

> **Why do these drugs suddenly stop working their magic?**

Medications are added to medications to eliminate the side effects, and we begin seeing a child psychiatrist who guides us through the medicinal maze. There is Tenex to deal with the rebound effect of the Focalin wearing off, but the timing of this new pill must be so precise that we rarely use it. Melatonin, coupled with an anti-anxiety drug that encourages sleep and appetite, becomes part of our child's nightly ritual.

I worry about the long term effects of all these medications and whether we are dosing our child for the right reasons. What about weekends and holidays when she does not need to sit for hours and listen to a teacher? Why do we give pills to her then? Is it because the medication makes her more malleable, more willing to listen to us, and more pleasant to deal with? Are these legitimate reasons to give her stimulants—because we like her better when she takes them? Can I only deal with my child when she is medicated or sleeping?

A couple of years ago I read a book in which a father admitted that he only liked his daughter with autism when she was asleep at night. During the day, with her multiple needs, she was a burden to him, he frankly admitted. Though he took care of her needs, he did it without joy or love. He moved through each day awaiting the blessed moments of peace that came only when she fell asleep.

I too feel more relaxed and competent—less edgy—when I can manage Lia; when she is compliant like her little sister, when she does what I ask her to do when I ask her to do it. I feel badly about this, terribly twisted inside my heart and my mind by my conflicting feelings. Aren't I supposed to accept my daughter "as is?" But I don't. I help her mood and her mind along with the best that the drug companies have to offer.

Because I cannot always deal with "Lia Unplugged"—as I've come to think of her without pharmaceuticals—I feel like a horrible mother. I use drugs to make Lia into the daughter she *should* have been. I am tortured by my thoughts; that I put myself first, that I need to control Lia, and that since reason and loving guidance don't work I use medicine.

What about Lia's right to be who she is?

What about the mother she *should* have had? Where is the mother who would know how to calm the rages and how to bring out the best in her child? There are so many times that I feel like a total failure. Nights when I cry over her small form while she sleeps and tell her that she deserves better than me; that I will find someone more loving, more patient, and more accepting to take care of her. We are in crisis.

When Lia is nearly eight years old I begin studying Applied Behavior Analysis (ABA) looking for anything that might help my daughter. ABA is a well-studied treatment for autism, and perhaps I can use some of its techniques to help Lia. I take five online courses and earn a certificate in the field. Armed with this new education I leave the corporate world behind and begin working with young children on the autism spectrum. ABA is all about antecedents, behavior, and consequences.

What precedes a person's negative behavior? With my daughter it can be hard to pinpoint a distinct trigger.

What consequences does the person receive for the behavior? I smile when I think what my professors of behavior analysis would say about my latest method of soothing Lia's fury. They would say I was rewarding her for throwing tantrums by giving her what she wants—undivided attention and pleasing physical sensations—but I know better. The stroking and soft murmurs help regulate her; they bring her back to a point of equilibrium. Without balance in her system she flies through space like a shot arrow. Besides, Lia gets attention and sensory input whenever she wants them, not just when she has a meltdown.

> Because I cannot always deal with "Lia Unplugged" —as I've come to think of her without pharmaceuticals—I feel like a horrible mother. I use drugs to make Lia into the daughter she *should* have been.

The years pass. At work I see how ABA can help a child with autism progress. The child is not "fixed" or "cured" but has more functional skills and behaviors. The child is not perfect but is better, and I accept that "better" is good enough.

At home we have good days and bad. There are days when Lia comes home beaming, with a good grade on a spelling test or a math quiz. Math is especially difficult for her, and we fall all over ourselves to praise her hard work. There are days when the pills seem to do nothing at all and tantrums and rages take over. Then I pull out other tools from my ever-growing kit. I have learned from books, magazines, the Internet, classes, and from trial and error. My toolbox is large.

The best thing I can do when Lia rages is to keep her close to me and ask her what she needs. I will take a walk with her, which seems to help. I will envelope her in gentle physical sensations; place her on a cushion, softly stroke her arms, speak quietly to her. I will let her snuggle with her dog and cry into the dog's soft body, burrowing into her poodle-like soothing curls. I will let Lia be until the furies are spent.

Nothing and no one is perfect, I have learned. Medication may or may not work. Experts may have advice that I can use or advice that I find useless. I've learned to trust my instincts, remembering the old chestnut "the doctor reads the charts; the parent reads the child."

Being a "good enough" parent rather than a paragon of perfection is my new goal. It is more achievable and not as anxiety provoking. I no longer strive to "fix" my child, or myself. We just keep walking the path, learning as we go.

The author says:

This essay honors the strong women who have marked my life: my mother Lucille, who had the patience and fortitude to raise me, who showed me how to balance work and family with a smile, and whose belief in me makes me believe in myself; my grandmother Dina, may she rest in peace, who experienced much hardship but never complained and who adored me, and my Aunt Etta, a fearless advocate for the disabled, who has never let her own disability stand in the way of living life to the fullest.

Owner and Director, Central Iowa Psychological Services and Senior Lecturer, Department of Psychology, Iowa State University

Q. There is anecdotal evidence from parents that medications for ADHD sometimes work quite well for a period of time, and then suddenly stop working. Does research support these reports? What are some possible explanations for why this happens?

A. I have worked with many children and families where ADHD presents a notable struggle, and sometimes gift, in their lives. Although the most effective treatment, thus far, still appears to be psychostimulant medication there are occasions when these medications may not work in the ways that parents hope or expect. In particular, many parents experience frustration when they find a medication that appears to be helpful to their child and then after several months or, sometimes years, notice that the medication is losing its effectiveness. While there is some research to support the presence of this changing effectiveness, the reasons for it still remain somewhat unclear and are likely quite varied in nature.

The developing human body, of course, is quite complex. We know, for example, that as children get older their physiology and metabolism changes and they gain weight and may need a higher dose in order to maintain the same therapeutic effect. There is also some reorganization of neural connections in the prefrontal cortex of the brain (an area highly involved in the presence of ADHD symptoms) that occurs as children move into adolescence. All of these normal developmental changes can have an impact on ADHD symptoms and on the ways that the medications work. We also know that children's activity and exercise level, maintaining a balanced diet, and getting enough sleep has an impact on attention, impulse control, memory, and learning. Thus, there are several factors that may influence both children's ADHD symptoms and the effectiveness of the psychostimulant medications.

Q. Parents are always looking for tools, treatments, and therapies to use either instead of or in addition to ADHD medications, and we want to know if research suggests these approaches are effective. Would it be accurate to state that research has shown medication is the most effective treatment? Many other treatments have been suggested or are being studied. Which, if any, look promising?

A. While it is true that parents and families frequently search for alternative or adjunctive treatment to psychostimulant medication for ADHD, the research remains clear that stimulant medications are still the most effective treatment for ADHD symptoms. However, there are many other approaches that, when combined with psychostimulant medication, can be quite effective at helping children, adolescents, and adults with ADHD to function more effectively and learn how to turn ADHD into a gift rather than a disability.

For example, many common forms of psychotherapy such as cognitive behavioral therapy and interpersonal therapy are highly effective for adolescents and adults with ADHD, as they help individuals improve their organizational skills, pay closer attention to self-control, and combat negative thoughts that lead to anxiety, depression, or low self-esteem. These approaches also help adolescents and adults with ADHD to learn and practice appropriate social skills, conflict resolution skills, and listening skills that can be of tremendous assistance in their interpersonal relationships.

Behavior management and parent training programs are also well-supported interventions for parents of children with ADHD. These interventions help parents make modifications necessary to remain consistent, patient, and effective in their parenting with children who can certainly present unique challenges.

In addition to these well-established forms of psychotherapy there are many adjunctive approaches that are gradually getting more research scrutiny and, at some point, could be promising interventions as well. For example, EEG biofeedback/neurofeedback and working memory training now have some mixed research support for their effectiveness as an adjunct/add-on therapeutic tool (but not as an alternative to medication or standard treatments) for ADHD.

Q. Could you please give a brief layperson's introduction to self-regulation and executive function as they relate to ADHD?

A. The concepts of self-regulation and executive function are, of course, at the core of ADHD through the lifespan. Self-regulation is the general term used for one's ability to control impulses and regulate emotions. Thus, self-regulation involves the ability to consider consequences before speaking or behaving and soothe oneself when distressed. Executive function involves the ability to plan and think ahead, organize activities, be aware of and make appropriate judgments about time, and simultaneously attend to and act on information. For example, to attend a classroom lecture a student needs to make sure they bring the necessary materials for the lecture, arrive to the lecture on time, and then simultaneously pay attention to the oral presentation and any visual aids being utilized (e.g., PowerPoint presentation), relate this information to their own experiences and knowledge-base to give it meaning, and then produce understandable written notes. Thus, self-regulation and executive function are involved in most, if not all, of our daily activities.

Dominoes
by Adrienne Ehlert Bashista

"Butthole dickhead asshole poopy head." My eight-year-old son turns over the dominoes. "Asshole son-of-a-bitch my butt is big buttcrack. I'M DONE!" he yells. "COME PLAY!"

"Just a minute," I say. "I need to finish up dinner."

"NO, YOU SON-OF-A-BITCH!"

I don't say anything. I wait a beat.

"Sorry. Sorry, Mommy. You're not a son-of-a-bitch."

No, I'm not, I think to myself. Your grandma's not a bitch, and I'm not her son, anyway. I'm her daughter. And what's the definition of a son-of-a-bitch anyway? I mean, besides the literal? Asking him to wait 10 minutes before playing dominoes does not make me a son-of-a-bitch. I just think this. I don't say anything. I try to focus on chopping the carrots, and only the carrots. I've learned that the best reaction is no reaction. Expression, flinching, telling him to stop—all only encourage the child on the best of days. And on the worst of days he needs no encouragement at all.

Today is one of the worst of days.

My son, Little J, is not your average bear. He has a variety of diagnoses, none of which describe him exactly, but together paint a portrait of what we've been dealing with for the seven years since we adopted him from Russia at 15 months. According to various doctors and specialists, he has ADHD (attention deficit HYPERACTIVITY disorder – caps mine), ODD (oppositional defiant disorder), SID (sensory integration disorder), PDD (pervasive developmental disorder, which is on the autism spectrum but which our doctor says in my son's case does not apply. Not very helpful, but whatever.), borderline intelligence (but only due to the aforementioned ADHD, SID, and PDD; otherwise they think he's actually highly intelligent), and some kind of mood disorder, NOS (NOS meaning not otherwise specified. Translation: the doctors don't really know). All of this due to probable fetal alcohol exposure, malnutrition, institutionalization, and possibly genetics.

That's how he looks on paper, but in real life I use different words to describe him. Words like: wide open. Out there. Loud. Sweet. Loving. Angry. Happy. Sad. Irritated. Irritating. Funny. Too clever by half. A pain in the butt. Big trouble. Into everything. Affectionate. Gorgeous. My heart. A serious challenge.

> **He tells me he just wants to be a normal kid.**

He can spend hours creating a race car out of an appliance box but minutes destroying it in anger. He wants a kiss on the lips at bedtime. He has the worst potty mouth I've ever heard and the best giggle, though I don't hear it very often. Until he was seven he destroyed every birthday gift he received by the end of the day. He loves glitter, two hour baths, and eggs over easy. Some days he screams all day long. Some days he makes me so angry that I shake. Some days I want to get in my car and drive away. He has the most beautiful green eyes you'll ever see. He's tough. He doesn't feel pain the same as you and me.

He tells me he just wants to be a normal kid.

Over the years we've tried a number of different techniques to try to help Little J move past the behavioral age of two, which is where he seemed to sit for six straight years. Our natural parenting instincts, the ones that worked so well for our older son, didn't work as well with Little J. Expecting the kid to be good, then giving some kind of consequence when he wasn't didn't have much of an impact on him, no matter how big, small, wonderful, or horrible. When a child is overcome by impulsivity to the degree that Little J is, cause and effect has little impact. Neither do rewards, sticker charts, natural outcomes, sympathy, empathy, physical punishments, time in, time out, appeals to logic, or bribery. It took us five years to figure out the best thing for him and us: calm parents, reasonable (i.e. lowered) expectations, and appropriate medication.

The day of the dominoes was missing one of these elements. The most important one. The meds.

Little J was without his stimulant medication because his doctors, his dad, and I felt his dose of stimulants was too high. We'd increased it because of problems in school: he was unable to sit and listen and concentrate and he was bothering the other students. Essentially, we'd doubled it. Instead of giving it to him when he woke up and hoping it'd last the school day, his dad and I now took turns getting up at 5:30, waking him enough to swallow the pills, and then hoping he'd go back to sleep. At school they gave him a second dose just before lunch. The increase in medicine put his daily dosage at 50% more than the maximum dosage for anyone, including adults three times his size.

Increasing his medication allowed him to sit still and do his worksheets to a greater extent, but it hadn't taken care of all his issues in school, and in the five weeks since we'd increased the dose he'd quit eating any meals except breakfast, lost five pounds, become more and more irritable, and vomited several times. Oh, and had taken to waking up at 2:00 a.m. and watching infomercials with the sound turned down so we wouldn't catch him doing it.

We liked that he was having an easier time in school. But the rest of the stuff we couldn't live with.

The doctor had given us a schedule to try to wean him off his medication; lower it bit by bit so after a couple of weeks he'd be medicine free. Then she'd see him again and we'd come up with a new plan of action. Sounds great, except that once we got down low enough all bets were off. He simply had no self-control.

Bad things happen on the meds. But good things happen, too. Our constant worry since he was first diagnosed at four has been: what is working? What isn't? What's stopped working? Why? What else is there?

I finish chopping carrots. In 15 minutes dinner will be ready. Little J has spread the dominoes out on our dining room table and is jumping from chair to chair, waiting for me to play. His dad, Mark, is in the living room watching television. It's literally the one free hour he's had all week. Little J has been forbidden from watching with his father because he already used up all his screen time for the day playing some kind of futuristic car-racing-shooting-bad-guys game on the computer.

> **Bad things happen on the meds. But good things happen, too.**

It's the end of a holiday weekend. He's hungry. He's tired. He's angry because of the television restriction. He's had to wait 10 whole minutes for me to play with him. And he's medication free.

I sit down and collect my tiles. The objective of the game is to get rid of all one's dominoes by matching them to the domino in the center. Little J lays down a non-matching domino.

"You need to match the number, honey."

"I'M NOT PLAYING THAT WAY!"

"But those are the rules of the game," I say. I know arguing with him in this state is pointless, but I also had really hoped to play the game, not just toss dominoes in a pile.

"THE RULES ARE ASSHOLES."

I sigh. I wait. A beat goes by.

"I'm sorry. I'm sorry. How do I play?"

I explain the rules for the fifth time in three days. Click clack click clack click clack go the dominoes on the glass table top as I'm talking. CLICK CLACK CLICK CLACK. He sees me getting distracted, irritated. CLICK CLACK CLICK CLACK.

"Stop. Please stop."

"I'm not playing this way!" One by one, he throws dominoes—at me, at his brother Jacob, who is reading at the end of the table, and out the door into the hallway.

I hope I still look calm, although I can feel a familiar ache in my jaw where I'm clenching my teeth.

"Pick those up. We'll put it away. I can't play with you if you do that."

He throws himself on the floor and screams.

"I JUST WANT TO PLAY! WHY DOESN'T ANYONE WANT TO PLAY WITH ME?"

I start to put the dominoes back in the container and he pops up off the floor like a jack-in-the box and sweeps his hand across the table, knocking the remaining black and white tiles onto the floor.

I grab him, pull him into the kitchen, and sit him in a chair.

"Stay there."

He doesn't. He gets off the chair and lies down, bangs his head on the hardwood floor, and weeps.

I finish picking up.

"BUTTHEAD!" he yells. "I HATE YOU."

I place the dominoes in their wooden box, one by one, slide the top on and place it on a shelf. Simple, neat, contained.

The buzzer on the stove goes off. Dinner. Little J turns over onto his back and waves his arms and legs back and forth.

"I'm a snow angel," he says to my husband, who has just walked into the kitchen.

"Get up off the floor and quit acting so crazy."

"I AM NOT ACTING CRAZY! YOU ARE A SON-OF-A-BITCH!"

A beat. A very long beat in which I consider my options.

> **I look at his tearstained face, decorated with the smug expression of a child who knows better than his parent.**

I switch off the stove and grab Little J, lifting him off the floor and standing him upright in a single motion. I can be calm Zen mommy as long as I'm the only one involved but never, ever, go after my man.

I pull him so his face is inches from mine.

"Stop the snotty mouth with Daddy! Stop it! Stop it! Stop it!" Spit flies from my mouth onto his face. I'm shaking. Little J is screaming. "Stop it!"

"Mommy, where's the jelly?" Jacob, unfazed by a scene he's seen too many times to count, stands next to the refrigerator, door wide open.

"Where's the jelly?" I ask. "Where's the jelly? Find the damn jelly yourself!"

"Oooooh, Mommy said 'damn'," says Little J, completely recovered. I look at his tearstained face, decorated with the smug expression of a child who knows better than his parent. My hand still tightly grips his arm.

"Don't swear, Mommy," he says. "Swearing is bad."

I let go of his arm and laugh. A real, honest, from-the-gut laugh. Because yes, swearing is bad, and in this one, small comment—a comment that could be interpreted by some as the utmost in mouthiness, in disrespect—Little J has demonstrated to us where he's coming from: a place where the rules are the rules but where nothing he, nor I, nor his dad, nor his brother can do to make him follow them. At least not when unmedicated. At least not today.

The author says:

While we've managed to reduce Little J's medication, managing it, and him, continues to be a work-in-progress. Each day I'm becoming more and more aware of what's within my child's control and what isn't. For years we thought he was being rude and defiant and oppositional, but now we've come to the understanding that these are ways he impulsively expresses his lack of understanding or control. It will be very interesting to see how all of this changes (oh, how I hope it changes!) as he gets older.

In My Heart
by Kathy Stump

From this day on, now and forever more, you'll be in my heart.

Every child holds the key to unlock his mother's heart, but the truth is, some turn that key more effortlessly than others. Parenting a special needs child made me realize that sometimes love lodges in your heart in ways that you cannot predict.

Erica was conceived in the proverbial last-ditch effort, the cycle that marked the end of nearly five agonizing years of infertility treatment. She brought my husband, Phil, and me more joy than we ever imagined was possible, and we wanted to give her everything. However, we knew we could not repeat the infertility treatments in order to give her a sibling. That realization opened our eyes, and our hearts, to adoption.

The idea of adoption was sometimes on and sometimes off the table during our efforts to conceive. Shortly after our daughter's birth in 1996, we finally completed the application process through Catholic Charities. Less than two years later, we were offered the opportunity to adopt a newborn boy. We were thrilled! The wait had been shorter than we expected, and we were surprised a birth mother selected us since we had a biological child already.

The baby seemed healthy; seven pounds 10 ounces with a normal delivery, despite the birth mother having no prenatal care during the pregnancy. She admitted to binge drinking before she realized she was pregnant, toward the end of the first trimester. Knowing that alcohol can cause harm in utero we researched fetal alcohol syndrome (FASD/FAS) on the Internet. Based on what we learned, we concluded that if this baby was affected by FAS we were prepared to handle the outcome.

Our adoption agency allowed us to arrange for a well-baby check and an HIV/AIDS test before we took temporary custody. The baby screamed throughout the entire exam, but I was finally able to calm him as we walked out of the hospital. Phil and I both believed he would be fine once he adjusted to us. After all, he was barely three weeks old and was away from the familiar sounds of his birth mother's womb, had been moved to a wonderful, but unfamiliar foster home, then to us, and now, here he was in a brightly lit, noisy hospital. That's a lot for any newborn to adjust to. Little did I know that would be the last time I could calm him for nearly two years.

Come stop your crying, it will be all right …

We obtained temporary custody and brought Mason home—and the screaming continued. Mason's foster mother had documented how much he screamed and what strategies she'd used to try to calm him in a daily journal she kept while he was in her care. Early on I learned what she had experienced: *nothing* calmed him! I began to feel desperate, anxious, and wondered whether my husband felt the same way.

> Little did I know that would be the last time I could calm him for nearly two years.

"Do you feel as isolated as I do?" I asked him. "Have you bonded with him in any way, like you did with Erica?"

I worried that Mason's distress was my fault. I didn't yet feel the same connection to him that I had felt when our daughter was an infant. In fact, I didn't feel connected to him at all. There were *no* cuddly moments. Even while we fed him or changed his diapers he didn't look at us, or give us those adorable, gassy smiles that break every parent's heart. Instead, he pushed his way out of our arms. Touch actually seemed to cause him pain. It seemed screaming was the only sound he made. I felt barren, useless, and emotionally and physically drained.

A social worker visited regularly, and her visits were nerve-wracking. I actually worried that she would think we were abusing him. We prayed that Mason would be somewhat calm during her visits, and we shared our struggles with her. She reassured us, just as everyone else we knew did, that he would grow out of it, that it was just colic, which sometimes lasts longer than nine months. *Longer than nine months?* I didn't have nine months of strength or stamina in me. I couldn't possibly hold on that long.

This baby was tearing our family apart. We couldn't go anywhere together because Mason screamed and fussed the entire time. Yet we couldn't stay home all of the time either. We had an active, social four-year-old who needed interaction and our attention. I felt schizophrenic most days. Erica's affection and highly imaginative play brought me great joy, while the baby's screams dragged me to dark depths of emotions, the likes of which I had never before experienced. How could such a small person have such an enormous impact on me, my faith, my family life?

> This baby was tearing our family apart. How could such a small person have such an enormous impact on me, my faith, my family life?

For one so small, you seem so strong …

Our pediatrician checked Mason over many times, and finding nothing else wrong, concluded that he had colic. We switched formulas, endlessly rocked and walked him, and tried every other remedy we could find. But our efforts were to no avail. Finally, after Mason screamed for what seemed like an eternity during an office visit, the pediatrician referred us to a gastro-intestinal (GI) specialist at Children's Mercy

Hospital in Kansas City, Missouri, a wonderful facility where we would end up seeing many specialists.

The GI specialist diagnosed Mason with severe abnormal reflux, and at about four months old he had to spend a night at the hospital to complete a GI scope. A nurse strapped his squirming body and flailing arms to a metal crib and he wailed the entire time. As upset as I was for Mason—I knew lying on his back was extremely painful—I could not bring myself to stay with him. Phil spent a sleepless night beside him in his tiny room, unable to pick him up or offer him any relief. I spent the night worrying about both of them, but guiltily enjoyed a peaceful evening with Erica, the first in many months.

My arms will hold you, keep you safe and warm…

During his first year, Mason was subjected to more medicine than I have taken in my 40-plus years. Food was a major problem for his digestive system and the apparent cause of much of his screaming. We removed the offending foods from his diet—initially dairy, acidic fruits and juices, later eggs and nuts—and treated his environmental and seasonal allergies.

But I still felt something else was wrong, something was missing. Mason still didn't make direct eye contact nor respond to us like a typical infant. He had not developed a way to communicate, not ma-ma or da-da, not a word or sound for Erica, his favorite playmate, or for anything he wanted. No matter what we tried, we could not satisfy his needs. I felt we were failing. Parents are supposed to take care of their children. Everyone was extremely frustrated.

Finally, I called Children's Mercy to make an appointment for Mason to be evaluated for fetal alcohol syndrome and autism.

"You are either the most honest mother I've ever met, or you are his adoptive mother," the nurse on the other end of the phone commented.

"Yes, I am his adoptive mother," I said. But I didn't feel like his mother, and I was afraid that was the crux of the problem: we could not connect with one another as mother and son. Despite my desperate desire we did not yet love each other.

This bond between us can't be broken, I will be here, don't you cry...

I thought this evaluation, though many months away, would be the answer to our prayers. We gritted our way through the next four or five months, hoping for a cancellation so we could get in sooner. And, we hoped for some change, some improvement in Mason's symptoms as we waited. Mason was around two years of age when the evaluation finally took place. The psychologist diagnosed Mason with fetal alcohol effects (FASD/FAE), a milder form of fetal alcohol syndrome. The diagnosis was helpful. It opened the doors for several beneficial therapies: speech, occupational, and sensory integration. But it didn't solve all of our problems.

But I still felt something else was wrong, something was missing.

This was a very difficult time for us. The therapies were hard on Mason, so he was crankier than ever. Two moms in my playgroup—one a close friend—adopted children from China, and my sister adopted a one-year-old boy from Russia. Rather than sharing their joy, my reaction was bittersweet. Their adoption processes were much more difficult than ours had been, but their children's adjustments were seamless. I did not wish our struggles on anyone, but I wondered: *What had I done wrong? Was it too late to "fix" it?*

No matter what they say, you'll be in my heart ...

I began to withdraw. I knew people were tired of hearing about therapies, delays, ear infections, asthma attacks, and food allergies. I was exhausted from trying to learn more about all of these issues, meet with therapists, find sitters for Erica, take her to activities and preschool, *and* meet Mason's demanding needs. Most days, by bedtime, I had nothing left to give my daughter or my spouse. There was nothing left of *me.* Mason's needs were completely overwhelming.

I felt pulled in two opposing directions. I ping-ponged between the joy of spending time with Erica, who marveled at everything around her, and dreading when I had to tend to Mason's needs, which included a strict feeding schedule, therapeutic brushing and rubbing, and coaxing him to walk and play. It was hard to think of this as "therapeutic caregiving" when everything turned into a battle.

Several months after Mason started occupational therapy we began to see progress. Mason could tolerate more sensations—the swinging motion that once terrified him became bearable, finger paint and shaving cream were fun. During one session I confided to the occupational therapist that although we tried to do as much at-home therapy as possible, I knew we should be doing more.

"Your job is to be his mom, not his therapist," she reassured me. Her comment made me stop and think; maybe we could exhale a little bit. After all, he *seemed* to be getting better.

And, for a while, we did have a reprieve. Mason was more engaged and interactive. He seemed to have adapted to his routine. But then, when Mason turned three, the occupational therapy program ended. His speech therapy continued, but those sessions weren't fun, like the play-centered occupational therapy. His crankiness and irritability escalated. I was back to battling doctors and nurses for help, for any recommendations; back to trying to be Mason's therapist.

A cousin in the medical field helped us with research, served as a sounding board, and as a last minute babysitter/respite caregiver. Although she could not understand the depth of the sadness, grief, anger, and desperation parents feel when their child has disabilities, she helped me to think, question, and experiment. When I truly felt I could not take it anymore she would lift me up with a funny card, take me to a movie, or send me more information. I know we would not have made the strides we have without her help.

I may not be with you, but you got to hold on ...

School has been a roller coaster for Mason, to say the least. There have been some wonderful moments—like the preschool Mother's Day tea when Mason sat beside me, smiled, and seemed to know I was there—while other experiences left me wondering whether he even remembered me. Of course, there has also been the "typical boy" stuff: playground fights, classroom disruptions, and too many visits to the principal's office.

School grows progressively challenging for Mason each year. As concepts become increasingly abstract, responsibilities grow, and the need to organize becomes more important, the depth of his disability becomes more apparent. He has gone from enjoying school to hating it and wanting to quit. Initially we had resisted using medications with uncertain outcomes and unknown long-term effects, but we were forced to reconsider. How do you let your child continue to suffer?

> There was nothing left of *me*. Mason's needs were completely overwhelming.

Mason's immaturity and social ineptness are also becoming more and more apparent, affecting his friendships. I worry what these qualities will look like when Mason is in middle school, high school. How will we manage his behavior then? The questions seem endless and the answers are hard to take: expect three years delay in his ability to accept responsibility and in his overall level of maturity. Forever. *Really?*

'Cause you'll be in my heart, just look over your shoulder ...

Ten years and 13 doctors later we're still puzzling out his diagnoses. In addition to FAE, ADD is confirmed, but we're still wondering:

are Mason's irritability and dramatic mood swings depression, over-medication, lack of sleep, or something else entirely? I feel as if we're still at square one: same basic behaviors, different means of expression. Bottom line: are we helping him? I still don't know, and despite my own therapy I'm just as frustrated, angry, and tired as ever.

However, that anger and frustration fuel my efforts to help Mason unlock his full potential. They compel me to keep asking questions. I feel that I understand his world a little better, and as I learn to separate the behavior caused by his disability from his actual personality, I'm more compassionate toward him and am able to respond with more patience—and, finally—love.

I'll be there for you, Mason... *just look over your shoulder. I'll be with you, always and always.*

The author says:

Mason describes himself as a "funny and playful" fifth grader. His varied interests include sports, video/Wii games and nearly any 3-D movie. He dreams of being an astronaut. His favorite books are the Diary of a Wimpy Kid *series, which he enjoys with any Black Eyed Peas song. Mason is quite a creative writer and enjoys participating in his school's art club. Mom and Dad attribute his new-found confidence and contentedness to attending a public school that both understands and is able to accommodate his learning needs.*

Tell Us More: Expert Q & A with Lucy Jane Miller, Ph.D., OTR

Founder and Executive Director, Sensory Processing Disorder Foundation and Director of the STAR (Sensory Therapies And Research) Center, Greenwood Village, Colorado

Q. Several of our parent-authors write that sensory processing issues were the first clue that their children were wired differently. Those children, who were later diagnosed with ADD/ADHD or another disorder were, as infants: unusually sensitive to stimulation, poor sleepers, and difficult or impossible for parents to calm. Pediatricians typically said the infants were just colicky. Does this very early presentation match with your experience and research?

A. If only I could get funding for a "fussy baby" clinic! What is colic? What is a "fussy baby" or a "difficult child?" I think these likely are children with Sensory Processing Disorder. Yes, that matches with our experience at STAR Center so closely. We do see many infants and toddlers, and the children who come to us at later ages invariably have in their histories early indicators of difficulties processing sensation. The only exception is one of the six subtypes called Sensory Under-Responsive. These kids are more likely to be "ever-so-quiet" and are reportedly "good babies" because of their processing difficulties. They are more on the unaware spectrum than the over-responsive spectrum.

Q. How common is SPD? How often does it overlap with ADHD in particular?

A. There are only two prevalence studies of SPD to my knowledge. One study surveyed parents of kindergarten students in a Colorado school district and published in 2004 (Ahn, Miller et al.). We found a 5% prevalence rate calculating very conservatively. Dr. Alice Carter and her team at Yale and University of Massachusetts/Boston, completed an extremely rigorous epidemiology study. They studied every baby born in and around New Haven from birth to age eight and found that 16.5% of the children had significant sensory symptoms. What is most important about her studies is that none of those children had autism spectrum disorders or developmental disabilities and 75% did not meet criteria for any psychological or psychiatric (e.g., DSM) condition. This is the most convincing data that exists suggesting that SPD is a valid separate syndrome.

Some children with ADHD have sensory challenges, however many do not. Our data show 40% of children with ADHD have sensory symptoms.

Q. So far, SPD hasn't been listed in the Diagnostic and Statistical Manual of Mental Disorders (DSM-IV-TR). Will SPD appear in the next edition, the DSM-5 (May, 2013)?

A. The process for getting SPD or any new diagnosis is somewhat of a black box. A final submission of requested material was completed in July 2011. SPD can get into the DSM in one of three ways: as a new diagnosis, as a subtype of an existing diagnosis, or as a novel diagnosis, which needs additional research before it can be validated as a new condition. Any of these options would be outstanding as far as we are concerned; a step in the right direction!

Q. Does the ability to tolerate sensory stimuli tend to improve with age for our kids?

A. Children with SPD tend to "look" better over time. Whether they are actually better seems (personal opinion, no data on this point) to revolve around them receiving an accurate diagnosis (including SPD subtype), getting appropriate treatment, and the family acquiring strategies to manage daily life challenges independently. We feel strongly that an intensive model of treatment is much more effective for most children than a once a week model.

Breathe

by Robin Rhodes

"How are you feeling, Lucais?" Dr. Anna asks my eight-year-old son.

"I'm not sleeping well."

"Why is this?"

"I'm afraid an assassin will try to kill me."

I spin my head around to face my son, blown away by this comment that came from nowhere. I avert my eyes from Dr. Anna, afraid of what she is thinking.

"Why would you think something like this?" She continues in her formal tone of voice.

"Because I hear the footsteps outside my door at night."

"That's just Dad and me walking down the hall," I interject. I had been pacing at night again. That had to be what was making the noise.

"How's his weight?" I ask, changing the subject, not wanting to get started on Lucais' strange, irrational fears. The doctor flips through her chart and murmurs some things in her native language of Romanian. I wait, wondering what she is thinking.

"The weight is up again. 111 pounds."

I cringe. I can't begin to imagine what it is like to be an eight-year-old and weigh as much as I did in high school. I knew Lucais' clothes were tight again, but didn't want to admit that we may need to start shopping in the men's section. Dr. Anna shakes her head, still looking at the paperwork.

"It's not the Geodine. That doesn't cause weight gain."

No, she's right. It's not the meds. It's the disease. My son has early onset bipolar disorder, and for him one of the byproducts of the disorder is an insatiable need for food. He can't seem to get enough food, specifically carbs and sweets. We have been talking about getting a lock box for the snack cabinet. It wouldn't be fair to his siblings though. But then not much about life in our family is.

"How is the anger?"

Dr. Grundle, Lucais' therapist, says Lucais needs to be practicing his breathing more: *Every day, just for a little while.*

I nod. I know it's important to make him sit still for 15 minutes every day and practice this anger management technique, but it's not easy. I want him to be a normal boy, to come home from school and play with his friends. But the truth is that he isn't normal. He has anger issues that we have to work on.

"He tries," I tell her. "He hasn't had any major outbursts this month."

This is good. Lucais sometimes explodes for no apparent reason and becomes violent. He punches his brother without cause or kicks his sister for something she said or did. Sometimes he throws a toy or game controller across the room. But we're lucky. He's never seriously hurt himself or anyone else.

After these episodes, when he's damaged something or hurt his brother or sister, he'll break down, saying he hates himself, that he's an awful person. I do the only thing I know to do. I hold him and tell him he's wrong, with tears of my own rolling down my face. You see, he's not the only person in our family with bipolar disorder. I have it too. I am the one who passed the gene to Lucais. That is a hard thing for a parent to be burdened with. I remind myself every day that I inherited the predisposition for the disease, just like him, and am not to blame. But my own insecurities continue to torment me. For many years I was determined not to have children or even burden a partner with my unexpected outbursts and irrational behavior. But I met Lucais' father and all I wanted was to have a family. Does that make me a selfish person? I once believed so.

"How is school?" Dr. Anna pulls me from my thoughts.

"Good. Always good. He brought home his report card—all good grades except handwriting. He's still rushing."

School is one of the things that made getting an accurate diagnosis so hard. Lucais learned from me early in life to hide his problems. Except for an occasional glimpse of emotions, to the outside world, he's a good kid who loves school. Mostly he saves his outbursts for at home.

> **You see, he's not the only person in our family with bipolar disorder. I have it too.**

Before we found Dr. Anna we worked with Children's Hospital of Milwaukee. Luc was only three when I first noticed his inability to handle much stimulation and his short temper. The doctors at Children's diagnosed him with a mood disorder, which could be situational rather than foreshadowing that a diagnosis of bipolar disorder was to come. Because of this it took months for me to convince the doctors to try medications. I felt a sense of doom all around me. I saw hints of myself as a child in Lucais and couldn't bear the thought of him living through the emotional rollercoaster I rode as a child. When I was young there was no such thing as early onset bipolar disorder. I was labeled with depression and drugged on antidepressants only, leading me to many years of manic cycles; of not sleeping for days, skipping meals, and suffering from constant paranoia. I knew that the play therapy sessions the psychiatrist at Children's insisted on were a waste of time and money. Lucais needed more than a playmate. He needed someone to talk to and to be chemically balanced. That meant he needed drugs.

"He did have a small episode a few weeks ago when he took his Geodine later than normal and spent the next morning in a daze. He had to sleep it off in the school nurse's office."

"He needs to take the meds at dinner," she reminds me.

"Yes, I know."

In order for Lucais' medications to work he must follow precise instructions. The Geodine must be taken with food and at exactly the same time every day. If he takes it too late he doesn't sleep well and spends the next day in a fog. If he forgets his other meds he gets edgy and may have an outburst. If the doses are too close together he suffers other side effects.

"I think we should add another drug. It will help with the weight and it will act as a mood stabilizer."

"Will it replace any of the others?"

"We'll see how he responds to it."

Another drug. Sometimes I think I opened a can of worms when I demanded meds for Lucais. I sign the paperwork acknowledging the risks involved with the new medication. Dr. Anna writes the new prescription and refills of the others and hands them to me.

"When is his next appointment with Dr. Grundle?" she asks.

"Next Monday," I reply.

Dr. Grundle is a godsend. He's Lucais' fifth therapist and the first one that has made progress with him. Rather than play therapy, which only seemed to distract Lucais, Dr. Grundle teaches him life skills, anger management, and good decision making.

Satisfied that everything is in order Dr. Anna stands and opens her door. She looks at Lucais who has been quiet most of the appointment.

"Make sure you practice your breathing and take your pills," she reminds him.

He nods and walks past her out the door. I follow behind.

Luc climbs into the backseat of the car, and as I settle in the driver's seat, his eyes meet mine in the rearview mirror.

"Did I do okay?"

> Another drug. Sometimes I think I opened a can of worms when I demanded meds for Lucais.

I stare back at him, confused at first by what he means. And then I realize he was trying to appease the doctor—and me—with his silence. It scares me sometimes how well he can read me. He sensed my nervousness, knew I'd changed the topic when he brought up his irrational thoughts. I scold myself for letting my own paranoia of what people think get in the way of helping my son.

"You have to be honest with her. She can't help you if you aren't." The reminder is as much for me as it is for Luc.

"Will I always have to go to her?"

This is the part that I hate, when he has a realization that is far too deep for an eight-year-old to have. My stomach clenches.

"Not necessarily her, but yes, you will always need to see someone, just like I do."

"Why?"

"Because we have a disease that there isn't a cure for. It's like Grandma's diabetes. She has to see a doctor on a regular basis for that too." I try to emphasize that our disorder is as physical as any other.

"Why can't they find a cure?" he asks, looking out the window as we make our way back to school.

"Maybe someday they will. But for now, there isn't one."

"That sucks."

"I know," I reply. There really is nothing else to say. This disease is something that we both will have to live with for the rest of our lives, so we deal with it the best way we can.

We pull up to the drop-off zone at the grade school and I walk Luc into the office. We follow this routine about every other week, so there is no need for any conversation between the secretary and me as she writes out Luc's pass to class. I find myself wondering what she thinks about my son. I used to work for the school, so I know that the office staff knows—and talks about—everything. I try to tamp down my urges to defend Luc and myself, to tell them there is nothing wrong with us, but it is a constant inner battle. Luc grabs me into a tight embrace and gives me a kiss.

"I love you, mom. I'll see you after school."

A small smile crosses my face.

"Love you too. Be good."

I watch him walk through the door and into the main section of the school and the smile slips away. Without another look toward anyone in the office I turn and head back outside. I climb behind the steering wheel and sit quietly for a moment. Before I realize it, tears start to fall down my face. I love my son with all my heart, though he tries my patience and self-control constantly. I swipe at the tears and remind myself that everything I do for him is in the hopes that he can have a better childhood than mine.

I wasn't diagnosed and treated until I was eighteen. The irrational thoughts and feelings of paranoia and constantly feeling not good enough were left to fester inside of me for years. I understand the importance of early detection of bipolar and other neurological disorders. Even though I fight against the urge to pretend that everything is normal with Lucais, I'm determined to get him help. Instead of seeing his outbursts as childish temper tantrums, as everyone thought mine were, I see them for what they are—symptoms of a disorder he can't control. Hopefully, by the time Luc is an adult he will be well equipped to function in the world and not have to fight a constant battle within himself like I do.

> **Instead of seeing his outbursts as childish temper tantrums, as everyone thought mine were, I see them for what they are—symptoms of a disorder he can't control.**

As I drive home I realize that this is my greatest wish for my son. I dream of Luc being happy and in control of his life. In this way, I am just like any other parent.

And really, can any parent hope for anything more?

The author says:

Our beloved Luc is nine years old and is ever changing, ever a challenge, but he is also the most loving and intelligent child a mother could ask for. I often wonder why I was blessed with a child who is at times infuriating—like when he shattered my laptop in a fit of manic fury (while I was writing this essay!)—but who loves me unconditionally, despite all my own flaws. I want to dedicate this essay to parents who, like me, have walked in our children's shoes, while still learning to walk in our own. Those shoes may have gotten bigger, but when we see our children's pain, we grow into them quickly.

Tell Us More: Expert Q & A with Kathy Flaminio

Founder, 1000 Petals LLC

Q. In this essay, Lucais practices deep breathing as a way to manage his temper. Deep breathing is one aspect of mindfulness. What is mindfulness, and how does it relate to ADHD or other conditions, such as mood disorders? Is there research about this?

A. Mindfulness, according to Jon Kabit Zinn, means: "…paying attention in a particular way; on purpose, in the present moment, and nonjudgmentally." When we pay attention in a mindful way, experiencing the present moment, this creates a physiological change in the body which impacts the way we think and how we relate to others. (*The Mindful Brain: Reflection and Attunement in the Cultivation of Well-Being*; Daniel Siegel; W.W. Norton, 2007)

Teaching mindfulness techniques to children actually teaches the skill of paying attention and focusing. It literally gives children the experience of what it means to pay attention to the present moment. As a yoga therapist at the Minnesota Amplatz Children's Hospital, I have seen profound changes in children gaining insight into their behavior and finding wisdom from within. We call this type of work "working from the inside out." This facilitates a profound shift in their mindset from depression and saying "I can't/I won't/I'm not" to saying "YES!" to life. These shifts have occurred with the integration of mindfulness, Yoga-based activities, and breathing exercises.

Using yoga-based movement and mindfulness techniques with children not only teaches movement that regulates the nervous system, it gives them a new perspective of who they are. Every person wants to feel whole and connected. Children with ADD/HD often feel scattered and disconnected. The ability to learn what it feels like to be centered and calm is life changing for many. Children begin to shift how they perceive themselves from distracted and impulsive to focused and in control. The yoga postures provide children the tangible skills and experience of being still, grounded, and connected. They learn the connection between the mind, body, and heart by infusing the cognitive and emotional skills with the physical postures. When the balancing poses and inversions are connected to self-talk ("I am strong, I can do this") and the emotional connection of feeling steady, the children learn at their inner core what it means to be grounded and connected.

According to G. Seilier (as cited in *Elementary School Guidance and Counseling Journal* 12 (4), 229-237), "Yoga for children is a relaxation technique that has been found to reduce stress and tension, dissipate excess energy, relieve tiredness, lengthen attention span, improve physical health, sharpen concentration, enhance mental clarity, and cultivate better interpersonal relationships." Children who participated in mindfulness programs have shown an increase in attention, relaxation, as well as decreased conduct and anger management problems (Sines, 2009).

To address the need for a holistic approach to therapy, Yoga Calm® integrates mindfulness, yoga-based movement, and nervous system regulation with social/emotional skill development. This approach helps children on all levels—physically, emotionally, and mentally.

References:

Gillen, J., and Gillen, L. (2007). *Yoga Calm for Children: Educating Heart, Mind and Body*. Portland, Oregon.

Peck, H. L., Kehle, T. J., Bray, M. A., & Theodore, L. A. (2005). Yoga as an Intervention for Children with Attention Problems. *School Psychology Review*, 34(3), 415-424.

Seiler, G., & Renshaw, K. (1978). Yoga for Kids. *Elementary School Guidance and Counseling, 12*(4), 229-237.

Siegel, Daniel (2007). *The Mindful Brain: Reflection and Attunement in the Cultivation of Well-Being*.

Sines, Julie Shupe (2009). Ohio State University. *The Perceptions of Children Following Participation in a Yoga and Mindfulness Program: A Qualitative Study.*

White, L.. (2009). Yoga for Children. *Pediatric Nursing*, 35(5), 277-83, 295.

Clearing the Haze
by Maureen Sherbondy

I am giving my 15-year-old speed.

This thought jolts me as I drive from the gym to the coffee shop. Soon I will be sipping java—my own form of speed. Lately I drink coffee because without it I can't wake up; I drift around in a cloudy haze, unable to string words together into coherent sentences. My son's form of speed is 15 milligrams of Adderall, a medication for attention deficit disorder (ADD). Monday through Friday for the last two years (with summers and vacations off) he swallows the capsule down with juice.

I hate giving my child medication of any kind. I rarely take pills. My own mom was a firm believer in chicken soup, rest, and fluids. I don't recall taking pills or liquids to cure my childhood colds or infections, let alone my up and down moods. If you had asked me three years ago what I thought of ADD, or the medications associated with the condition, I'd have shaken my head, told you ADD was an excuse used by moms who had very active boys—moms who didn't know how to handle their children. That the kids should just buckle down and get their homework done. That there are no excuses for laziness.

But then something changed. Two years ago my older son, Jacob, became cranky, emotional, forgetful. He began receiving terrible grades. His marks had gradually declined in middle school, and then suddenly he brought home C's and D's. Jacob would complete his homework and then forget to hand it in. Or he wouldn't write down the entire assignment and he'd get partial credit. His self-esteem became very low. He's a smart kid, but his grades no longer reflected that picture to the world. He couldn't make sense of the gap in this fact, and neither could we. Had he become suddenly stupid?

Jacob knew he had a problem, but didn't understand how to communicate it to us. On a sheet of doodles and scribbles tucked in a drawer in his messy room he wrote a question in sloppy red ink: *Learning Disorder?*

Jacob later told us that as far back as elementary school he had trouble following instructions, remembering to hand in assignments, and finishing tests. He dealt with his confusion by creating alternative methods. If he couldn't add like the teacher was adding he would invent a way that worked for him. That's probably why we didn't pick up on the clues sooner; he is a bright, creative kid who found ways to compensate for his problems. Math and reading took him longer to finish than other subjects. He could do well on tests and quizzes if he had enough time, but there was never enough time. He had been frustrated for years.

Jacob started having outbursts of anger. He'd scream at me, slam his bedroom door. He cried easily, and got frustrated very quickly. My husband, Anthony, and I decided to consult with a psychologist who specialized in children and adolescents. She began counseling Jacob, working on his emotional outbursts, his anger.

The psychologist, a mature and experienced woman who had treated hundreds of kids, suggested early on that we test Jacob for ADD. Anthony and I stared at her blankly. Was she talking about our son? We shook our heads. ADD? Jacob?

We wouldn't agree to the testing at first, we were so sure that Jacob didn't have this problem. We even wondered: was this a ploy to make extra money?

While Jacob continued to meet with the psychologist and talk about his feelings, Anthony and I kept returning to the ADD question. Could

Jacob have it? Maybe? Finally, reluctantly, we agreed to pay the large fee and have our son take the test—just to rule out that possibility.

Much to our surprise the psychologist's suspicion was validated. Our son had ADD, as well as processing issues in both math and language arts. Yes he was very bright, but he needed extra time to process information, and, to treat the lack of focus that kept him from writing down and handing in assignments, he probably also needed medication.

I was very reluctant to give Jacob drugs. But as I started reading about ADD I learned that accommodations alone—allowing extra time to complete tests, sitting in the front row, and getting copies of class notes—were often not enough. Medication made the biggest difference. I also learned that there are several categories of medications, and they all have their side effects. One category could cause liver damage. One type might cause heart problems. But the percentage of people who suffer these negative effects is very low. I consciously shelved my worry gene, and we decided to have Jacob give medication a try. Within two months my son was getting straight A's. Wow. What a difference.

> **Anthony and I kept returning to the ADD question. Could Jacob have it? Maybe?**

But there were side effects to the medication. Jacob said he felt "funny." And being a creative kid he hated how focused the medication made him. He said it prevented him from daydreaming, from accessing his "rooms" of creativity. He felt like he was in a large house with hundreds of rooms to explore, but the medicine forced him to stay on one path—the long hallway that would take him to the end of the house. It would not allow him to peek inside those fun, mysterious, exciting rooms filled with flashing lights, bright colors, music, and murals.

"The rooms are still there, they are waiting for you," I said. "When the medicine wears off at 6:00 in the evening, have at it. You can explore those other rooms all you want."

Every once in a while when a new study is released that suggests an ADD medication is dangerous—that this or that drug causes death in a very low percentage of the people who take it—I force myself to refocus on how much better Jacob is doing in school. His grades are in sync with how he perceives himself. And, he's a happier kid now.

In the future maybe he'll only take the medication on exam days—for midterms and finals, or when taking the SAT's. But if he has to take medication every day he's at school then that's the way it will be.

No, I don't like the fact that my kid takes a drug every day. And I still feel a tinge of guilt on days like today, when I think about Jacob while I drink my large java. But as my caffeine-clarity kicks in I imagine my son's medicine clearing away his mental fog. With each sip of coffee I swallow, the doubts I once had about medicating my son slip away. I've woken up to the fact that in the end, my son will be a happier kid—and a more successful adult—with medication than without it.

The author says:

Jacob, now 20, is a college student at UNC-Chapel Hill.

"Please, someone show me these hordes of children who are zombie-shuffling through their days in a haze of behavior-stilting 'chemicals.' Please. Show them to me. Now. Because all I know for certain is that my child is vivacious, chatty, funny, and compassionate about 35 minutes after he swallows his medication every morning. Before that dose kicks in, he displays all of those qualities, along with moodiness, impulsivity, and over-sensitivity. I've yet to meet a robot, but I have met children who are drowning in their disorder while adults stand back and crow about spankings and discipline—as though those are new concepts to exhausted parents like me."

Kelly Quiñones Miller, mom of Javier (ADHD)

Part 4: The Village

A Virtual Village
by Robbi Nester

A sturdy golden haired child, about three years old, stands on the grass of a sunlit playground, one hand pushed as far as it will go into his mouth while the other tugs at his earlobe. This was my son, Jeremy. Now, at 20, he is lean and handsome, almost a man.

I used to ponder whether anyone would become a parent if she really knew what the job entails. We all start out trusting and blissfully ignorant, sure in the knowledge that it has all been done, albeit with varying degrees of competence, countless times before. So when we look down at the tiny helpless being entrusted to us, splayed like a starfish and wriggling its four perfect limbs, we feel nothing but love, and the certainty that we will puzzle it all out. And should we hit a snag, well, there are always the countless doctors, experts, and the wisdom of the generations to fall back on. But sometimes even all of that is not enough.

When people don't understand a phenomenon or when the feelings it invokes in them are too painful, they prefer not to see it. This was true of my son's difficulties. He had some pretty heavy neurological baggage: Tourette syndrome (TS), obsessive-compulsive disorder (OCD), attention deficit hyperactivity disorder (ADHD), anxiety, and bipolar disorder were the fruits of my family tree, and Jeremy, we eventually learned, had inherited all of them.

Instead of recognizing and treating these disorders early on however, Jeremy's doctors and teachers and the community around us seemed invested in the idea that, in the words of one clueless neighbor, my son was simply a "bad apple," with parents who had caused his problems by inconsistent or absent discipline. His first grade teachers apparently agreed. When Jeremy flipped the bird at another first grader the teachers were shocked, assuming that the gesture represented something he was seeing around the house. Jeremy's knowing comments about sex, uttered in the hearing of a classmate's mother, strengthened the impression that he was learning the wrong things at home, where we must, people reasoned, behave in an altogether different way than we did in public.

Jeremy's aggression toward other children was also a matter of discussion among teachers and parents in the community. The director of his preschool asked that we please not permit him to watch action cartoons like "The Power Rangers" because he was imitating what he saw on the screen. I agreed to control what he viewed more carefully, only to find that it made no difference—unless Thomas the Tank Engine also breeds violence. When I bought him a set of miniature trains to encourage more peaceable play, he re-envisioned a small iron model of a caboose as an airborne weapon, knocking me nearly silly.

> I used to ponder whether anyone would become a parent if she really knew what the job entails. We all start out trusting and blissfully ignorant, sure in the knowledge that it has all been done, albeit with varying degrees of competence, countless times before.

Family elders shook their heads at Jeremy's behavior and the expressions on the faces of people in the supermarket shamed me when he acted out in the aisles. The implication was that I in particular, the mother, was responsible for Jeremy's problematic behavior. And I knew I was, if only genetically. I lay awake many nights questioning my parenting skills, wondering whether through my own patterns of behavior I was somehow causing him to act out.

I looked for evidence of my poor parenting skills. The many books on childrearing I bought during that period still pack the shelves around me, some titles politely tiptoeing around the problem, others forthrightly naming it. My husband, Richard, and I applied behavioral methods as elaborate as plans for the invasion of a small country, all to no avail.

Jeremy's problems worsened. Around the ages of four and five, he refused to have bowel movements for weeks at a time. His face would grow white and drawn, with dark circles around the eyes. He squirmed unceasingly, in evident pain. I tried to get him to eat fruit and drink more juices, but still, no go. He seemed to regard the toilet as a sort of torture chamber, and it was only by resorting to bribery—bags of M&Ms and other treats—that we could get him to sit on it at all.

> The implication was that I in particular, the mother, was responsible for Jeremy's problematic behavior.

At the same time he refused to eat (lest he have bowel movements), seemed never to sleep, and would rage and cry uncontrollably, apropos of nothing at all. Mealtimes were particularly stressful. We had long ago given up asking him to sit down and eat at the table. Instead, we provided a child-sized table and chair in the center of the living room, where we placed his food. He would grab handfuls of noodles or a half a sandwich as he ran through the room, an unstoppable whirlwind, seldom stopping to sit down, even to watch a favorite show on television.

The pediatrician grew tired of my calls and visits. He thought I was making a big deal out of nothing, particularly since Jeremy's problematic behaviors were episodic. Much of the time he was a happy little chap, athletic and popular with children his own age, full of energy and charisma. Because of that it was not until Jeremy was about seven years old and had developed his first obvious tic—a dry cough that would not go away—that a doctor paid any attention at all.

The cough had begun as a lung infection, so Jeremy was treated by a specialist and spent hours sucking white smoke through a plastic tube, medication meant to open his airways. But when the infection subsided the cough persisted. The steroids the doctor prescribed caused sustained rages—screaming, violent fits that scared us silly. One time he shrieked and wept uncontrollably for two hours, battering holes in the wall with his furious fists. It would not be the last time that doctors' "cures" turned out to be much worse than the symptoms they were intended to treat.

I begged Jeremy's doctor for a referral to a psychiatrist and he finally agreed. Jeremy was eight years old when we met with the psychiatrist. We described to her his steadily worsening behavior problems, the continued cough, then in its third year, and the bowel problems. By then Jeremy had also developed a complex arm tic that still occasionally surfaces to this day, a quick flex of his arm that looks like a chicken flapping its wing, a movement the doctor noted immediately. She diagnosed Tourette's, along with ADHD, OCD, and a mood disorder, and prescribed a low dose of Tenex, a blood pressure medication that is frequently given as a first-line defense against tics. She also referred us to a support group sponsored by the Tourette Syndrome Association (TSA).

At first I denied the possibility that Jeremy could have Tourette's. Like many people I thought of this disorder as being characterized mainly by the uncontrollable shouting of obscenities (coprolalia). Actually, I learned, only a comparatively small percentage of people with the disorder manifest this symptom. Despite the challenges presented by the disorder, which was poorly understood and seldom recognized, we were grateful to know that this problem had a name.

Richard, Jeremy, and I attended a meeting of the support group, where we met people of all kinds and ages: adults with the disorder, as well as children and their parents. Some told stories of how they went from doctor to doctor only to be told they were imagining the problem. One parent described taking her daughter to 15 doctors before she finally found one who recognized her Tourette's for what it was.

As parents unburdened themselves at the support group meeting we learned that others had even less support than we did. Parents of other children and even their own family members shunned them and their children, and many had no medical insurance.

Sitting in that room listening to the testimony of parents and adults who had weathered this nightmare, my husband, Richard, reddened and choked up, and tears marked their way down his face. He cried for our pain and for Jeremy's, for the injustice that all the people in this room had suffered. Yet we both felt relief: anything with a name has been studied and categorized, thus could probably be treated. Best of all we were no longer to blame.

> My husband, Richard, and I applied behavioral methods as elaborate as plans for the invasion of a small country, all to no avail.

The stories we heard at the support group meeting convinced me that either Richard or I must become a scholar of the disorder, to gather and archive the latest research on Tourette syndrome and the comorbid conditions Jeremy had been diagnosed with. Armed with this information we would request the latest medication or therapy from Jeremy's doctors. Since I worked only part-time I decided to become our family's self-made expert.

There is something inherently wrong with the system when, in order to receive a correct diagnosis and effective treatment, a parent must know more than the doctors. TS isn't all that uncommon (the latest estimates suggest that about 3% of the general population has some level of the disorder), but doctors tend to know almost nothing about it, and what they do know they have been taught by parents like me. If I had ever harbored the belief, fed by reruns of crinkly-eyed Dr. Welby, in the benevolent and all-knowing wisdom of the medical establishment, I gave it up now that my son's education, medical treatment, and social well-being depended entirely upon my own advocacy.

Over time the doctor changed Jeremy's medication, prescribing an SSRI (selective serotonin reuptake inhibitor), Paxil, to help him with his OCD symptoms, like his need for certain things to be "just right." For instance, when I tied his shoes he'd fall apart if the two loops of the bow were not perfectly symmetrical.

Meanwhile I wrangled on a regular basis with Jeremy's teachers, the principal, and the district, who insisted simultaneously and entirely irrationally that our son, intelligent and articulate as he was, didn't need any special services, while at the same time they complained that he was unmanageable. When Jeremy was in second grade one teacher (a narrow, biased woman who had seemingly returned from retirement solely to torture Jeremy) left him in a corner facing away from the other children in the class every day for two months, except during my weekly visits as a volunteer, when like the other students he faced the board.

When another parent volunteer finally told me what was really happening I charged into the principal's office and demanded that this treatment stop. She shook her head ruefully and insisted I was making a mistake. Jeremy was simply being given consequences for his negative behavior, something that he clearly was not receiving at home. Angry at her ignorance, I said, "No. You're the one who is making a mistake." It was only threat of legal action—and the presence of Jeremy's doctor, a well-known local expert in childhood ADHD at a school meeting—

that stopped the school from continuing this deplorable form of discipline.

By then the punishment had taken its toll. Jeremy had grown hollow-eyed and despondent. Every day after school, facing torturous hours of homework, he would turn to me and say, "I want to die."

Fearing a suicide attempt Richard and I took Jeremy to the psychiatrist's office, only to have him flee her office and scale two twisting flights of stairs in a single jump. We pursued him, but it took two security guards to subdue him, a thin and wiry boy of 10, and bring him back to the office. The doctor looked at him for a few seconds and turned to me.

> It would not be the last time that doctors' "cures" turned out to be much worse than the symptoms they were intended to treat.

"It might be a good idea to hospitalize him," she said. Jeremy begged me not to leave him there, and the thought of doing that horrified me as well. Eventually Jeremy promised not to hurt himself, and I promised to lock all the knives and scissors and other dangerous tools away safely, and we turned for home, a prescription for an increased dose of Paxil clutched in my hand.

For a while things looked up. During the summer after Jeremy finished fourth grade we flew to San Francisco for a rare family vacation. Jeremy had never tolerated change well so we usually avoided travel. However, the increased dose of Paxil appeared to be working. Jeremy's behavior had quieted. He was sleeping more soundly and eating well, so we set off on our trip.

We had some lovely and memorable moments standing by the Golden Gate Bridge, crawling through tunnels at the science museum, wandering the damp paths under gigantic redwoods at the Muir National

Monument, but as quickly as the tics and behaviors had waned they began again, this time worse than before. Once again, Jeremy began to have violent meltdowns and his depression became more profound. Clearly the medication was not working. In fact, I believed it was part of the problem.

In search of verification of this from experts on the subject we traveled to San Diego, where Jeremy took part in a TSA research study. I was told that the medication could not be the problem. My insistence that Jeremy's behavior had changed radically dating from the time the doctor had prescribed Paxil had no effect on anyone's judgment.

Desperate to solve the problem and to prove that medication could indeed be its cause I searched through the stacks at the library for works on the subject of Tourette's and rage. I found none. I asked the reference librarian if the library owned any books on the subject, but she looked at me blankly. As I stood there weeping, feeling helpless, a woman I did not know approached me.

"I overheard you ask for books about rage and Tourette's," she said. "My son has both and it was other parents who gave us the help we needed. Do you have a computer?" she asked, and handed me a small slip of paper with a URL scrawled on it. It was the address for TS-parents2, a Yahoo group composed mostly of parents of kids with Tourette's plus comorbid disorders who turned to each other for the help they could not get elsewhere.

Eager to connect with these parents I joined the online group. That proved to be the best thing I had ever done, for Richard, Jeremy, and me. The group was a solid and generous source of advice, information, wisdom, and support—even friendship—from people who well understood our experiences. Some of the other member's children had also been prescribed Paxil or other SSRI's and had suddenly changed, become depressed, suicidal—even homicidal. When the medications were discontinued it became obvious that they had caused the changes, as I had suspected. Such anecdotal reports eventually led to the famous black box warnings these medications now bear.

I called Jeremy's psychiatrist and made an appointment. I told her about the parents I had met online and their experiences with SSRI's. Despite her skepticism the doctor stopped the medication. Improvement was slow. Although the pharmacist insisted the medication would be out of Jeremy's bloodstream in a few days it took months for his brain chemistry to return to normal. That was a long, painful period, but if it had not been for the generosity of my online community things could have had a far worse ending.

> **There is something inherently wrong with the system when, in order to receive a correct diagnosis and effective treatment, a parent must know more than the doctors.**

From this experience I learned that there were thousands of invisible others in cyberspace who had to deal every day with their children's (and sometimes their own) irrational obsessions and bizarre symptoms, like a friend whose brilliant daughter, gifted intellectually and artistically, insisted there were gremlins in the toilet, or the parent who was nearly killed several times by her psychotic child. From these parents Richard and I learned how lucky we are to have a child with comparatively mild symptoms, to be capable of advocating for him, and to have insurance and access to a doctor who recognized the disorders Jeremy had. Others I met online were not as lucky. The options available to the poor, uneducated, and uninsured are shockingly few and far worse than inadequate, bordering sometimes on the criminal, with children as young as 10 being sent to juvenile hall for exhibiting symptoms of neurological disorders that they cannot control.

When my father, who recently died at the age of 93, was a child and showed what we now know were signs of severe Tourette's, he was completely abandoned by his family. He was thrown out of school for having outbursts of bizarre behavior and sent to reform school. Recognizing that his behavior was not criminal the family moved my father to a charity hospital, where he languished for months at a time without visitors because people feared his strange behaviors resulted from a contagious disease.

Though psychiatric treatment has changed in myriad ways since then, things are still far from ideal. Many parents are offered no assistance paying for the very expensive medications their children need (and which still, unfortunately, often return uncertain benefits) and are given no respite to regain their own spent energy. I have heard of such parents turning their children over to the state in the mistaken belief that this will get the children the help the parents themselves could not afford. Indeed, in the years I have participated in the TS-Parents group on Yahoo these problems seem to have proliferated, not lessened, in either frequency or difficulty.

Yet at the same time many parents feel hope. I speak with old friends from the difficult early days and learn that their children, like mine, are finding their own ways in the world. With the help of new medications— Risperdal, an atypical antipsychotic, and Wellbutrin, an SSRI, in our case—and for some new dietary and alternative treatments, as well as cognitive behavioral therapy, our children are going to college, working, starting families, and learning to cope with their disorders.

Jeremy is now off medications, his tics almost completely quelled, and though he still can sometimes still be a bit prickly he has grown into a compassionate and kind young man. He shares an apartment with several roommates and attends the community college where I teach.

In the process of his difficult journey Jeremy has developed an impressive sensitivity to others. In particular he has a gift for understanding and working with children and for mediating interpersonal conflicts. He hopes someday to become a therapist or counselor so that others like his earlier self—that toddler on the playground, so full of tics and quirks—may benefit from what he has learned.

I too have learned many things from this experience, among them that beyond passing along certain genes, I was not to blame for Jeremy's conditions. Regardless of what teachers, neighbors, and strangers in the grocery store thought, I never was at the core of the problem; in fact, I was always integral to its solution. My persistence in finding help for Jeremy paid off. I now encourage parents in the TS-parents2 group to persevere, even when others doubt them. I give them permission to arm themselves with information and to respectfully question the experts, or to seek multiple opinions if a practitioner is not open to their participation in the treatment process. I tell them that no amount of struggle in service to another is ever wasted, that their efforts will reap rewards in the long run.

> Regardless of what teachers, neighbors, and strangers in the grocery store thought, I never was at the core of the problem; in fact, I was always integral to its solution.

As for me, watching my warm, handsome son make his way in the world is all the reward I need.

The author says:

This essay is dedicated to my wonderful friend Linda Dann, who is the most significant to me of all the people I have met online. Besides serving via telephone and Internet as an advocate for my son during his schooling, she has been a great support to me, and quite literally saved my elderly parents' lives when my father had a stroke.

Author of *Stimeyland* (http://www.stimeyland.com/), *AutMont* (http://www.autmont.com/), and *Autism Unexpected* (http://communities.washingtontimes.com/neighborhood/autism-unexpected/)

Q. What role do you see social media playing in the lives of people parenting children who have special needs?

A. Social media is all the rage these days. Twitter, Facebook, Foursquare, Digg, StumbleUpon, Kirtsy, blogs, and the myriad of other ways that individuals around the world connect online has changed the face of the world.

It's easy to make fun of social media. How many ways do you need to broadcast what you are doing right this second? For parents of children with special needs and people with special needs themselves, however, social media can be a lifesaving conduit to a social world that is too difficult to interact with IRL—in real life. For people like this, social media is real life.

Having a child with special needs can be extremely isolating. Friends who don't understand what you're going through or who don't want to be around a difficult child may fall away. It's hard to take an unpredictable child into public. It can be hard to plan play dates ahead of time if you don't know how your child will be feeling at a specific time in the future.

Activities that typical kids enjoy may be too over-stimulating for a child with certain conditions. Sometimes even when your child wants to and is capable of participating in the social sphere, the invites just don't come. Some days it is just too hard to face the stares and judgments of onlookers, so parents end up staying home.

This is where the beauty of social media lies. When there is no one in your life to turn to in the middle of the day (or the middle of the night), Twitter is there. When you have a question about a treatment and you want to know others' experiences, blogs are there. When you just need some adult contact to take your mind off of all that is so difficult, Facebook steps up.

For people with special needs themselves, online communication eliminates the pressure to respond immediately in conversation and lets an individual choose which conversations they want to take part in. Web conversation is much more black and white than in-person interaction, reducing the need to understand all the non-verbal parts of communication that can be so difficult for those with certain disorders, such as autism.

Q. How did you get involved in social media?

A. I started blogging coincidentally at almost the same time I started to suspect that my son, Jack, was autistic. I know for a fact that my and Jack's paths would have been radically different without the social media to which my blogging introduced me. Social media helped me get to the accepting, knowledgeable place where I am far more quickly than I could have gotten there myself.

There is a lot of division in the autism community—and the autism social media community is no different. Much of what I initially found online terrified me. But more than that, I found people like me. I found women going through exactly what I was going through. Even more importantly, I found women who were a few steps ahead of me in the autism journey.

These people are there for nearly every special needs community. Not only can you find support for yourself if you put yourself out there, you will often find that you are offering comfort to those who follow you.

There are a tremendous number of special needs bloggers who offer comfort, ideas, and practical advice. While I would not recommend taking as gospel anything that you read online in terms of treatment or medical advice, I will say that with a little bit of work you can find a supportive group of parents who can help hold you up.

Q. How has social media helped you, personally, as the mother of a child with autism?

A. There have been times that I haven't felt confident in my knowledge about developmental disabilities and have had my tribe of online friends reassure me and offer me practical advice. There have been times I have felt destroyed by something that happened at my son's school and have had that same community help me hold it together. Some days that happens on my blog, some days it happens on Twitter, but regardless, I know that if I need someone who gets—really gets—what I am going through, they are there almost immediately. This is something that is very hard to find in real life.

Q. Are there any drawbacks to using social media to connect with other parents and people going through similar situations?

A. There are, of course, dangers with publishing so much information online. You have to be careful about your own privacy and that of your child. Many people write anonymously for this very reason. Needless to say, you should assume that anything you write online, even without your name attached, will be found and attributed to you. Just as the best things about social media are its sense of community and interconnectedness, those very things can turn into negatives if you write things you wouldn't say to someone in person.

I try to write as if the person I am writing about is standing behind me, reading over my shoulder. This includes teachers, administrators, and a potential court of law. In a few years, when your child is older, his friends will be able to read your words about what he does today. Understand that if you do take advantage of this incredible online resource, your words are permanently available should you have need to sue the school district or even go through a divorce.

I believe that the down sides are strongly outweighed by the benefits if you use these social media tools carefully. In a very real way, social media matters. Blogging, Twitter, Facebook, and the others can be very real lifelines that are inaccessible in your concrete life. Online friends are real friends. Sometimes the fact that you spend time and effort invested in these social media arenas without tangible paybacks obscures the fact that you are getting something far more valuable: community and support.

Anchored
by Delayne Ryms

A car accident in my first year of college left me paralyzed, but not defeated. I grew used to overcoming barriers, objections, and challenges, and went on to complete both my undergraduate and graduate degrees. So when at the age of 40 I decided to have a child, I was determined to have a successful pregnancy. Looking back it now seems like a kind of madness, but at the time I felt intuitively certain that I could manage pregnancy and motherhood. With the blind self-confidence that comes from living what I consider a charmed life—despite the unfortunate accident and resulting paraplegia—I'd conduct this grand experiment from the inconvenience of a wheelchair.

In the wake of the accident, and through transient episodes of depression, I spent a year and a half in physical therapy. I learned how to move my legs with my arms in order to dress myself, to transfer into and out of my wheelchair, to use the toilet independently, and to manage other activities of daily living. I learned to drive a van with hand controls and I drove long distances across country. I relearned how to swim in my new, cumbersome body; a slow, awkward half side stroke.

Over the course of 13 years I pushed my heavy chair across the campuses of several universities. While teaching a course at the University of New Mexico I met my future husband, Jaymz, 10 years my junior. I tumbled irrevocably into love with this man who wanted to be "the last man" in my life.

After five years of marriage, on the verge of 40, I told Jaymz that I wanted to have a baby. He left the decision up to me—completely—and promised to support either choice. Jaymz and I both understood that mine would be a high risk pregnancy, but I was too purposeful to fear anything other than the fat belly and the problems I might have in returning to my petite size (a small body is much easier to transport and transfer than a large one). I imagined waiting for a nascent body to migrate from my womb into our world, with only the vaguest idea of how to be its mother.

I waited three months before telling my family and friends that I was pregnant. I wanted to reach the end of my first trimester before sharing the news to be sure that I had maintained a healthy pregnancy that far. I also knew that some of my family and friends would object to my decision on the grounds that pregnancy could jeopardize my own health and/or that I could not physically take care of a child.

When I phoned my mother and told her our news there was a "pregnant" pause that seemed to stretch on interminably. The flat, "Oh," that finally followed stifled my hope that we would share smiles long distance.

My mother passed the phone to my grandmother and I told her that I was pregnant.

"Well, I wish you weren't," came her terse reply. "The doctors told you not to."

(No, they hadn't.)

Finally, my brother got on the phone.

"If nobody else is going to say it, I will: Congratulations!"

Avery-Jorin was born six weeks premature but otherwise robust. He spent his first few days in an incubator adding some fat to his four pound body for warmth. He was blonde-tufted, ocean-eyed, and skinny, unlike the plump full term newborns I had seen. He curled in the crook of my arm like a child's doll, but instead of the rubbery odor of a baby doll he smelled cottony, faintly botanical, and carnal, somehow different from anything I had ever smelled. Mine. Like a wild animal I knew that I could recognize him by his soft musk.

I accomplished a vaginal delivery, but not without complications. While delivering the placenta I hemorrhaged and lost 75% of my blood volume, and was kept alive only to refuse a blood transfusion. Consequently, for the next month or two I was severely anemic, exhausted, overwhelmed, and mystified by this baby, this tiny gift we called Jorin.

At four months he was still not breastfeeding properly, so I returned to pumping milk as I had done in the hospital. I stumbled through his early months in a maternal fog, focused on nothing but my infant: feeding, changing diapers, comforting.

When he outgrew the elongated basket that I first used to hold him, I carried him everywhere on a pillow in my lap. I could not set him in a play pen or lay him on a blanket on the floor, because I could not scoop

> I teetered on the edge of collapse, wanting instead to be strong and self-sufficient. I was desperate to make this mothering job look easy for the benefit of my detractors.

him up with both hands like most able-bodied people. My inability to use my abdominal muscles prevents me from bending over without holding onto my chair with one arm. Eventually Jorin used a bouncy contraption and other devices that safely supported and held him.

I found that my fantasy of strapping him into a front pack and returning to my active, though modified, lifestyle was pure wishful thinking. Even when my hematocrit level improved and I was a little less fatigued, it required a colossal amount of energy to pack him in front of me and then unpack him into a car seat in the van, and then perform the reverse actions, simply to visit a friend. I couldn't take him grocery shopping without help. Afraid of hearing "I told you so" I did not complain to others of my frustration, nor did I reveal my level of tiredness. I teetered on the edge of collapse, wanting instead to be strong and self-sufficient. I was desperate to make this mothering job look easy for the benefit of my detractors.

Jorin developed according to most of the normal developmental milestones. He rolled over and sat up, then crawled, then walked at 12 months. He didn't talk appropriately until he was three years old, and his daycare providers were concerned that he might have a hearing problem or some cognitive delay, perhaps deficit. We scheduled developmental screening tests with the early intervention program and we were on the cusp of the first meeting when Jaymz and I cancelled. It was clear to us that Jorin could hear and could understand directions, and sure enough he soon began to speak in sentences.

In early childhood my youngster seemed everything a happy child should be. He was active, smiled and laughed, and was innocuously mischievous; a little boy who simply sparkled. Nothing in his early development prepared us for the changes to come.

Jorin was already exhibiting some sleep disturbance by the age of one. He cried inconsolably in the middle of the night, and I held him and stroked his forehead for what seemed like hours until he could calm himself and sleep. Trying to get him to nap was usually futile, and he had no trouble staying up with the adults until two in the morning. His episodes of nighttime waking evolved into night terrors by the age of three. Jaymz and I often awoke in the middle of the night to screams.

When Jorin began school he invariably woke up in the mornings grumpy and angry. School mornings were battlegrounds on which I struggled and fought his opposition. Getting him ready for school and out the door on time was a difficult ordeal. I pushed him to get dressed, eat breakfast, and brush his teeth, while I watched the clock. Time and urgency meant nothing in Jorin's universe.

By that time Jorin often demonstrated his temper and frustration with toys that did not behave according to his rules. With manic fury he banged them on the floor or threw them, yelling incoherently. I ached at the inner turmoil he suffered and that I could not alleviate. I sometimes reacted to his outbursts with my own anger. In the midst of a tantrum I was not always placid, unruffled, like I wanted to be. I did not understand why he was so horribly upset and it unnerved me.

He also grew defiant as he began to realize that my physical condition sometimes interfered with my attempts at immediate, meaningful consequences. By necessity consequences to his actions sometimes occurred well after the fact, and by that time he could not connect the consequence with his actions. When I have to use the bathroom I can't "just hold it," and the process takes some time. If he chose that inopportune time to misbehave, by the time I returned he had already forgotten the event and was on to something else, so any discipline I applied made no sense. To him my firm words were random, unpredictable.

> In the midst of a tantrum I was not always placid, unruffled, like I wanted to be. I did not understand why he was so horribly upset and it unnerved me.

Inevitably, he learned that he could run and jump just out my reach. When he was three he loved to quickly slink under a rack of clothes in a department store, and hide with a great big grin on his face while I called him. He'd move stealthily from rack to rack, hiding, satisfying his need for adventure and stimulation. To him it was a fun game. To the department store staff and to me, his panicked mother, having to lock down the store and search for a lost child wasn't funny.

The consensus of those around me seemed to be that Jorin was nothing more than a "normal boy" who just needed more discipline from his mother, a sentiment I heard and sensed repeatedly. Barbs like: "Well, that's not what I would do with him!" flew my way. I felt judged, criticized, and discredited. But even I sometimes wondered: *Why can't I control my child?* Why did Jorin, in contrast, obey Jaymz so well? Was it the superiority born of height, the tenor and volume of a man's voice, the more limited amount of time Jaymz spent with Jorin?

We moved from New Mexico to Georgia when Jorin was six months old and were able to spend more time with my mother in Florida, and with my father and step-mother in Georgia. I soon learned that even my own family members, operating from spare-the-rod child rearing positions, assumed that Jorin's emerging behavioral problems were due to faulty mothering. Assumptions grew like mushrooms after monsoons. My mother said that I was far too lenient, from manners to punishment. Few people understood that with so many battles to fight, and with my body's limited weapons and defenses, I chose my battles carefully. The behaviors they found offensive were, in the scheme of things, low on my list of priorities. Even those who understood how my physical restrictions contributed to Jorin's misbehavior did so from a judgmental rather than supportive position.

> The consensus of those around me seemed to be that Jorin was nothing more than a "normal boy" who just needed more discipline from his mother.

The glares and stares I received in grocery stores, Cub Scout meetings, libraries, and parks oozed disapproval. I sunk under these unspoken judgments and a monolithic amount of maternal guilt. After all, I did lack many of the skills that other able-bodied bipedal mothers naturally possess. And, though I knew better, I *was* admittedly sometimes inconsistent, the big whammy of inadequate parenting. I operated under the liability of self-doubt, and it seemed that many of the rules of love and logic eluded me.

My daily activities are more complicated and time-consuming than most people realize. Beyond the obvious fact that I can't carry a baby on one hip, with one arm, while navigating through my day, or push my son in a stroller or a shopping cart, paraplegia adds lesser-known challenges to every aspect of my day. Each morning before crawling out of bed I perform range of motion exercises to maintain flexibility in my joints and to prevent drop-foot. (However, these exercises do not stall the atrophy or shrinking of muscles.) Performing these exercises daily is nonnegotiable, and they require a half hour of precious time. Spinal cord injury causes the kidneys and urinary tract to be prone to infections, so each morning I must drink volumes of water in order to flush out my kidneys, and deal with the multiple trips to the bathroom that result. As my paralysis affects my urinary continence, I have to remain near an accessible bathroom most of the day. It's crucial to maintain a bowel routine that works as well. Every evening I try to stand for an hour in a pair of long-leg braces, weight-bearing exercise for my bones, in hopes of staving off the osteoporosis that results from disuse, to improve circulation, and to allow my internal organs to hang as intended. Obviously, housework (when I get around to it) is time consuming as well. Thus, with a child in the household, the time and energy I put toward activities of daily living grew to monstrous proportions. Clearly some of Jorin's disciplinary problems were related to my physical disability, but surely not all of them. There had to be more.

As Jorin grew from a baby to a toddler so did my suspicion that something wasn't quite right. Although Jorin seemed, for the most part, happy, he was sometimes hyperactive, inattentive, and fidgety. He was easily frustrated and prone to tantruming after hearing that intractable word: "No!" He seemed overly reactive to sensory stimulation. Once he turned up the volume on the stereo and then screamed as if he had been mortally wounded. He ran from the room in a panic at the mere sight of the vacuum cleaner. His socks had to have a particular texture and his shoes had to be tied very tightly to create just the right amount of tension. He absolutely hated getting water on his face, which delayed his learning to shower properly and to swim. He often responded to such sensory assaults with rage.

When Jorin was three years old we moved from the country to a house in the suburbs, and I still can't quite believe that the neighbors never called Child Protective Services. Jorin's screams were impressive. He yelped, howled, and growled, sounding like an abused animal in the throes of pain. He was often tormented by frustration because he hadn't yet acquired the intellectual or physical capability to do many of the things he wanted to. If he couldn't figure out the physics of building a toy airplane, or if he didn't know how to attach the horn to his bicycle, if he could not find the correct Lego with which to construct a skyscraper, he'd rage violently. He'd flail his arms, crush his toys, kick the walls, and slam doors, destroying things with tornadic intensity. He'd kick my wheelchair if nothing else was available.

> As Jorin grew from a baby to a toddler so did my suspicion that something wasn't quite right.

Jorin was being unfairly misunderstood by me, by my parents, and by others who did not "get it." The adults in Jorin's world believed that any display of temper by a child should be squelched with punishment. I became less reactive to Jorin's rages once I recognized that they were triggered by frustration, but because others still saw them as narcissistic I'm-not-getting-my-way tantrums, the fault of a mother who didn't set limits, they still embarrassed and humiliated me.

It's my perception that even well-intentioned people respond to a mother in a wheelchair with less restraint than they would an able-bodied, more *competent* mother. As Jorin and I filed through a checkout line one afternoon, Jorin kicked my chair in a pre-tantrum. I consciously allowed him this level of release because I knew from experience that it would probably circumvent a full rage. But the woman behind the register turned on my son with fiery eyes and yelled, "Don't do that to your mother! You stop that!"

Another time a well-meaning mother chastised me for threatening to remove Jorin from a party for bullying her son. He had repeatedly invaded the boy's space trying to take a coveted item from him. She informed me that it wasn't Jorin's fault, rather, the red dye in the party treats was affecting his behavior, and she urged me to calm down. Would she have questioned an able-bodied mother who imposed the same consequence?

Jorin had difficulty making transitions. He veered from being silly and goofy to irritable, to enraged, to being consumed by a project. In his silly, goofy moods he jumped onto people, made faces and noises, and moved with frenetic energy. He seemed to have delayed empathy and was sometime rough with our dog or cat when excited or angry. Later he'd express regret, but then turn around and do the same thing again.

In social situations he behaved immaturely, constantly invading children's personal spaces and always insisting on being the leader. Others stopped inviting him to parties, play dates, and sleepovers. I worried when I hired babysitters. What would they do if he had a tantrum?

Although I loved mine no less, I found that I did not enjoy my child as much as most mothers seemed to enjoy their children. Other mothers took their kids to story time and held them lovingly while they listened. They watched proudly as their kids "played nice" with other kids in the sandbox at the park. Jorin scrambled out of my lap, made too much noise, and made a fuss when reprimanded. He didn't comprehend the reciprocity of play, taking turns.

This was not the wonderfully compliant fantasy child I had conjured before and during my pregnancy, nor was I the fantasy mother I had conceived I would be. I was too impatient and had a capacity for yelling that I'd never before considered. I yelled when he yelled. Sometimes my reactions to Jorin were akin to throwing fire on pine straw.

It wasn't until Jorin reached first grade that I began to seriously research what I had started to think of as symptoms of some kind of disorder, and I began with attention deficit hyperactivity disorder (ADHD). It seemed to be a fitting start as he embodied so many of the symptoms. Jorin's second grade teacher also suspected he had ADHD, and said she wouldn't be surprised if Jorin grew up to be a "juvenile delinquent." She also said that Jorin transferred his wild behavior with me to her in the classroom.

By this time Jorin was seeing a therapist who suggested that we transfer him to another class, and in retrospect I think we should have. This teacher constantly sent home litanies of his unacceptable school behavior. *He just walked around taking things right out of other students' hands. He could not finish his assignments even after he was prohibited from recess. He refused to sit still... refused to do his work...was sent to the office for in-school suspension.*

> **Although I loved mine no less, I found that I did not enjoy my child as much as most mothers seemed to enjoy their children.**

Like the teacher, my husband and I saw many of Jorin's actions as flagrant opposition, but no amount of discipline, time outs, sticker charts or incentives, or even spanking improved his behavior. But if Jorin was simply defiant, why did he frequently cry in an agony of remorse?

During that school year he wrote a story describing himself in the third person as a little boy who got in trouble all the time, at home and at school. The boy finally found a way to make his parents proud, and he "lernt" his lesson to be good; he would be good from now on. His crooked logic had him finding and reporting dirty words on the boys' bathroom stalls. This tale of heroism illustrated that Jorin did not want to be a problem child and did not understand his behavior any more than we did. We had to find a way to help our son live within the rules and mores of society. If only we could find that elusive *something*.

It was during second grade that I found Jorin hiding under his bed and he made the heart-chilling proclamation: *I wish I was dead.* In that moment I felt as if a bullet had pierced a picture window, and the glass hung intact for a long slow-motion delay before shattering into a thousand tiny fragments and falling to the ground. I felt shattered myself, and bled for him, but soon my shock coagulated into a firm resolve to help him.

Jorin sometimes played with our neighborhood children, including a girl a year or two older. This girl, Karah, had been hospitalized and diagnosed with bipolar disorder. Karah's mom and I walked our children to the bus stop each morning and we occasionally discussed our "problem" children. One morning Karah's mother brought along a book: *The Bipolar Child: The Definitive and Reassuring Guide to Childhood's Most Misunderstood Disorder.* She handed it to me with the uneasy suggestion that Jorin shared many of Karah's traits. She said the book had been a treasure trove of information for her and her husband.

I made the first appointment I could arrange with a psychologist, who in turn recommended a full evaluation by a neuropsychologist. She said she suspected Jorin had a mood disorder.

I set up an appointment with a neuropsychologist, and after a fierce insurance battle he was finally able to see Jorin for an evaluation. He concluded that Jorin had a simple uncomplicated case of ADHD and recommended we talk to Jorin's pediatrician about medication.

When I informed Jorin's elementary school counselor of his ADHD diagnosis she loaned us a copy of a children's book about ADHD, which Jorin and I read together. He identified with what he learned from the book. After that he began pretending that objects around our house had

ADHD; his hyperactive shampoo bottle repeatedly jumped into the tub while he splashed in his bath. He took apart toys and reassembled the pieces in odd, abstract ways, creating toys that had ADHD. His projections of ADHD traits onto inanimate things were his way of assimilating his new knowledge. He and I both felt better by giving the problem a name.

Still, I could not quell the pesky thought that Jorin's ADHD-like symptoms might be part of a mood disorder. I had joined a listserv of parents of children with bipolar disorder, some of whom, after hearing of Jorin's characteristics and symptoms, agreed that Jorin sounded very much like their children. Jorin seemed to exhibit more irritability, mood lability, and sleep disturbance than simple uncomplicated ADHD would warrant.

> Like the teacher, my husband and I saw many of Jorin's actions as flagrant opposition, but no amount of discipline, time outs, sticker charts or incentives, or even spanking improved his behavior. But if Jorin was simply defiant, why did he frequently cry in an agony of remorse?

Jaymz and I had resisted giving Jorin medication thus far. I loathed the idea of altering the brain chemistry of my growing child. But the neuropsychologist had recommended medication, and who was I to question a professional? With much trepidation I contacted Jorin's pediatrician. Jorin began taking a low dose of Adderal during the summer before third grade.

Adderall increased Jorin's distractibility, mood swings, and hyperactivity. It induced what I now know as rapid cycling, or ultradian cycling of moods, the most common indicator of prepubertal bipolar disorder. His behavior became even more erratic and extreme than usual.

Pressured, incessant speech, flight of ideas, inconsolable crying, and uninterruptable goal-oriented behavior emerged.

For most of the first day he chattered nonstop. He flitted between his movie, Legos, magnets, and getting right in my face to describe all the exploding, careening, crashing thoughts in his head. The next day he built what looked like a giant spider web in his room with twine attached intricately from the bed, to the armoire, to the chest of drawers, and elsewhere. When his creation didn't turn out exactly as he wanted he sobbed relentlessly. The next day he tried some experiment with a soda can and kept yelling, red-faced, "It's not working! It's not working! It's never going to work!" while stomping, kicking, and thrashing his arms. Finally, he made sure it would never work by smashing it with his foot. He banged a door repeatedly until he'd knocked a hole the size of a doorknob in our foyer wall. For a full hour he suffered what I now know was what clinicians call an "affective storm," and as a last resort I maneuvered him into the shower to cool down.

Afterward he was very contrite. Such tumultuous fury and frustration was nothing new to our house, but he'd never had such a prolonged, intense episode of rage. Jaymz made the understatement to end all understatements: "I don't think this is how the medication is supposed to work." Jorin's pediatrician had us stop the Adderall after only four days and "prescribed" a psychiatrist.

The psychiatrist to whom I took Jorin diagnosed pediatric bipolar disorder. Even though I'd suspected Jorin had a mood disorder I was stupefied by anguish. The diagnosis was not an easy one to digest.

I vowed to obtain a second opinion and turned to a highly recommended child psychiatrist who practiced in our area. He concurred with the diagnosis of early onset bipolar disorder. Jorin's stimulant trial had apparently produced classic childhood bipolar symptoms. This reaction to stimulants cemented the diagnosis. At the same time that we learned that Jorin couldn't take stimulants for fear of activating his underlying bipolar illness, we were told that he may also have ADHD, that up to 95% of children with bipolar disorder have co-existing ADHD. The psychiatrist said we would revisit the ADHD issue once Jorin's mood was stabilized. He prescribed a mood stabilizer and an antipsychotic medication.

Jorin's new diagnosis began to make sense to me. After a few months the medications, although imperfect, seemed to be effective in reducing the bipolar symptoms. His behavior improved and he raged less often and with less intensity. I felt more confident that we were finally on the right track.

Also during the summer before third grade, friends of ours, a family with a boy Jorin's age, moved in with us due to unfortunate circumstances. Todd, Elia, and Carlitos became welcome additions to our family. Carlitos and Jorin attended the same school in the third grade, in different classes. Temperamentally the two boys are polar opposites. Carlitos is mild-mannered, neat, compliant, and docile; in other words, a "good boy." He took Jorin's need for dominance and control in stride, understanding that Jorin was "different," and he metamorphosed into something like the brother of a mentally ill sibling. I was amazed at Carlitos' maturity towards his sometimes abusive surrogate brother.

This living arrangement, which lasted three years, was a positive experience for all of us, but it was especially beneficial for Jorin, who learned some of the fundamentals of maintaining peer relationships. Throughout this merged-family existence I felt like a weight had ascended. I was liberated by the fact that others observed Jorin at home, and could appreciate the demanding reality of rearing him. And, I was grateful for the daily support that Todd and Elia provided.

Jorin's third grade teacher, Mrs. Higgins, was an incredible ally and advocate for Jorin. She emailed me every day throughout Jorin's entire third grade year, sharing her thoughts about how his environment affected him, how and what he was doing each day, and how she might be able to help. What a stark difference from the second grade teacher who had badgered us with toxic negativity.

The school counselor, Mrs. Uttley, was also an ally. Once, Jorin was aggravated, upset, unhinged, in a desk-toppling rage. Mrs. Higgins moved him into the hallway and called the counselor. When Jorin saw Mrs. Uttley he just slumped down. His entire demeanor changed. The fight in him evaporated. Mrs. Uttley had worked with Jorin since kindergarten. She seemed to love Jorin, and was able to see the uncomfortable little boy inside a raging body, and Jorin sensed that. Both women believed that he was brighter than any test would reveal. I grew tearful when Mrs. Higgins related this story. I appreciated both of these women immensely.

Although my parents knew that Jorin had been diagnosed with bipolar disorder prior to third grade, they were skeptical that such disorders as ADHD or bipolar disorder actually existed, or if they did exist, they believed Jorin couldn't possibly have them.

> **To them he was simply a difficult boy, and I was the culprit behind his misbehavior.**

This distressed and disappointed me. To them he was simply a difficult boy, and I was the culprit behind his misbehavior. However, something happened to change my father's mind. Jorin spent the summer after third grade and the first month of fourth living with my father and step-mother in Brazil, and the two homeschooled him during the month he missed school.

After Jorin's visit, my father, having enjoyed the full Jorin experience, said, "If I was Jorin's teacher, I'd retire tomorrow!"

I felt validated, even vindicated, that one of my parents finally understood my challenge.

In fourth grade Jorin was forever losing assignments, but his grades were decent and his moods were somewhat controlled. His teacher held a Master's degree in special education, and she was able to handle Jorin's episodes of defiance, impulsivity, and fury quite well. This teacher, laughing, conveyed an amusing incident. She found a folder tucked away in Jorin's desk that he had labeled "LOST." In this folder were all the "lost" handouts, assignments, and papers that Jorin had either not told Jaymz and me about, or had told us and his teacher that he could not find, proving he knew damn well where they were the whole time!

Jorin was eventually officially "awarded" the secondary diagnosis of ADHD. We waited until midway into Jorin's fifth grade year, when we felt confident his mood was fairly stable, to again try a stimulant to treat his ADHD. His math teacher exclaimed that it was as if Jorin was attending school for the first time. Again, I felt a small weight disappear. I was overjoyed. The stimulant was not a miracle pill. Jorin still wrestled with obstacles and difficulties, but they were less pronounced, and every little bit of improvement is worth celebrating.

> I know I'm not a perfect mother, but I believe I am a good one. I'm learning to trust my maternal instincts.

This year Jorin transitioned from fifth grade to sixth—from elementary school to middle school—and the change overwhelmed him. The strange environment with new people and higher expectations was a nightmare. The hustle and bustle and frenzy in that environment were more stimulation than Jorin could handle. He was teased and bullied on the bus, and he arrived home in tears more often than not. Jorin was not sleeping well. Many times Jaymz and I awakened to find him standing beside our bed wrapped in a blanket, crying. He told us that he "saw things," or that some object in his bedroom was moving, or that he felt something touch him. He was terrified and exhausted. Several times at school Jorin was found curled in a fetal position under a desk, sobbing and rocking. He became depressed. He begged to be homeschooled. His self-esteem plunged into a deep, murky lake.

I gave Jorin a small journal in which he drew and wrote stories. Jorin frequently drew pictures of himself, "mood faces" that depicted his vast array of moods. His faces became more sophisticated, with enormous expressive eyes, and tears dripping down the pages. I ached for him. When Jorin showed me pictures that he had drawn of himself with a noose around his neck, hanging on a gallows, with others laughing—"Ha, ha, Jorin's dead"—my heart dropped from its hammock of ribs and my blood froze in swooshing darkness. I called Jorin's psychiatrist, and he called a psychiatric hospital to reserve a bed. Since Jaymz was working and I was too anxious to drive, a great friend, Nan, drove me and Jorin to the psychiatric hospital. Jaymz and I had already discussed with Jorin the possibility that he may need to go to a hospital that would help him feel better, and with his favorite stuffed animal in hand he was ready to go. The hospital placed him on suicide watch, readjusted the dosages of his medications, and provided other psychological treatments.

Jorin was released mid-school year and we transferred him to a different public school in our district, one that offers a self-contained classroom in which he could feel safe and transition into other classes at his own pace. The new classroom is not a cure-all, but it helps. Jorin still suffers anxiety attacks at school, and he was suspended for a week for shoving a paraprofessional, but he is no longer suicidally depressed. I still jump every time the phone rings, hoping that school isn't calling, but the requests for me to pick him up because he's unable to function have ceased. He looks forward to going to school. He even enjoys riding the bus.

At home Jorin still rages, although he's better able to control his "madness" (what he calls anger) and impulsivity. He has developed a fine sense of humor like his daddy, and we laugh with him, give him the freedom to play, the freedom to be himself.

I strive to remain stormless; in my wheelchair, I am a serene anchor for Jorin during troubled times. I know I'm not a perfect mother, but I believe I am a good one. I'm learning to trust my maternal instincts. My imperfect parenting did not bring on Jorin's brain disease, nor was the view from my chair skewed when I recognized Jorin's frustration and depression. I wasn't defeated by becoming a paraplegic, and I'm surviving the intense challenge of parenting a mentally ill child. No, I'm not perfect, but I am able, as a woman, as a wife, and as a mother.

The author says:

Jorin, on the cusp of 13, is progressing well in his new middle school. He is currently transitioning into several regular classes from his special education program with the goal of becoming completely integrated into all regular classes. The school program into which he transferred after hospitalization has been a life-saver. He has not experienced another suicidal depression, and his teacher assures us that his self-control has improved tremendously at school. Jorin's mood disorder and ADHD are still treated with a combination of medications and he appears to be fairly stable as he completes seventh grade and lurches into the mysterious universe of teens and puberty.

I cannot imagine dedicating my essay to anyone other than Jorin who has created a complex fugue of innocence and responsibility, who details the intimacy and ultimate alienness of relations, even between child and mother, but without whom I would not have experienced the voyage of love—both wrenching and exhilarating—on which we have embarked.

Tell Us More: Expert Q & A with Judy Winter

Author of *Breakthrough Parenting for Children with Special Needs: Raising the Bar of Expectations*

Q. In Delayne Ryms' essay about her experiences parenting her son, Jorin, eventually diagnosed with ADHD and mood disorder, she says that everyone around her felt that her son was just a "normal boy" who needed more discipline from his mother. This made her feel judged and discredited as a parent. Is this a common experience for parents of children with "invisible" special needs: differences that manifest themselves in behavior but may not be evident by simply looking at the child?

A. Unfortunately, what you've described is all too common for many parents of children with specific needs not readily visible to the eye—and yes, blaming the parent for poor discipline and less-than-stellar parenting decisions is often the resulting, often unfair judgment. People seem quicker to harshly judge children whose needs may involve acting-out behaviors and/or mental health issues, in part, because of fear. On the other hand, parents of children with more obvious physical needs face tough judgment of their own. Based on what's seen, their kids are often viewed as more disabled than they really are and less may be expected of them as a result. That was the case with my own son who had cerebral palsy and used a wheelchair. Whether or not your child's needs are visible, it helps to understand that many people react to your child out of emotion, ignorance, lack of experience, or fear. Forgive them. Educate them. Move on. You become your child's greatest advocate when you use such unnerving moments to help others see your child's value, potential, and yes, their challenges, more clearly and accurately. Our children are great teachers.

Q. Do most parents experience a tipping point that forces them to start ignoring others and start trusting their own parenting instincts? Or does it tend to be a gradual thing?

A. There's no simple answer to this question because every child and family, in all its rich complexity, is different, and the degree of disability facing these children can vary greatly. But in the 20 years I've been writing and speaking on special needs parenting issues, I've discovered that as parents become more comfortable in their own parenting skin, they are better able to connect with and more easily fall in love with their children, a moment that tips the scale.

Some of the finest parents I've ever met have children with special needs who are willing to step up and do what it takes to improve the lives of their children, always. The result—true unconditional love— is amazing to witness. Reaching that point takes time, support and education, and a boatload of tears, and the reality is that some people may never get there, especially if they become isolated and refuse to reach out for support. Most of these outstanding parents have not traveled an easy road or reached this pivotal parenting place overnight, including me. Acceptance of your child and confidence in your ability to handle this challenging role successfully is often gradual, and because new and unexpected challenges always wait just around the uncertain parenting corner, acceptance is often an on-going, life-long process, especially as your child misses important developmental and social milestones. Having previous parenting experience under your belt may help parents realize this adjustment more quickly, but having a child with special needs still takes parenting to a whole new level. It's not for the meek of mind or heart. Patience and a fierce commitment to your child is required 24/7. During the toughest moments, you must believe in your child's value, no matter what. It will fuel you on.

One special note: It's crucial that parents work through tough grief issues about not having the son/daughter they'd hoped for, so they can more fully embrace, nurture, and celebrate the child they do have. It's okay to seek out professional support to better take on this demanding role—and that includes for siblings, the unsung heroes in special needs families. It's healthy to ask for help.

Q. What advice would you give parents who are surrounded by family and friends who give well-meaning but misinformed advice?

A. Fake a smile and thank them for their concern—and respectfully set them straight. Family support can be lifesaving to special needs families, but communication is key in helping others better understand and appreciate the demands you and your child face. I suggest parents view every seemingly hurtful action or comment by others as an opportunity to better educate and inform them about your child. Set up regular family meetings to do just that and ask for the support you need. Pick your battles well, and never lose your sense of humor, especially at the most absurd moments, and they will be many. Laughter is a great stress release.

Q. What advice would you give parents who are being told one thing by a doctor or therapist, but have the niggling feeling that those experts are wrong?

A. Trust your gut. It's rarely wrong. If you feel uncomfortable with the professionals you've entrusted with your child's care, despite your best efforts to work together well, find new team members or at the very least get another opinion. Experts are human, just like us, and like us, they are sometimes wrong. No one knows a child better than a loving, involved parent. Others should be in awe of you.

A Tale of Two Brothers

by Laura Shumaker

It was an icy cold morning in our northern California town. I tapped lightly on my son, Andy's, door to wake him for an early morning flight back to the east coast, where he is a freshman in college. During his three week winter break, my husband and I were struck by how little time he needed to spend with us. Though he was perfectly pleasant, he was always in a hurry to be anywhere but home.

"Have you had a meaningful conversation with him?" I asked my husband after a week and a half. "I sure haven't."

"No," he sighed, "but he's thrown me a few lines."

Paranoid that we had gone wrong somewhere along the way, we polled our friends in similar circumstances, and they assured us that his behavior was normal.

"Join the club," they laughed, so we relaxed and made ourselves available for conversation and meals, and were grateful for the scraps that came our way.

It was clear, however, that Andy couldn't wait to get back to school, so much so that I was ready for him to leave.

Just as I took a quick swig of coffee before our trip to the airport Andy stepped out fully dressed, packed and ready to go. The night before, he had printed out his boarding pass and arranged for a ride from JFK to his school in Connecticut. *Amazing.*

It was quite a different scene one week earlier, when Andy's 20-year-old brother Matthew, who is autistic, prepared for his trip back to Pennsylvania, where he attends a special school.

"Mom," he had said the night before his trip, "I need to make pancakes in the morning."

His flight was at 7:10.

"Of course," I said. It was an outrageous request, but one I'd anticipated. Travel days were hard for Matthew, and sticking to his routine would increase the odds of the day being a successful one. So we were up at 4:15, setting his place at the table and warming the griddle. After breakfast, he counted the money that he had earned during the break doing garden work, and left it piled neatly in the drawer next to his bed. It was no use telling him to put it in a wallet or the bank.

"I like the dollars stacked," he said, "and we're not going to talk about it anymore."

> While painfully aware of his disability, Matthew has always wanted to be a regular guy attending a regular school.

I looked to see if he had cut his bangs the night before, another one of his pre-travel rituals. *Oh, man, he sure did.*

Matthew is high functioning but socially inept, and it's necessary for him to fly with a helper. Today, he would be flying back to school with a young woman who worked at his school. She had flown Matthew home and had been touring California during his stay.

Sending Matthew to a residential school was the last thing that my husband and I thought we would ever do. While painfully aware of his disability, Matthew has always wanted to be a regular guy attending a regular school. But just a few days into his fifteenth year, he decided that he should drive a car like a regular guy and drove my car through the front wall in our garage.

There were other unsettling episodes. One day, during his freshman year at our local high school, he observed a guy pushing his girlfriend flirtatiously and then tapping her on the head. When Matthew tried the same move on her friend with a little too much force, I was summoned to his school to find him crying in the principal's office. "Joe did it to Sue, and she liked it!"

Just when we thought things were calming down from the incident at school, a letter arrived from an attorney asking us to contact him about the bicycle accident involving Matthew. It turned out that a month before, while riding his bike, Matthew had run into a young boy on his bike.

> It seemed unfathomable to me that after all of the years of struggling through school meetings, countless hours of therapy and damage control with neighbors— it had come to this.

"Matthew? What's this about a bike accident?"

"Who told you?"

"Someone sent me a letter. Was the boy you bumped into hurt?"

"Pretty much."

Dear God. "Was he bleeding?"

"Probably. Am I in trouble?"

It became clear that Matthew was no longer safe in the community he had grown up in, and his impulsive actions were putting others in danger. He needed more supervision, more than we or the local school could provide. It seemed unfathomable to me that after all of the years of struggling through school meetings, countless hours of therapy and damage control with neighbors—it had come to this. I felt incredibly sad and defeated, but too exhausted to keep fighting.

So the search began, and we were lucky to find a great place, Camphill Special School near Philadelphia. There, Matthew learned that he had a purpose, and he was an important part of the community of disabled people with whom he lived.

During visits home, Matthew, a self-proclaimed landscape specialist, is obsessed with garden work—mowing, blowing, and edging with precision. When he is not doing it himself, he studies garden crews in our neighborhood and around town. They all know him and are kind to him, as are the neighbors for whom they work.

This year, after three or four days, he grew tired of gardening and announced that he was ready to hang out with his friends. The only problem is he has no friends.

"You can go to the movies with me and my friends," Andy offered as he always does, but Matthew refused.

"I have my own friends," he said proudly, and proceeded to call people who had been kind to him five years ago during his first and only year in public high school.

He called them over and over and over. Their mothers took most of the calls, and I'm sure they wondered why I didn't put a stop to his obsessive behavior.

"Matthew," I said, "calling once or twice is fine, but if you keep calling, that's bothering, and you'll make people angry." I told him that when I was his age, a guy I liked called me too much and it drove me away.

"But did you still think he was nice?" Matthew asked, his lip quivering.

Before I could answer, the sound of a lawnmower around the corner distracted him, and with the promise of a friendly garden crew he was off with a grin. I could exhale for the moment, but I remained constantly on edge until delivering him into the hands of his travel companion for his flight back to school.

"Having a brother like Matthew will make Andy a better person," said well-meaning friends when Matthew was first diagnosed with autism at age three. While their words were meant to comfort and encourage me, they implied that tough times were ahead for baby Andy, which strengthened my resolve to protect him.

Andy was five when I first noticed playmates in the park teasing him about his brother's hand flapping, and I flew to his side, ready to take on the little jerks.

"He has a brain problem," Andy was explaining to them cheerfully. "He can't help it."

The boys nodded anxiously and backed away.

"Andy," I said with a lump in my throat, "I'm so proud of you. That was very loyal."

"Thank you," he said, "I'm proud of you, too."

It wasn't long, though, until the novelty of educating his peers wore off, and by the time he was seven, I watched Andy's exuberant explanations turn defensive, and I swooped in with suggestions of snappy comeback lines for him to use in a pinch. *Takes one to know one.* *WHATever.* And Andy's favorite: *Get a life!*

But by the time he was twelve and entering his middle school years, Andy got tired of using all of the clever lines as Matthew's impulsive behavior and public meltdowns increased.

"Andy needs a break," I told my husband. "Why don't you go to his game today, and I'll stay home with Matthew." Andy seemed pleased with this arrangement, but when he came home, he looked strangely sad for a boy who had scored three goals.

"I had such a great game," he said. "I wish you could have been there."

Soon after, Andy stopped having friends over and started refusing invitations.

"The last time I went to a friend's house," he said, "they asked me why we never hang out at *my* house. I don't want to say 'because I'm tired of apologizing for my brother.'"

"Would you like to talk to someone?" I asked. "Or maybe join some kind of a sibling support group?"

"Or could I just talk to you sometimes," he replied quietly, "and sometimes can we do stuff—just you and me—without Matthew?"

"Oh, of course!" I said, choking up. And, wouldn't you know it, the next day Andy had a slight fever, but we decided he was well enough to go to nearby San Francisco for the day.

The next few years with Matthew were especially hard, and Andy prided himself on being one of the few people in the world who could calm Matthew down when he was upset, and on being the one who could make Matthew laugh the hardest.

"I've got him," he would say when Matthew climbed off the yellow school bus in tears. The two would go out to the mulberry tree in the back and sit on opposite branches until Andy got Matthew to smile.

When they walked back in the house, Andy flashed me a secret victorious smile, and I put my hand over my heart in reply.

When I was having doubts about whether or not to send Matthew to a residential school, it was an innocent comment from Andy that helped me make my decision.

"If he goes, maybe both you and Dad can go to my games."

A month to the day after that Matthew left for his school in Pennsylvania, Andy, who was now in ninth grade, burst into the house after school looking nervous but exhilarated. He asked if I could help him clean up the house—*now.*

"Luke and Greg are on their way over!"

I couldn't even remember the last time he'd had friends over. Within minutes, the clutter of the house was stacked on my bed, the house was vacuumed, and the toilets cleaned. I was shoving the mop back in the closet when the doorbell rang.

"Hi, guys," I said, grinning like a modern June Cleaver. "He's back in his room."

Before I could bake the cookies that I had thrown together in my manic state, the boys rushed out laughing and announced they were walking downtown. They flew out the front door, and I burst into tears.

The morning Andy was born, I still thought Matthew was just a regular two-year-old, and I worried whether I could ever love this second baby as much as I did the first. The feeling evaporated the moment I was alone with Andy for the first time in my hospital room, kissing his fuzzy baby head and studying his chubby hands.

Now I had not just Matthew, but brothers, and I imagined the two growing up together. Andy would look up to Matthew, and learn from him. When they were in school, the teachers would say, "Oh, you're

Matthew Shumaker's brother!" and Andy would beam. They would drive around together as teenagers, have the same friends, and I would raise them to be loyal to one another. They might go to different colleges; that would be healthy. But wouldn't it be great if they lived near each other as men and if their wives were friends?

I could never have known that Andy and Matthew would blossom at about the same time—3000 miles apart. I couldn't have imagined that Matthew would be an autistic young man, and that I'd be grateful that he was living and learning with teachers who understood him and valued him.

And I could never have guessed that Andy, after suffering through his reclusive period, would experience a joyous rebirth as he entered high school and that he would reclaim the class clown status that had eroded since grammar school. He would enjoy sports, friends, and classes. By senior year, his homebody stage would be a distant memory as he made plans to go to college at

> "I love you, Mom. Thanks for everything. And don't worry so much about Matthew. He'll find his way. And you know I'll always look out for him."

Yale. When I drove Andy to the airport after winter break, he asked me if I had heard Matthew speak Spanish.

"No. He speaks Spanish?"

"He pretends to speak Spanish," Andy said with a smile, "when he hangs out with some of the garden crews."

"Oh, no, that's terrible!" I said. "They must think he's racist or something!"

"Come on, Mom," he laughed. "They think it's hilarious. They can tell he's...*you* know..."

Andy jumped out of the car, dragging his huge duffle bag behind him.

"I love you, Mom. Thanks for everything. And don't worry so much about Matthew. He'll find his way. And you know I'll always look out for him."

He walked into the airport, and I drove away, conscious that my 18-year-old son had just thrown me a line. But he meant it.

And I grabbed it gratefully.

This essay first appeared in Literary Mama, *February 2009.*

The author says:

Matthew lives in a Camphill Community in Santa Cruz, California and is pursuing his dream of becoming a gardener.

Andy graduated from Yale University May, 2010 and is teaching English in France for a year.

Baby brother John (not named in the piece, but perhaps the nicest of them all) is a senior in high school.

Seeing Emma
by Penny Williams

My daughter, Emma, is a middle schooler. She is smart, funny, persistent, passionate, athletic, and beautiful. And right now she feels completely invisible in our house. She believes her eight-year-old brother, Luke, is all Daddy and I see.

Luke has attention deficit hyperactivity disorder (ADHD), and Emma is having a really hard time with what that means for our family. She feels there's an inequity in our household, in the amount of time and attention—even love—we give her and her brother. Instead of being able to step back, analyze the situation, and realize there's a concrete and valid reason why Luke gets more of our attention, she, in all her tween-queen glory, believes we simply love him more.

> **The fact is that Luke needs more from me to achieve the same success Emma achieves with "the basics."**

She considers herself second to him in our eyes. Not even second, really. I think she feels we'd cast her off completely if we could find the time.

I am heartbroken to think she feels we don't love her as much as her brother. I don't think it's possible to love one child more than another. Of course we love them equally, but it's also true that I ache for Luke, for all he endures under the cloud of ADHD. Emma certainly picks up on that.

She sees that I take Luke to occupational therapy. She sees me purchase special things for him, like pencil grips and a weighted lap pad to help him with motor and sensory issues in school. Even though she knows Luke doesn't even want these things, because they make him look different from the other kids at school, she is clearly jealous when he gets anything that she doesn't.

The fact is that Luke needs more from me to achieve the same success Emma achieves with "the basics." Emma does well in school; she's a solid A-B student. I am available to her for homework and projects, but she's pretty self-sufficient with that. Luke, on the other hand, needs constant supervision and nagging to get even the smallest amount of homework done. I have to literally stand over him and talk him through every single infinitesimal step. Emma wouldn't want me to do that, yet she sees the extra time with Luke as extra love for Luke.

Emma is a Little League softball star around here. She is emotionally invested in doing well in the game and it comes quite naturally to her. Luke wants to play baseball, but just can't muster the focus and quick thinking it requires. So I spend each of his practices and games draped over the fence, intently watching, nudging, and protecting. Again, Emma sees that extra time spent with Luke, no matter how strained and stressed it is, as extra love. Luke doesn't want me hovering, neither does Emma. She's jealous of something nobody wants, nonetheless.

I try to explain to Emma that I don't have a choice in the matter. We would all change the situation if we could. She knows the extra attention is mandatory when she thinks about it. She knows Luke can't finish his homework without my constant presence. She knows Luke needs occupational therapy for his handwriting so he can get by in school. She knows these things are absolute. And yet, she judges the situation with her heart instead of her head.

I brought this up so many times in sessions with Luke's counselor that she suggested Emma get some counseling as well. Emma's first counseling session was a real eye-opener.

"What is going on at home that you don't like, Emma?" the counselor asked.

Emma crossed her arms and released a belabored sigh. "Everything's about LUKE!"

The counselor dug for more. "What? What's 'everything'?"

"Just everything. Mom spends all her time with Luke. And Daddy spends all his time at home talking to mom about Luke."

I'm writhing in my chair, trying to hold my tongue. The counselor raises her open hand to me, signaling that she also wants me to hold my tongue.

"One day I'm going to go home, and there's going to be a big altar with statues of Luke right in the living room." Emma swings her arms wide to gesture how grand this altar will be. "And Momma and Daddy will be there worshipping it."

"Give me a break Emma! That's ridiculous."

The counselor urges me to hear her out. "This is how Emma feels. It's important to know how she feels, whether her feelings are justified or not."

> **Emma sees that extra time spent with Luke, no matter how strained and stressed it is, as extra love.**

That was the most uncomfortable of all our counseling sessions, which are still ongoing after 15 months. At first it was unnerving to hear Emma spout off about my parenting. Then heartbreak set in. I realized she truly believes we don't love her as much as we love her brother.

I know I love her with all my heart. I know I'd take a bullet if it meant saving her. I know I couldn't live without her. I tell her all the time, but I know showing her is key. It's up to me to make her feel it.

In that first counseling session, we agreed that Emma and I would start having more time together, just us girls. And for a while we did.

For our first "Momma & Me" trip, we decided to eat lots of chocolate. Sitting at a café table in the bakery, sipping hot chocolate, and nibbling on fancy chocolate cake made Miss Emma feel so grown up.

Lots of chocolate. Lots of laughs. Lots of girl fun. And not one word about Luke, the only mention of our boys was to say we'd take something home for them too. I had great fun and Emma was over the moon. Just a few hours alone—and $35 worth of chocolate, pastries, and coffee—was all it took to bring the bright smile back to my sweet girl.

I was watching a television show about a family with a child with Asperger's shortly after. The older teen sister was telling her dad about all the things that had been different about her life because of her little brother's disorder, while her dad was trying to apologize for missing her championship soccer game. I caught a glimpse right then of how Emma feels. My mind started racing back to all the things she couldn't do, the outings cut short, the embarrassing public moments she'd suffered due to her brother's ADHD. For as long as she can remember, Luke's behavior has driven our plans, our conversations, our lives.

> "Mom spends all her time with Luke. And Daddy spends all his time at home talking to mom about Luke."

While we planned to have "Momma & Me" time at least once a month, life has once again hijacked my schedule. I'm afraid I let it. I will get back to planning recurrent girl-time with Emma very soon. It's time—again—to restore that bright smile.

Someday, we'll truly live the notion that our family is so much more than ADHD.

The author says:

This essay is for my sweet girl, Emma, to read when she's all grown up—see, Momma loves you bunches and bunches too.

Tell Us More: Expert Q & A with Don Meyer

Director, Sibling Support Project

Q. Several of our parent-authors express concern over meeting various needs of the siblings of their challenging child. What would you say to these parents?

A. In the United States, there are over 4.5 million people who have special health, developmental, and mental health concerns. Most of these people have typically-developing brothers and sisters. Throughout their lives, these brothers and sisters share many of the concerns that parents of children with special needs experience, including isolation, a need for information, guilt, concerns about the future, and caregiving demands. Brothers and sisters also face issues that are uniquely theirs including resentment, peer issues, embarrassment, and pressure to achieve. Here are some things siblings would like parents to know:

- The basic right of siblings to their *own* lives must always be remembered.

- Like parents, brothers and sisters will experience a wide array of often ambivalent emotions regarding the impact of their siblings' special needs, and these will change over time. These feelings should be both expected and acknowledged by parents, other family members, and service providers.

- Some typically-developing brothers and sisters react to their siblings' issues by setting unrealistically high expectations for themselves, or feel they must somehow compensate for their siblings' special needs. Parents can help their typically-developing children by conveying clear expectations and unconditional support.

- Teasing, name-calling, and arguing are common among most brothers and sisters—even when one has special needs—but typical sibling conflict is more likely to result in feelings of guilt when one sibling has special health or developmental needs. Typically-developing siblings deserve a life where they, like other children, sometimes misbehave, get angry, and fight with their siblings.

- To the extent possible, parents should have the same expectations for the child with special needs regarding chores and personal responsibility as they do for their typically-developing children. Similar expectations will minimize the resentment expressed by siblings when there are two sets of rules—one for them, and another for their sibs who have special needs.

- During episodes of challenging behavior, remember that siblings deserve to have their own personal safety given as much importance as the family member who has special needs.

- Children need to know from their parents' deeds and words that their parents care about them as individuals. When parents carve time out of a busy schedule for their typically-developing children, it conveys a message that parents are "there" for them as well, and provides an excellent opportunity to talk about a wide range of topics.

- Many educational, health care, and social service agencies profess a desire to offer family-centered services, but continue to overlook the sisters and brothers of the child with special needs. When brothers and sisters receive the considerations and services they deserve, agencies can claim to offer "family-centered"—instead of "parent-centered"—services.

- Parents and agency personnel should consider inviting (but not requiring) brothers and sisters to attend informational meetings, IEP meetings, and clinic visits. Siblings frequently have legitimate questions that can be answered by service providers. Brothers and sisters also have informed opinions and perspectives and can make positive contributions to the child's team.

- Like their parents, brothers and sisters benefit from talking with others who "get it." Sibshops and other programs for preschool, school-age, teen, and adult siblings are growing in number. The Sibling Support Project maintains a database of over 200 Sibshops and other sibling programs.

Stretching

by Pamela Fagan Hutchins

Before a marathon, any good coach will advise his runner to stretch her muscles for the physical test of running 26.2 miles. Stretching, done correctly, can have significant benefits. Stretching hurts like the dickens, though. Stretching takes time and effort. And, stretching, done wrong, can cause injury.

In my professional life, I'm a Type A, slightly OCD writer and attorney, but in my athletic life, I am a marathoner. I love the endurance required. I enjoy the mental and physical test; I even like the pain. And, before I run, I stretch; I stretch my middle-aged, talentless muscles carefully and for a very long time.

> **Parenting a child with ADHD...stretches the love we feel for each other into something bigger, better, and stronger.**

I can also see the value of the stretch in my personal life. Parenting a child with attention deficit hyperactivity disorder (ADHD) is a long, hard road which requires my very best. Mothering Clark stretches me; weathering Clark's struggles with him hurts, but through them and with him I grow, not just as a mother, but also as a more resourceful and sensitive human being.

Parenting a child with ADHD also stretched my troubled marriage to Clark's father, Edward, right past its point of endurance, as it turned out. And it stretches my relationship with my husband Eric as well, but in the best sense; it stretches the love we feel for each other into something bigger, better, and stronger.

Clark's ADHD was not the reason Edward and I failed to finish our marriage-marathon, but ADHD played a role. Because there is a genetic component to ADHD, often, one parent of an ADHD child will have ADHD himself, and the other will not. In our case, Edward is the slightly less symptomatic, older version of Clark. Edward was undiagnosed, too, at that time. I was the neurotypical odd (wo)man out, the "How can God pair a woman like me with a child like this?" mismatch. The characteristics that drove me absolutely insane about Edward were magnified in the innocent actions of our as-yet undiagnosed little boy, which made me angrier than ever at Edward. Getting either of them to start, let alone finish, a task? Challenging, at its best. Pulling either of them off a computer screen? Heaven help me.

Some of their similar behaviors were positive ones, though still maddening. I often accused my ex of traipsing through life wearing rose-colored glasses, like the red ones I wore to run in. The world looked awfully good through their scarlet lenses. Edward could forget the reasons for an argument and let go of the feelings that precipitated it almost before it was over; Clark could forgive his mom her flash of anger in the same way. Yet, I realized that it was exactly this trait that made both father and son so resilient; they each snapped back in a flash from events or slights that would have left me huddled in bed for days. I leaned on this trait in Edward during some tough times, and I was grateful to him for it.

In parenting our kids, Edward and I made a pretty dysfunctional marital team. I am doggedly consistent. OK, I am so ~~consistent~~ rigid with enforcement of rules and decisions that I border on militaristic, and it ain't pretty. Edward is not. Edward is not only inconsistent in his parenting choices, largely due to his ADHD, but he is infuriatingly inconsistent with my parenting actions. I enforce homework time in the same location and at the same time each day; Edward does not. When I say "no screens," the answer is still "no" 15 minutes later, and I follow up to make sure Clark hasn't snuck onto his laptop. Edward often not only forgets to monitor, but he forgets his original answer, so inconsistency results. With our neurotypical daughter, Samantha, this presents only minor issues. She can handle lapses in routine; she is wired for flexibility. With Clark, inconsistency leads to chaotic results, like incomplete homework, and temper tantrums on the withdrawal end of unsupervised screen binges. So, while our divorce resulted from problems that pre-dated Clark's birth, that even pre-dated our marriage, skirmishes over parenting became a focal point. Now, years after the divorce, those difficult moments continue, but without the vitriol they once had; with something more like resigned frustration.

Clark was about seven years old when Edward and I first talked about seeking a diagnosis for Clark, and making that decision was a painful stretch for us. Edward feared someone would label Clark. In retrospect, I suspect Edward feared someone would label *him* for something he perceived as a negative. But at that time, I did not understand. And I secretly feared Clark had, not ADHD, but autism.

> So, while our divorce resulted from problems that pre-dated Clark's birth, that even pre-dated our marriage, skirmishes over parenting became a focal point. Now, years after the divorce, those difficult moments continue, but without the vitriol they once had; with something more like resigned frustration.

My father is a physician, and Clark had a good pediatrician, so, like an ostrich, I went about my busy life and assumed I didn't need to ask questions. Someone would tell us if Clark had any issues we should worry about—issues like the ones I saw every day. Clark waggled his left hand incessantly, ran in circles to the left, and he would sometimes draw a long gasping breath, eyes wide with excitement, rather than speak. He did not engage with other kids as I expected him to, or as his little sister did. He wanted to be *around* other kids, but he didn't want to play *with* them. He had terrors. Terrors that you might expect, but bigger. Terrors of roller coasters. Terrors of scary scenes in TV shows. Terrors of loud noises. When the terrors got to him, he would run around, fluttering his left hand, with the other hand over his ears or eyes.

During fifth grade, Clark's school asked to test him for ADHD, citing example behaviors including reading *Harry Potter* while all the other kids took a test, tapping his pencil while bouncing his foot, wiggling in his seat and bobbing his head, and leaving questions half answered in his assignments. Edward resisted the school's request, and I deferred to Edward. He reiterated his fear of labeling, and he added a distrust of medication and aversion to its side effects. He told the story of how he had to utilize his own life skills to succeed in college, without a pill to lean on as a crutch, and how hard it was for him. He wanted Clark to learn to cope with life in the same way.

> **We took opposite ends of this rope and pulled until our hands were raw.**

Out of naiveté about ADHD, I concurred and assumed that through structured parenting we could help Clark enough that he could succeed. We took Clark to a counselor who had a reputation for diagnosing conservatively, rather than risking a quick and dirty diagnosis by a school psychologist. The counselor found that Clark had a genius IQ. He said that diagnosis of ADHD was fairly subjective, and that Clark definitely fell somewhere in that "spectrum," but he could not say conclusively that he had ADHD. We heard "Clark does not have ADHD," and we hung on to it.

Even though the counselor did not diagnose ADHD, Edward and I sought out materials on the ADHD we insisted to others that Clark did not have, and we studied up on how to parent him. None of the techniques we learned—everything from support groups to teaching organizational skills to sticker charts and game boards—worked well then, and they worked less well with every passing year.

Whether or not some of Clark's behaviors resulted from ADHD or choice became a point of contention, even competition between Edward and me. We took opposite ends of this rope and pulled until our hands were raw. Edward insisted that Clark could not control behaviors that I saw as choice-driven. And here I must confess Edward was usually right, and I was so, so wrong. Edward saw Clark's "refusal" to write down his homework assignments as an overwhelmed mind that simply crawled into its hidey-hole when faced with a task too complex for it to handle. I believed Clark was defying a direct instruction to write words on a piece of paper, and I couldn't understand why. We both saw Clark's addiction to computer games and angry withdrawal when forced to remove himself from them as brain-related. Neither of us knew what to make of his chronic untruthfulness.

Edward was right about another thing, too. My frustration and, at my weakest times, my anger over ADHD behaviors I saw as Clark's choices made the situation worse. It saddens me to think of the perspective a diagnosis (and acceptance of it) would have given me.

By this time, the marriage had reached its low point, and Edward and I divorced. In racing terms, we turned in a DNF (Did Not Finish)— because of our own issues, not because of Clark's. But, like any couple that endures a difficult time with a child's disability, we lived under more pressure than we had expected when we said "I do." We will never know what, if any, lessening of pressure might have occurred within our marriage had we pursued a more comprehensive diagnosis for Clark, sought and obtained accommodations from his school, and had him take appropriate meds. Yet, isn't there always *something* in our lives?

The DNF of our marriage raised new issues. We would continue co-parenting our two children, but how? Neither of us wanted to deprive the kids of time with the other parent, nor deprive the other parent of time with the kids. I, however, worried about Edward's parental inconsistency, especially with Clark. He, in turn, worried about my inability to understand Clark's ADHD, and the frustration I felt and displayed that he, Edward, did not. Eventually—two years into the divorce—we agreed we would trust each other and stay flexible. This worked well for a few years. Until it didn't. (Hold that thought.)

The divorce had an immediate positive effect on Clark. Nope, I'm not living in a dream world. The divorce broke his heart, and it had negative impacts, but it also helped him. First, Clark, more than his sister, hated conflict, and he especially couldn't tolerate raised voices. Picture him as a small child running off from the sounds of our angry, fighting voices with his hands over his ears, slowing down to flutter his left hand and run in a circle, then resume his flight. The conflict from his unhappy parents ended. Full stop. Big sigh of collective relief.

Another benefit to him was that my frustration with ADHD was no longer exponential. Once I was no longer living with Edward, I stopped feeling angry at Clark because he acted like Edward. The other positive impact for Clark was the post-divorce counseling we sought for the kids. He had counseling in the past, but that relationship had lapsed. We secured a new counselor to ensure the children had support in a difficult emotional time, but for Clark, the sessions quickly turned into life skills and organizational assistance, as well as an outlet for his non-divorce-related feelings about middle school (a horrible time for any ADHD kid). Through this counselor, we ultimately were given and accepted a diagnosis of ADHD, and found the doctor who prescribed the meds that changed Clark's life.

Onto our team came new members: Clark acquired a step-dad when I married my husband Eric, plus three step-siblings. Now I had to teach another neurotypical adult about ADHD. Or so I thought. Clark taught Eric about himself, all by himself. The most shocking thing about their relationship, really, was how quickly Clark adapted to Eric: there's that resiliency trait I mentioned earlier. Eric, for his part, promised to help me be the best "me" I could for Clark, to step in when I got frustrated, to calm me and center me; an unmet need in my prior marriage. He succeeds brilliantly.

Eric, as step-dad, also became the only person able to tutor Clark. Maybe he has less emotional skin in the race, or maybe Clark doesn't feel the same need to push-pull that he did with his father and me. He certainly can't trick Eric like he did the paid tutors we had hired in the past. Whatever it is, Eric is the saint who goes through Clark's backpack and organizer and helps him throw out the trash and keep what he needs, and helps me pull Clark off the computer at two a.m. and send him to bed. Eric shares my frustration, but he lets it stretch him, not make him unhappy. And, when the times come that I hurt for Clark, or cheer for him, or worry for him, Eric is with me stride for stride.

Edward's chance to stretch came in Clark's high school days, when one of the negatives to Clark of the divorce reared its head. For years, the kids had split time equally, week by week, at our houses, which are within walking distance of each other. For Samantha, the arrangement worked fine. It didn't work as well for Clark. Clark had enough trouble organizing himself in one space. Transitioning week by week was too hard for him. We tried to set up environments requiring him to tote as little as possible back and forth, but we couldn't anticipate every situation. Does he have his worksheet from Algebra? Today is a debate tournament—did he leave his suit at the other house? It was clear the strain of preparing to transition, transitioning, and failing in the transition stressed him out.

> **Ah, how the heart can stretch, with love. I think we're all going to finish this race strong, after all.**

Edward came to me in Clark's sophomore year and told me the time had come to let Clark maintain primary residence at my house, and see his father every other weekend. Edward had finally accepted that he has ADHD himself, and because of that, his is not the better household to provide the stability and consistency Clark needs. Now, we have far fewer fire drills and less running back and forth between houses, unable to determine at which one Clark left/lost what—his meds, his sandals, or his backpack. He does his homework in the same place at the same time with the same rules and the same endless prompts from his non-ADHD momma every day: "So Clark, what do you think you should do next? And then? And how about now? Did you write it down? Could you write it down? If I begged you on bended knee would you consider writing it down? Would you just pretend to write it down so I could have a moment of peace? Thanks."

Does everything go perfectly now? Of course not. Recently, Eric and I busted Clark in an elaborate scheme to avoid mowing the lawn. Clark sat at the table with us as we meted out his punishment.

"Honey, is it me, am I a terrible mom?" I asked my husband, after we finished the dirty work.

Eric smiled at me, his face earnest and supportive. "No more than it's me when both of your kids are doing great and all three of mine implode."

"I want to be a lawyer when I grow up," Clark broke in, changing topics in classic ADHD fashion.

Eric turned to me and shook his head. "I take it back. It appears it's you after all."

Ah, how the heart can stretch, with love. I think we're all going to finish this race strong, after all.

Self-Reflection
by Penny Williams

I have trouble looking in the mirror these days. It's not that the reflection is shocking. I've grown used to the gray hair and the extra 25 pounds I've been packing around since having children. I just don't recognize the person staring back at me.

I trudge along now under this heavy, thick armor I've slowly twisted and melded around my likeness. It started as a defense mechanism, to hide from judgment when Luke began having problems in school. Then it thickened to protect me from the guilt of not being able to fix my child. Then it grew even heavier when I decided I'd have to change the world to accept my child, since I cannot change my child's neurology.

And now, here I am, a shell of myself, under an enormous protective coating, banging around in a life that is no longer my own. The weight of all this armor has caused me to shrink and cower, and rarely be seen as anything but "Mom."

I am a *wife* to support my husband.

I am a *mom* to nurture, teach, love, and protect my children.

I am an *ADHD crusader* to shield my son and countless others like him.

Somewhere along the line though, these responsibilities became the things that define me, despite all the reasons why they shouldn't. These are just roles that are part of my life; they are not who I am entirely. I have interests that nurture my soul; interests I've neglected for the good of others. I love to write and dream of publishing a book someday. I like to take photographs and want to learn more about the art and improve my skills. I like to create and wish for the time to develop my sewing skills and try my hand at painting.

It's not that my family demands that I neglect myself. My husband would be happy for me to spend some time on creative endeavors. My children, not so much, but they don't mean to be selfish. And ADHD is just the elephant in the room whose consistent denial absorbs all our energies. Not a denial that Luke has ADHD. Not a denial resulting from shame or disbelief, but a denial that it controls our lives.

ADHD does control much of our lives, and my identity. It requires research, attention, creative parenting. It requires doctor, therapy, and OT appointments. It requires that much more of my time is spent on children and family than on self-preservation.

> **And now, here I am, a shell of myself, under an enormous protective coating, banging around in a life that is no longer my own.**

Please don't get me wrong. I have accepted my new motherhood. I am not resentful and I certainly don't begrudge my son. This is the life I was given and I am happy to live it. In fact, I am happy much of the time, because I choose to be. There's a lot of joy in loving Daddy and raising these two beautiful kids.

Recognizing that I am losing myself is half the battle, I suspect. Now I am prepared to fight to let my individuality shine through. I am going to make a conscious effort to spend some time on myself, doing things I like to do, alone, and just for me.

My heart melts when those two little people call me "Momma," but I have other names too.

A version of this essay first appeared on the blog: a mom's view of ADHD {everyday life with our ADHD kids} (http://www.amomsviewofadhd.com/).

Eve Speaks:

"My son's ADHD requires my analysis and patience and work and juggling and attention. I don't spend nearly the same amount of time working on my marriage as I do working on my child—despite knowing that, statistically, marriages in families with a special needs child are highly likely to end in divorce. I allow everything else to come first."

Kelly Quiñones Miller, mom of Javier (ADHD)

Part 5: Acceptance

Coming Out
by Rachel Penn Hannah

I'm chaperoning a school field trip to a local science museum, when
the young grandmother of one of my daughter's classmates walks over
to me and tells me that *she was there* the previous month *when Sarah lost
it* during the class holiday party. *She was there*, she says, *and it was really,
really frightening to watch.*

What exactly did she mean by that? I wonder, troubled by her
comments. *Does she think my daughter is a monster?*

The holiday party was held the Friday before winter break. Sarah's
tension had been building for days. She was clearly on edge about the
"holiday sing" her class would perform in front of several hundred
parents, and overly excited about the class party. Most kids were excited
about the day, but for Sarah the change in routine and energy level was
overwhelming.

I attended the "sing" but not the party. Big mistake. I should have
known that Sarah needed me there as a buffer; that I couldn't leave her in
the care of her uninitiated teacher and other parents.

Sarah knew that the class would be making gingerbread houses with
graham crackers and canned frosting, and when the day of the party
arrived, she insisted on bringing a bag of candy to share for decorating
the houses. When it was time to decorate the gingerbread houses a
parent-helper poured the candy Sarah brought into a bowl and handed
it to a child at one end of the classroom, who took some and passed it to
the next child. By the time the bowl got to Sarah the candy was gone.

This was not the scenario she'd pictured. This was wrong! Panicking, Sarah started to yell. She ran from desk to desk taking candy off of other children's houses, shouting at them to give her the candy back. Sarah's sweet, young, first-year teacher could not stop her, so she took her by the arm and insisted that she had to go to the principal's office to calm down. Sarah resisted, screaming and crying, and the teacher, seeing no other alternative, literally dragged her across campus to the office, passing by the hundreds of parents still congregated outside of the auditorium along the way. Once in the office the situation only got worse. In the aftermath, Sarah, as well as her dad and I, were left raw and scared.

It's a month later and we're on the field trip. I am already tight with fear and anticipation, afraid that Sarah will have another outburst, when this well-meaning grandmother, a former teacher and current psychotherapist, approaches me as we casually walk with the kids from one science exhibit to another, to tell me that *she was there when Sarah lost it* and that *it was really, really frightening to watch.*

> I'm coming out. I'm coming out as an imperfect mom of imperfect children.

Why is she telling me this? What does she think about Sarah? Does she think I'm a terrible mother? She knows I'm an adolescent psychologist. Is she judging my professional skills too?

I'm tired of hiding the situation we are in. Tired of feeling judged. *That's it,* I think. *I can't do this anymore.*

I'm coming out. I'm coming out as an imperfect mom of imperfect children. I'm tired of pretending that my children are fine when sometimes they are not, that I know what I am doing, when, even though I'm a psychologist, I often don't. I am flawed and so are they. As any child with special needs can tell you, in our perfectionistic culture, flawed is a lonely way to be.

My nine-year-old daughter, Sarah, has attention deficit hyperactivity disorder (ADHD) and a mood disorder, which basically means that her psychiatrist thinks she may have bipolar disorder, but isn't quite ready to say so. Since day one of her young life Sarah has been different, challenging her dad and me into states of pervasive exhaustion, while at the same time enchanting us with the unique way she perceives life. We see the whole of her, not just her differences, but that's not how others see her.

Since kindergarten Sarah has frequented the principal's office at school. Her zero-to-ten-in-seconds flight or fight response causes her to have over-the-top meltdowns on a regular basis. On the day of the holiday party, she was carried across campus screaming and resisting. During another incident she was restrained for over an hour by two adults, while her entire being drove her to run, to hide, to get away from everyone; every cell in her body pulsing with anger, humiliation, and fear. That's the "defiant" Sarah the teachers see, the "upsetting" Sarah the other kids see.

> **When Sarah has a meltdown she is suddenly experiencing a flight or fight response.**

Sarah's meltdowns are hard for most people to understand. When Sarah has a meltdown she is suddenly experiencing a flight or fight response. The frontal cortex (where logical thinking happens) shuts down and the limbic system (the home of pure emotion) lights up. In other words, her animal brain takes over. What is truly an inability to cope looks like defiance to her teachers and classmates.

How, I wonder, do the other kids' parents see me? I've walked through campus as the parents of girls Sarah's age turn away from me, avoiding my eyes as I avoid theirs. I've heard her classmates talk about the birthday parties she is never invited to, the mother-daughter book club we weren't told about, the soccer teams, dance classes, swim team, and so on. It seems Sarah and me are both outsiders.

I can't tolerate feeling ashamed and trying to hide anymore. I want out of the culture of moms who say *my kids are perfect and let me tell you all about them* or *my child is advanced and needs to be challenged.* The parents who imply that *since my child is such a well-behaved, high achieving, popular kid, I must be a stellar parent.*

I want to be around other parents of children who don't fit, the families who are nurturing the quirky kids. The parents who are utterly exhausted, like me. The parents who will go to any length, spend all their money and emotional effort, trying, hoping, *praying, praying, praying* for some small sign of forward movement, an indication that their child will be okay.

I am isolated and vulnerable. People expect me to have it together but I am filled with self-doubt. While the other moms worry that they ordered the wrong size costume for the dance recital or that their child does not have enough homework to be prepared for the next grade, I wonder: *Am I wrong to comfort Sarah after a meltdown, rather than punishing her? Did I give up too soon when I let her stay home because her stress level at school has been so high I can see a storm forming on the horizon? Will Sarah be able to stay in a regular school setting?*

While those other moms drive their kids to and from soccer practice, I spend most of my non-working hours driving Sarah to the psychiatrist or the learning specialist, the neuropsychologist, or the optometrist for visual integration problems. Or meeting with the teacher to explain, yet again, how, due to her learning differences, Sarah walks out of class feeling frustrated and defeated in some way every day. Helping them anticipate possible triggers such as social stress, transitions, unmet expectations, academic pressure, and embarrassment all in an effort to help Sarah, our sweet child, the baby I nursed for over two years because it was all that gave her comfort, the strong willed force of nature. Our girl.

I remind myself that I have been in this place before. When things seem out of control my own response is to pull in like a turtle into her shell. It is difficult for me to face others, to witness the normalcy in other people's lives, and it is easy for me to assume that no one wants to hear about our struggles with Sarah. They wouldn't understand, I assume. They might judge me, so I won't let myself take the risk. It is safer to stay alone.

> I want to be around other parents of children who don't fit, the families who are nurturing the quirky kids. The parents who are utterly exhausted, like me. The parents who will go to any length, spend all their money and emotional effort, trying, hoping, *praying, praying, praying* for some small sign of forward movement, an indication that their child will be okay.

Unfortunately, these thoughts reinforce my alienation. I forget about the good connections that are available to me. I have a solid marriage, good friends, and a couple of family members who will listen without criticism. I also know of a few women in our community who have children with special needs and, though I do not seek them out enough, just knowing that they are there is a comfort. I see a couple of these women in my book group. We have not talked much about our children, but I am hopeful about the future. I may even start a support group at some point.

I hear the grandmother's words on the field trip and I wish I could explain it all, to tell her how wonderful Sarah is despite the major challenges she faces. I want her to know how sensitive I am to her words, which I interpret as judgement. I don't want pity. I certainly don't want blame, though I fear it from those who have not walked down this path and I regularly inflict it on myself. I just want company, because to be alone with this is too much to bear. I want to say it like it is.

I'm coming out.

Tell Us More: Expert Q & A with Rachel Penn Hannah, Psy.D.

Q. Could you tell us more about the fight or flight response and how it relates to ADHD?

A. When a child who is neurologically atypical (such as those with ADHD, Asperger's, bipolar disorder, or OCD) has what we call a meltdown, a temper tantrum, or becomes aggressive, adults often interpret that behavior as within the child's control. In many cases, it isn't. What's really happening is that the fight or flight response is being triggered more easily in these children than their neurotypical peers.

> I don't want pity. I certainly don't want blame, though I fear it from those who have not walked down this path and I regularly inflict it on myself. I just want company, because to be alone with this is too much to bear.

Children who are prone to these episodes often lack the cognitive skills to cope with frustration and other emotionally charged situations. The regulation of arousal in their brains is under-developed compared to neurotypical children. When these children perceive some kind of threat, instead of being able to rely on the powers of the brain's frontal cortex to help with problem solving, they lose access to their cortex, and the limbic system (also known as the emotional or animal brain) is left in charge. Left on its own, the emotional center of the brain is unable to distinguish between real and perceived threats and automatically goes into survival mode, a primitive response to danger. The child responds by trying to escape (running or desperate avoidance) or with aggressive behavior (physical and/or verbal). These episodes can be frightening. They can be so intense that they leave children (and their parents/caregivers) exhausted. Some children don't even remember what happened afterwards.

Neurologically sensitive children perceive danger in situations that other children cope with easily, such as changes in routine, negative peer interactions, and being in environments with intense lighting or sounds. In these children, anything that is perceived as a threat or is anxiety provoking can trigger an extreme response. The fight or flight response is quite efficient in the right circumstances, say when there is real physical danger, but when it is triggered too easily, as it is for these children, the response is maladaptive. Adults in the child's environment often perceive the child's actions as defiance, and react in ways that make the situation worse.

Interventions need to be quiet and geared toward safety. The focus for adults is to avoid escalating the event (as we can do so easily) by engaging in power struggles, disciplining, touching the child who doesn't want to be touched, meeting the rigidity in the child with adult rigidity, and so on.

To outsiders, the child's reaction often seems to come out of the blue, but in most cases there are subtle warning signs, so learning to be a keen observer, learning the triggers and avoiding them whenever possible is important.

It is important to remember that these responses are not willful, but rather stem from neurological immaturity and underdeveloped coping skills. Episodes leave children depleted, demoralized, and embarrassed. No child would choose this.

Under the Rug
by Renee Perrone

I'm snuggled up against my son, sound asleep, my ear inches from his mouth, when he screams. His scream elevates my entire body out of bed, and although my body is up my legs are not. I land flat on my back, just inches away from hitting my head on our dresser—and one sniff away from my very old slippers. My legs slowly uncurl, and I pull myself up and back into bed. My son was just having one his nightmares.

I pull him close and hold him until he falls back to sleep. I know from experience not to ask him to talk about his nightmares. Doing so bumps his anxiety up higher than my body just elevated, making the chance that either of us will get back to sleep close to zero. We have a simple rule for dealing with nightmares: if he remembers them in the morning we will talk, if not we won't.

My son, Jimmy, is neither an infant nor a toddler. He is 14 years old. He has slept with Jim and me since birth. If he didn't he would never sleep. The fear that engulfs his body and mind—every day, and every night—wouldn't let him.

The next morning I grab a cup of coffee and sit down at the computer. I pull up Jimmy's mood chart and document last night's nightmare. Then my mind drifts off as I stare at the large area rug under my feet. *Under the rug*, I think.

We now know that Jimmy's fears stem from bipolar disorder, anxiety, and attention deficit hyperactivity disorder (ADHD), but for years we were left in the dark with those issues. *So many problems*, I contemplate, remembering. For years we swept all of them under the rug.

Jimmy's problems began immediately, at birth. A nurse told us Jimmy was the loudest baby on the unit. I remember begging the doctors, "Put him back! He isn't done!"

Jimmy hadn't been born early, but that was the only explanation I could come up with for his constant crying! He cried for 726 days straight. According to the pediatrician that was perfectly normal.

"He's just a very colicky butter ball," was always his response.

The colic was relentless, continuing into the terrible twos. Month after month it got worse, not better. The pediatrician thought we were exaggerating when we told him about Jimmy's temper tantrums, the non-stop crying, the sleepless nights, days without eating, his fears of everything, and his unbelievable energy.

If the doctor said it would pass, *well, then it will pass,* I told myself. Besides, things weren't always bad. As intense as he was with anger and rage, Jimmy was just as intense with his love and happiness. The goodness inside of Jimmy made the doctor's reassurances easier to believe.

> *So many problems*, I contemplate, remembering. For years we swept all of them under the rug.

I stare at the rug, lost in a memory so vivid that I can smell it. Jimmy was four. The day began with a huge temper tantrum—Jimmy torpedoed a pair of scissors across the room at me—but I was able to help him get his rage under control quickly. Quiet had settled over the house. Jimmy played in his bedroom. *A good sign,* I thought. He never played in his room by himself. What a luxury for me! I heard him talk as he played, probably to his army men. It was a rare moment, I thought. Jimmy was behaving like a typical four-year-old.

Then I smelled smoke. The world stopped for a moment, and then a wave of panic coursed through my body. I ran.

In Jimmy's room a beautifully arranged campfire, surrounded by rocks from my garden, burned.

"So the fire won't spread, Mommy. That would be dangerous." I hear that four year old voice like it was yesterday.

Later, as I cut the burnt layer of nylon fiber from the carpet in his room, that sweet voice explained, "The bwack man told me how to do it." The "bwack man" turned out to be a shadow.

I didn't tell the pediatrician about this incident. Why would I? I covered the black spot in the middle of Jimmy's room with a throw rug.

My eyes shift to the computer and then back down to the rug. I think the word: *school.*

No one understood the torture Jimmy suffered in his mind. No one knew that hallucinations, anger, and fear tormented him, leaving no room in his mind for ABC's or 1, 2, 3's. His teachers were baffled by his behavior and his lack of progress, and we were baffled as to what to tell them. We assured them we'd talked to his doctor, that nothing was wrong. We promised to work with him more at home, and we left it at that.

The day came when we knew we had to uncover the truth. No more hiding. Jimmy was a little more anxious than normal that morning, but not off the charts. I finished blow drying my hair and flipped the switch to off, just in time to hear a blood curdling scream. The scream came from Jimmy. My heart stopped, dropped, and rolled. My body ran towards him. I grabbed him. He was whiter than the towel that wrapped around him.

Jim jumped out of bed and we both reached Jimmy right before he fainted. After a few seconds he came to.

"Jimmy, what happened?"

Once he settled down he described the pirate, a skeleton-like creature that he saw coming toward him.

Jimmy had suffered long enough. He was not going to grow out of this. We couldn't continue to sweep it under the rug. It was time for us to demand real help.

We met with a child psychiatrist, a tall, gray-haired man that was recommended by our pediatrician. We bombarded him with Jimmy's problems—our problems—from infancy to the present and everything in between. The terrible visions that we later learned were hallucinations. The intense anger and temper tantrums. Eleven years of unbelievable events that this doctor actually believed. He put his very expensive pen to great use during that session.

The day came when we knew we had to uncover the truth. No more hiding.

Anxiety and ADHD were his official diagnoses. Jimmy's hallucinations were a product of anxiety, the doctor claimed, although he couldn't explain why Jimmy heard voices. The medicine trial and error—mostly error—began. The worst error, a combination of a stimulant and an antidepressant, led to a psychiatric hospitalization. The medical establishment was failing us yet again.

Jimmy was 14 when I found Kristen McClure, a licensed social worker, on the Internet. During our first appointment Kristen touched Jimmy's knee and looked straight into his eyes.

"I can help you, Jimmy. I talk with a lot of children who feel the same way you do, and I can help you, I promise."

231

I knew immediately that she was the right therapist for Jimmy. She's been our guardian angel ever since, guiding and directing us through Jimmy's treatment, every inch of the way. Without Kristen we would still be floundering in our search for answers.

With Kristen's help we finally found the right psychiatrist, and learned that for all of those years our son had been struggling with bipolar disorder, along with anxiety and ADHD. The diagnosis of bipolar disorder explained a lot—the hallucinations and intense moods—and it changed the course of Jimmy's treatment.

At 16 Jimmy is pretty stable. *Knock on wood*, I think, as I shut down the computer. The combination of medicines he takes currently seems to be working for him.

As Jim and I journey alongside Jimmy, through his life with bipolar disorder, we expect some bumps in the road. Those bumps are tough, but we are tougher. We face them head-on. We'll never again sweep them under the rug.

The author says:

Jimmy is now 17 and is a junior in high school. After many years of fighting the school system, he finally has an appropriate educational plan, and graduation is looking possible. He still has his daily struggles, but we all feel better equipped to handle them. Mary Ann Radmacher says it best: "Courage does not always roar. Sometimes it is a quiet voice at the end of day, saying...I will try again tomorrow."

Kristen McClure, M.S.W., L.C.S.W.

Psychotherapist in private practice, Charlotte, North Carolina

Q. Is bipolar disorder a relatively new diagnosis for children?

A. The first serious studies on bipolar disorder in children began about fifteen years ago. This is despite the fact that case studies in psychiatric literature dating as far back as the 1920's document cases of mania in children. The psychiatric profession is notoriously slow to recognize mental health issues in children. Beliefs get established in the profession and doctors are slow to change their minds, even when there is overwhelming evidence to the contrary. Usually mental health diagnoses are studied in adults, and then whatever is learned is applied to children.

Q. Does bipolar disorder in children differ from bipolar disorder in adults?

A. Many of the symptoms used to identify disorders in adults are not observed in children. The cycles of mania and depression are shorter and less easy to recognize. Unpleasant behaviors such as tantrums, inability to handle frustration, complaining, or crying are often seen. Hostility or aggressive behavior may also be present. Difficulties in attention and concentration, oppositional behavior, and anxiety are also all common symptoms seen in bipolar children. The behavioral symptoms often cause others to mistake bipolar children as intentionally engaging in bad behavior. The parents are then judged as overindulgent or ineffective. Thankfully, researchers are continuing to refine the diagnosis of bipolar in children.

Q. Will children with bipolar disorder necessarily have bipolar disorder as adults?

A. There is some evidence that a certain group of children who are diagnosed with bipolar symptoms "outgrow" the illness. However, it is very possible that these children were misdiagnosed. The process of diagnosis is so complex that children are frequently misdiagnosed.

Q. Will pediatric bipolar disorder be listed in the new version of *Diagnostic and Statistical Manual of Mental Disorders* (DSM-5, May 2013)?

A. There is no separate category in the DSM for bipolar children. Children are diagnosed under the adult classification, which is inaccurate. They will continue to be diagnosed by the adult criteria, unfortunately. Currently the only option is to diagnosis a child with bipolar disorder not otherwise specified (BP-NOS). There is a new category, temper dysregulation disorder, which is highly controversial. This diagnosis was created to prevent children who have irritability and no other symptom from being misdiagnosed as bipolar. Essentially all it does is make things even more complicated.

Q. Several of our contributors write about their children struggling for several years and being assigned several other diagnoses before being diagnosed with bipolar disorder. Once they receive that diagnosis they are finally prescribed medication that brings significant improvement. Is this delay in diagnosis a common pattern? What are some reasons that might happen?

A. This is incredibly frustrating and sad. Even the best, most highly trained diagnosticians struggle to accurately diagnosis bipolar disorder in children. In essence, the DSM has no category for childhood bipolar. In order to come close to accurately detecting this, practitioners need extensive training, and even then, there are many other diagnoses that look like bipolar in some way (attention deficit disorder, oppositional defiant disorder, depression, sleep disorders, anxiety disorders). With adults, where there are clearer diagnostic guidelines, the pattern is similar. On average it takes years to get a correct diagnosis. Adults are frequently diagnosed with depression when they have bipolar disorder.

Meeting Ed
by Marsha Partington

Meet Ed—the nickname for eating disorders.

Ed didn't look the way I thought it would. Ed is much more than a skinny, frail arm or pasty, sunken-eyed face. It hides deep in the crevices of a target, in the mind and the body of someone who may not know it is there, and is shielded behind denial, shame, and fear. Ed plays a tricky game of hide-and-seek, making its presence known and then receding again to a secret hiding place. This stranger lurked inside my daughter, robbing her of life for two years before it was identified and captured.

> **This stranger lurked inside my daughter, robbing her of life for two years before it was identified and captured.**

In the years before Ed arrived Cara and I often ate dinner together, sitting at our small kitchen table, cluttered with mail, sticky notes, and to-do lists, quickly catching up on our day before Cara dashed to soccer practice or orchestra rehearsals. We ate anything from peanut butter sandwiches or MacDonald's to simmering, spicy Crockpot dishes and casseroles.

When Cara was in ninth grade I noticed that she stopped eating with regularity. I packed lunches for both of us each morning, but when Cara returned at the end of the day her bag was still half-full. Meals that had been her favorites no longer held appeal. She moved food around her plate but consumed little, claiming she was not hungry. Our dinners became tense, unsatisfactory experiences.

Her body image absorbed more and more of her attention. Long fascinated by Meryl Streep as a role model and an actress, Cara dressed as Meryl had in her latest movie. She bought blue-tinted contact lenses that camouflaged her dark eyes and added blonde highlights to her brunette hair. She would stand in front of her mirror comparing herself to the picture of Meryl hanging next to it. Baffled by her behavior, I watched as these changes took place.

Cara had first shown the symptoms of obsessive-compulsive disorder (OCD) at the age of 6. She filled bottles with rocks and water, sealed them with electrician's tape, and hoarded them under her bed. She developed arduous bedtime rituals trying to combat irrational fears. Cara was terrified of walking down the hallway to her bedroom by herself. She pushed all her furniture against the wall nightly, making sure it was flush. She asked countless questions about safety.

"Is everything locked?" she asked. "Are the windows all shut? Will you go and check and come back and tell me after you make sure?"

This routine took two hours each night. I finally had to force myself to ignore her heart-wrenching cries.

"Mommy, can you come back, please, just one more time?"

She underwent hours of behavior modification therapy. Those years, until her diagnosis at age 11, were emotionally exhausting for me and my weariness was compounded by a difficult, heartbreaking divorce. I became Cara's primary parent and felt solely responsible for meeting her mental health needs.

There had not been a glimmer of any obsession with food or body image until Ed took up residency. When it moved in she changed. The half-eaten meals, calorie restricting, and excessive exercise that began unnoticed in eighth grade changed my bouncy, engaging, athletic child.

She frequently complained of being cold. She was chronically exhausted and her long, shiny hair turned dry and brittle. She had trouble remembering how to spell simple words for school assignments. She became listless, deadened. Seeing her get winded climbing the stairs to her loft bedroom reminded me of the pain I felt as she walked nearly frozen with fear down the hallway years before.

My parenting alert was again activated, but no one else seemed to notice these changes. Cara's dad, step-mother, teachers, and even her therapist looked at me blankly when I described her developing symptoms. My attempts to convince myself that this was typical adolescent development failed. *Why didn't anyone observe what I did? Was I going crazy?*

Early one November morning the school nurse phoned to express her concern.

"Cara is complaining of cold and exhaustion," the nurse told me. "She wants to lie down and rest before class." The nurse, her voice urgent said, "Something doesn't seem quite right. Cara's hands are blue."

> *Why didn't anyone observe what I did? Was I going crazy?*

With tears running down my cheeks I asked the universe for guidance to find the right course of action. Determined, I dialed the number for the Eating Disorder Institute at Methodist Hospital hoping they could help. Hearing that appointments were being scheduled for weeks out I kicked into panic mode. *What if she got sicker? What if her brain was being starved?* These questions exploded in my mind. Handed off to supervisor after supervisor I persisted in relaying the urgency I felt until we were scheduled for an intake a few days later. Then I prayed the Institute would have some answers.

Cara was assessed by Dr. Joel Jahraus, Executive Director of the Eating Disorder Institute (EDI) in St. Louis Park, Minnesota. He admitted her to the inpatient floor directly from the exam room. Cara cried.

"I'm not going to stay!"

Dr. Jahraus remained stalwart in his decision. Looking directly into Cara's eyes he told her, "Your vital signs are too unstable. I can't allow you to leave the building."

Relief washed over me. Somebody was going to do something. Then sadness hit hard as I realized how severely ill my daughter was. Then, more relief, her symptoms had a name, eating disorder. Thank God, I had made the right call.

I learned that an eating disorder is the only emotional disorder that is coupled with a physical component; the emotional turmoil of the disease manifests in a decline in physical health. It is typical for patients with eating disorders to also have some combination of attention deficit disorder (ADD), OCD, and anxiety disorders, and in time we learned that Cara had them all.

> **Relief washed over me. Somebody was going to do something.**

Cara spent the next 11 days in Methodist Hospital's rigorous inpatient program. Middle of the night blood pressure checks. Locked bathroom doors. Therapy sessions. Urine measurements. Meal planning classes. Occupational therapy. And tears, lots of tears. From both of us.

I spent those 11 days in emotional prison. Cara was behind a locked hospital ward door. I was locked behind invisible bars and imaginary guards stripped me of the ability to lessen my child's pain.

I fought against this powerlessness. I spent hours in the hospital lounge waiting for visiting hours to start. I drank cup after cup of horrible coffee, tried to read, threw down magazine after magazine. I was restless and unable to concentrate, but couldn't bear being home.

I made redundant appointments with Cara's therapists and dieticians so I could at least be near her. I even intruded on my ex-husband's meal planning session, afraid I would not remember what I had learned in my own.

Finally Cara earned a field trip to the cafeteria to practice how to re-feed herself. Then came a four hour pass from the hospital to do something "normal" with me. Frightened and feeling far from normal I cooked a dinner at home following the meal plan a nurse gave me, measuring portions fastidiously, rechecking, measuring again, endlessly reviewing the amount of protein, fats, and carbs Cara should be eating.

Hospital orders dictated that patients on the eating disorders floor watch only PG movies and disallowed any form of print media because of body image references, so knitting became the evening pastime in the hallway lounge. Another patient offered to teach Cara to knit. She jumped at the chance to learn and became part of a community.

The evening Cara spent with me on her pass we shopped at Michael's, a craft store, before returning to the hospital. Cara pushed her cart towards the knitting section and following the suggestion of the other knitters selected large neon orange needles. She chose chunky brown yarn, as well as navy, black, and a rainbow blend to share with the others. Lastly she threw a Nifty Knitter kit, designed to knit simple hats, into our cart. I felt as if I was watching someone I didn't know choose those knitting supplies. It was like being on a first date. Later when I left Cara back at the hospital among the rhythmic click-clack of needles I wondered if the date had gone well.

When Cara was discharged we continued getting to know one another. A three year journey filled with weekly check-ins with nutritionists, psychologists, and weigh-ins with a physician gave both of us a glimpse of the person she was becoming. Cara was, in fact, someone different after she left the hospital. While there she uncovered an important truth about herself. She is gay. Ed had served as a distraction—a way to avoid looking at who she really was. Unknowingly she was trying to look like the girls she was attracted to, blonde and blue-eyed like Meryl Streep. As she came to accept this realization during and after her hospitalization she gradually regained her health.

Today Cara and I continue our joint journey. Cara is learning to live in this world which is, too often, unkind and unfair to homosexuals. As a 19-year-old college sophomore she faced homophobia head-on from a potential roommate. We both knew it wouldn't be the only time.

I am learning to live with a different daughter than the one I drove to the hospital that day. Cara struggles with the challenges her sexual orientation brings, and I admit, I struggle too. Ed lingers in my mind. I have to force myself to keep from calling the college dining service to check how many meals she has eaten that week. When she walks in the door on school breaks I hug her, and then scan her face for color, her hair for brittleness.

> I am learning to live with a different daughter than the one I drove to the hospital that day.

As hard as that hospitalization was I came to realize it had to happen. Without it, rather than healing as we are now, we might still be living in denial. The pain was worth it. After all, if I'd never met Ed I wouldn't know Cara.

The author says:

My daughter, Cara, who inspired this essay, is a college student whose goal is to be an animal precinct officer. She is in recovery for the eating disorder that landed her in the hospital in high school. Passionate about equal rights for minority groups, she is often involved in social justice efforts creating awareness through education around GLBT issues.

This essay is dedicated to Ann Rubin, my dear friend and "first editor" for her endless encouragement and gentle, but honest critiques.

Handle with Care
by Mary Greene

When I was young I liked to fill hot dog shaped balloons with water, draw faces on them with markers, and dress them in doll clothes. Once transformed, I'd wrap my water-born creations in dishtowels and place them gingerly in breadbaskets. My best friend and I played with them in the backyard, usually some variant of "house." I loved my limbless babies and mourned each time one leaked, or even worse, burst into liquid oblivion.

Like all children, I was developing my sense of self, ordering my world, and establishing my expectations for the adult life that awaited me. The vision of motherhood I developed as I played with my "babies"— and stubbornly clung to through my mid-30's—did little to prepare me for the particular version of motherhood that I found myself living: the challenge of loving and reaching a child whose brain was damaged by unspeakable hardship and a young woman's poor prenatal judgment.

My child is an innocent whose odyssey began on August 4, 2001, when a lonely teenager gave birth in a filthy hospital in Birobidzhan, Russia. By all accounts the girl had neither the means nor inclination to mother a child. My husband, Pat, and I adopted Peter in late 2004, along with his biologically unrelated sister, Sophie. Peter was 39 months old, Sophie was 27. We would eventually learn that Peter suffers from fetal alcohol syndrome (FASD/FAS), autism, seizures, bipolar disorder, attention deficit hyperactivity disorder (ADHD), attachment issues, a mitochondrial disorder, and a myriad of other psychosocial, psychiatric, physical, and learning challenges. He is also strikingly beautiful, and when he's connected and his defenses are lowered, I'm struck by his equally beautiful, resilient spirit.

Parenting Peter isn't easy. In fact, there are times, such as when he urinates on the floor or bed for three months straight, or when he rages so uncontrollably that he throws himself head first into the side of our car, when I question whether I'm equipped to handle his needs. Every day I work hard to transform myself from that naïve, hopeful, make-believe mother into the kind of mother Peter, a child who often and actively resists the tug of intimate family life, needs. All the while I cling to the hope that somewhere there is a path that leads to a richer life for him.

When Pat and I first brought our children home, underweight, pale, and wobbly, we devoted every waking minute to improving their health and forming a healthy bond upon which to grow and thrive as a family. It's what all of us adoptive parents do, and it's especially critical for those of us who adopt children toddler-aged or older. Adopting two unrelated toddlers at once presents additional challenges, certainly, but the focus is no different. The minute we left Russia, our dazed and bleary-eyed children in tow, our hopes and hearts belonged to them.

> The vision of motherhood I developed as I played with my "babies"—and stubbornly clung to through my mid-30's—did little to prepare me for the particular version of motherhood that I found myself living: the challenge of loving and reaching a child whose brain was damaged by unspeakable hardship and a young woman's poor prenatal judgment.

Six and a half years later, our commitment to the children hasn't changed, but we've been forced to change our expectations of family life and our dreams for our children's futures. When we first met Peter I had

243

concerns. There's no denying that. At three years old he was a little bit like a wind-up doll, stiff and robotic in his movements but cute and interesting to watch. He also screamed whenever I came near him and repeated the same mumble jumble over and over. I remember biting my lip as I watched him stomp around the room in the orphanage, knees locked and arms stretched like airplane wings.

Autism had not occurred to me then. It would take nearly two years before I started researching that word on the Internet. Attachment issues seemed probable, but I naively thought time and love would heal those. Fetal alcohol syndrome came to mind right away but I pushed it aside. We had tried to determine if Peter showed symptoms of in utero alcohol exposure but our investigation came up short. He had some signs but not others. Our adoption pediatrician had asked for more information but our agency refused to provide it. In the end, Pat and I decided that Peter's unknown prenatal history would not prevent us from adopting him. Seizures? Two and a half years would pass before

> **Six and a half years later, our commitment to the children hasn't changed, but we've been forced to change our expectations of family life and our dreams for our children's futures.**

those were discovered. We started to suspect Peter had bipolar disorder around the time the seizures were diagnosed, but our suspicions weren't confirmed until he started taking Lithium in June 2009, and our world suddenly changed for the better.

Start with a dose of prenatal exposure to alcohol, and add a heaping scoop of institutional neglect, abuse, and deprivation into the mix and the end product is our beautiful, but damaged son. My "limbless" baby. Had I only known.

Adopting Peter was our decision to make, a decision we still sometimes struggle to accept and embrace. Funny how the ideal of motherhood can wreak havoc on the reality of parenting, especially a special needs child with significant and complex behavioral, attachment, and developmental issues. How easily the ways in which we perceive ourselves—in my case, confidence in my ability to traverse motherhood with grace, ease, and humor—can be derailed. It doesn't take long for a child who screams every time he sees you, says you stink, ransacks the house in the middle of the night, throws toys, scissors, and pieces of furniture at you, and intentionally vomits what you cook to rattle your self-assurance.

Peter has done all those things and more. But he's also taught me to recognize the value of fighting for what you want even when that means clawing, scratching, and crawling your way toward the prize. For Peter that prize is survival, and brief moments of feeling comfortable in his own skin. For me, the prize is my son's affection, and though his capacity to love and be loved is unique in both texture and terrain, it's a humbling gift more precious than any other I've ever received.

I've been swimming upstream toward my son since the day we met. I can honestly say now that I'm Peter's mother. I have earned the title. Even he, I think, would agree.

* * * * *

Though I've achieved the designation of "mother," it's come at a high cost. Some of those costs were unavoidable. Others were incurred as a result of fear and panic, and the reactionary decisions that arose from them. Sometimes it's hard to tease out the difference between the two. But one thing is clear: my husband and I cannot continue to sacrifice ourselves, our futures, what's left of our financial security, and our daughter Sophie's stability in exchange for a more hopeful outcome for our son. We have to corral our otherwise boundless commitment and do what's best for him within the existing means and confines of our family.

Is that a shocking thing to say? Is it a justifiable position? I don't know, but I need to think so. If Peter had a curable, physical disease that required months—even years—of constant attention and therapy, would his needs move to the forefront, ahead of everyone else's? Of course they would. But this is different. We now know that Peter's conditions can be improved but never cured, including his emotional wounds. When we started the journey to make him well, we didn't know that.

Peter was four and a half years old when we first accepted that his behavior patterns were abnormal, not just unusual. For over a year we took him to a wonderful adoption therapist, 60 miles from our home, once and sometimes twice a week. We also began seeing a psychiatric nurse practitioner to prescribe medication to calm him enough so that he could at least participate in therapy.

> **Start with a dose of prenatal exposure to alcohol, and add a heaping scoop of institutional neglect, abuse, and deprivation into the mix and the end product is our beautiful, but damaged son.**

When none of that worked, when the therapist said, with disappointment in her eyes, that she didn't think she was helping Peter, that his problems were likely neurologically based, we dipped even further into our dwindling savings and turned to an even more specialized expert. We spent more than $6000 taking Peter to see Dr. Ronald Federici, a renowned neuropsychologist who specializes in post-institutionalized children, especially those from Eastern European countries. After one day of testing and two days spent in intensive family therapy, we left armed with a map to decipher Peter's disabilities and a solid plan to address them, especially the attachment and trauma-based issues that were destroying our lives.

Taking Peter to Dr. Federici was the best and most important decision we ever made. Not only did he diagnose Peter properly, he gave us explicit instructions regarding how to tear down Peter's walls so that he could learn to accept direction, affection and build trust. Everything he asked us to do has worked. In fact, I doubt our son would be in our home today if it wasn't for Dr. Federici's expertise.

Spending $6000 to "save" a child may not sound extraordinary, but this was merely one expenditure among a never-ending series of possible solutions and interventions, whether medical, psychological, pharmacological, or rehabilitative. Keeping Peter healthy, and keeping Pat and myself one step ahead of the Peter-curve has drained our family of resources and put us in real financial jeopardy.

Retirement, family vacations, summer camp for our daughter—all of these things are no longer possible because of the expense associated with meeting our son's needs. To this day we spend more on our son than the rest of us combined. Financial strain—even ruin—is just one of the many realities of parenting a special needs child. Still, I'm grateful we didn't forego Dr. Federici, who, though expensive, gave us the tools that enable Peter to remain in our home. But as far as we've come, both as a family and as parents striving to heal a broken child, we have a long way to go.

Peter behaves remarkably well for strangers and acquaintances but falls apart in the privacy of our home or around people with whom he's emotionally connected. He will keep it together in school only to come home and scratch deep grooves in our furniture with his fingernails, make himself bleed by repeatedly gouging his nose, or throw himself against the wall so hard that he's left with a doorknob impression on the side of his face. He particularly targets his aggression toward Sophie and me, so it's often unsafe for us to leave Peter unattended with his younger sister. He continues to struggle with gross and fine motor control, speech and language delays, executive function problems, appropriate social skills, memory, hallucinations, and profound difficulties with self-regulation and impulse control.

To address these problems we've entertained a revolving door of occupational therapists, speech and language pathologists, physical therapists, Applied Behavior Analysis and Verbal Behavior (ABAVB) specialists, social workers, adoption therapists, and counselors, first in our home, and now at Peter's school. We hired a special education teacher certified in ABA/VB methodology to work with Peter after school. She is now an integral part of our support system and our family. Not only does she love Peter, she organizes his brain and demands that he reason and think for himself. He also receives school-based sensory integration therapy once a week to help calm his overzealous central nervous system.

> **That every day minutia is exhausting beyond what parents of "typical" kids can appreciate.**

When I say we're trying to make a conscious decision to redirect our family focus, I don't mean we'll stop doing any of the above. Those are things we must continue to do, as Peter's parents and as chief guardians of his hopes and dreams. We'll always be committed to helping him reach his potential; to improve his ability to grow and think, as well as his capacity to love and embrace genuine affection. All of these are nonnegotiable. What needs to change is our everyday focus, the minutia of the grand plan that dictates our family life and eats away at the edges of our family's very fabric.

That every day minutia is exhausting beyond what parents of "typical" kids can appreciate. Peter very often blends into a group of children, and people who don't know him well comment on how "normal" he looks. And he does, when he's not toe-walking, flapping his hands, spinning in circles, or walking with his tongue hanging out—physical traits he exhibits less with the passing of each therapy-packed year. In fact, he's a gorgeous child, with huge brown eyes and an athlete's muscular build.

He's polite and has a wonderfully contagious smile. That's what people see when they see Peter. They see his assets, which is wonderful.

But there's another side to our son, a darker side that robs his normally gentle heart of kindness and strips clean his already limited reasoning skills. That part of our son isn't gorgeous, and it can rear its ugly head without notice, or just as likely, with a slow but dreaded crescendo that eventually shatters any semblance of order, safety, or control we've managed to establish. Peter has stolen money from family and friends and from public places. He's stolen my jewelry, including my engagement ring, and hidden the stash so well that we believed him when he later said he buried it at the bottom of the garbage bin. In fact, he was so convincing that after tearing the house apart over the course of a year my husband bit the bullet and replaced the ring. We found it three years later.

Peter can be physically aggressive toward others, usually family members, and as I've described, he hurts himself. He pinches, punches, and spits at me. He also periodically pushes Sophie down the stairs, usually without provocation or warning. He scratches our furniture and our car upholstery like a cat, and he's pulled the seatbelts out of their holders and broken the headrests.

At nine and a half he still suffers from urinary incontinence. He knows how to use the bathroom but prefers to pee in his Pull-Up. There are times when he uses bodily waste as a weapon, peeing on the floor when he's angry or smearing feces all over himself or our belongings. In the middle of the night he's broken into the locked medicine cabinet and dumped the pills out of all the bottles, poured shampoos onto the floor, smeared cologne on the walls, tried to leave the house, stuffed the toilets with diapers and paper towels until they overflowed, and ripped disposable diapers to shreds, leaving a trail of confetti that took weeks to completely eliminate.

Despite these behaviors I know he's not a "bad" child. His heart is pure, I know this now, but his brain is damaged. He lacks the neural connections to self-regulate, to resist his more animal impulses, to understand cause and effect, or to problem-solve at even the most basic level. This means he can tantrum over the conundrum of opening a car door if he has a baseball in one hand and a glove in the other. He literally can't think to free up a hand. He can lie in the face of overwhelming evidence because he can't fathom that someone else can see through the fabrication. Peter will deny spilling milk, for instance, even though he's holding a cup in one hand and the milk carton in the other, standing in the puddle, and is the only person in the kitchen.

His must be a terribly confusing, scary world; a place where almost nothing makes sense, where only three out of 10 spoken words are processed and understood, but where people nonetheless will one day hold him accountable for his actions. It's this latter reality that motivates and compels us to improve his cognitive functioning and all-important life skills. We

> **Despite these behaviors I know he's not a "bad" child. His heart is pure, I know this now, but his brain is damaged.**

spend many a sleepless night fearing for our son's future. Who will take care of him? Will he be exploited? Will he commit some horrible offense because he can't resist his impulses? The fears are endless and the solutions limited. This paradox is what's driven us to seek answers, solutions, interventions, and endless types of therapy.

But it has to stop. There is no magic bullet, no magic therapy, and no single solution. Peter is brain-damaged. We can help him to learn coping skills, but we can't make him whole. We can work on trust and love and attachment, but we'll never completely conquer the damage suffered as a result of the conspiracy of institutional neglect and abuse and the prenatal alcohol exposure that robbed our son of his God-given potential. To some degree, we need to let go. Not give up, but let up.

We spent thousands of dollars on an education attorney only to have her tell us to move. We took her advice and relocated to a school district that we thought had better special education services. We put our beloved home up for sale and built a new one across the river. It took three years for the old house to sell due to the downturn in the economy and we lost our shirts financially. Our new home cost more to build than it's now worth. Nothing much changed in the new school either. In other words, much of what we sacrificed has been for naught. Educators simply do not understand children with complex presentations coming out of Eastern European institutions. This is especially true of kids like Peter, whose IQ puts him in the borderline intellectual functioning range, but whose adaptive and functional IQ is 25 points lower.

We are slowly changing, fighting the impulse to commit every resource—time, energy, and money—to Peter. We're no longer allowing his disabilities to hold us hostage. When he starts to tantrum we send him to his room. If he won't go, we escort him, and he is not allowed to rejoin the family until he has calmed himself down. We have an alarm on his door that alerts us if he leaves his room in the middle of the night. When he acts like the food I prepare will make him vomit, we ask him to leave the table. When he won't come down in the morning for school because he prefers to sit on the floor and toss Legos around his room, when he refuses to put his toys and books away, we require him to pack up his things and put them in the closet, which we then lock. He earns them back by coming downstairs within a reasonable amount of time in the morning, by making his bed, and by keeping his clothes at least somewhat accessible.

When he sits on the toilet for half an hour and won't get up, we turn the light off and close the door. When he destroys our property he makes amends by doing chores that benefit the family, like stacking wood, picking up dog poop in the yard, or sweeping the garage. Whether it takes him a half hour, like it should, or four hours because he's noncompliant, the choice is his and the rest of us try our best to move freely about our day.

We're trying to send Sophie and him the message that no one person rules the family. Life goes on with or without Peter, and he needs to adapt if he wants to join in. Our home is more peaceful now because of it. We can watch a movie as a family without multiple rounds of tears and without Sophie melting down in frustration because Peter is incapable of being quiet. If he can't control himself, he must leave the room. Plain and simple. We try very hard not to get angry or show any sign of upset because negative reactions are like candy to an attachment-disordered child. It's amazing how well this works when we manage to disengage and take our emotions out of the mix.

Just as we've stopped pouring all our emotional reserves into Peter, we've also stopped investing what's left of our financial resources toward his rehabilitation. Yes, we continue to advocate for appropriate and legally mandated school services. In fact, we recently won a due process hearing, which I conducted myself (to save money)

> There is no magic bullet, no magic therapy, and no single solution.

over the course of 3 months. The hearing officer ruled that our school district had failed to provide Peter with any educational benefit for the last three years and ordered that he be sent to a program for autistic children. He now attends a program modeled after the TEACCH methodology, with 5 children and three teachers. He's only been in the program for six weeks, but so far so good. And yes, we continue to seek and give him the best medical care possible. We'll also continue to pay for his ABA/VB home specialist and we'll continue to periodically take him to Dr. Federici for neuropsychological testing updates. But we've made a deliberate, conscious decision to stop searching for the specialized therapy, the cutting edge intervention, or the magic cure. We strive to remember that the rest of us have needs too. My husband needs his wife, and I need him. Our daughter needs two parents who are available to listen and who have enough emotional reserve to cope with her normal ups and downs. We need time alone as individuals, as a couple, and we need to be able to spend quality, uninterrupted time with Sophie. It's a difficult thing to admit, but it's true: we can't be properly attentive to our own needs or our daughter's in the presence of our demanding, all-encompassing son.

We know what we need; the trickier part is figuring out how to get it. How do we rehabilitate, heal, recharge, and replenish ourselves when Peter's always with us? We need to hire a caretaker who can be with him while we take time both for ourselves and with our daughter, but that's easier said than done. In order to do that I have to accept a fact that's very difficult for a mother to accept: that to help the three of us, we sometimes have to hurt Peter, at least a little. That's a very hard nut to swallow. Hiring yet another person also costs money, which we no longer have.

We came very close to leaving Peter behind while the rest of us enjoyed one day of a mini-vacation in Quebec over a long holiday weekend. His behavior was making it impossible for us to enjoy any of our planned activities. The receptionist at our hotel's front desk gave me the phone number of a babysitting agency they recommend to guests. I called the agency, spoke to a gentleman about our son's specific needs, and arranged for a retired special education teacher to spend the better portion of one of our three vacation days in the hotel room with Peter. In terms of her background, we couldn't have been any luckier. Sophie was ecstatic. She would be getting a break from her brother's menacing, unrelenting behavior while she received some well-deserved attention of her own.

But as the time grew closer, we couldn't do it. Neither Pat nor I had the heart to leave Peter behind for a set of offenses that weren't entirely within his control. We apologized to Sophie and managed the best we could with Peter, who was predictably difficult the rest of the day. At the time I felt we failed our daughter, as well as each other, but I've since let us off the hook, at least somewhat. After all, we did get close to following through on our new resolution, closer than we'd ever come before. So maybe, just maybe, next time when circumstances dictate, we'll have the necessary courage.

In some ways I think parenting an attachment disordered child must be similar to caring for a spouse or parent with Alzheimer's. You know the person isn't at fault, that the agitation and aggression is beyond his control and outside the realm of what his healthy personality would have ever allowed, but it hurts all the same. The sinister words, the rancor, the hate and disorientation in his eyes—all of it still hurts. Our son loves us the only way he knows how, which is conditionally and intermittently. He has no more control over this than an Alzheimer patient who thinks his loving and dedicated wife of 47 years is a prostitute. I know this, but it hurts. Mental illness—whether the result of brain eroding disease, prenatal alcohol exposure, traumatic injury, or psychiatric disorder—is painful to endure, both for the victims and their caregivers.

We have a long journey ahead. In the next few years we'll face puberty and a whole new set of challenges. Will Peter continue to improve or will he decline sharply? It's impossible to say. All I know is that we no longer can allow him to operate the rollercoaster that is our lives.

We've taken substantial and at times scary new steps in this direction. One day we'll clear the hurdle that will give the rest of us occasional freedom from Peter's demons. As Pat and I shift our mindsets toward a more healthful, sustainable future, I pray that we are doing the right thing, not just for us, or for our daughter, but also for Peter. I pray that my new, hard-won vision of motherhood is the right one for my real life "limbless" baby.

The author says:

Peter, now nine, continues to make progress overall, though he still experiences significant periods of regression. He is now at a residential treatment program. He is thriving in this new environment.

I believe that Peter, a former Russian orphan, now understands, deep in his heart, that my husband and I love him, and that he will never be abandoned again. And he led me to understand that love can blossom in even the most hostile terrain.

Tell Us More: Expert Q & A with Adrienne Ehlert

Co-editor of *Easy to Love but Hard to Raise*, mom to Little J, age nine, and Jacob, age 12, and an often thoroughly stressed-out parent

Q. In so many of our essays, parent-writers talk about the stress of parenting their "Easy to Love, but..." child. Besides the obvious difficulties of additional doctor and therapy visits, what other stressors are connected with parenting a child with behavioral issues?

A. Too many to count. The simple fact that our homes, the places where we should be most relaxed and off-guard, are a place we can never relax, is a huge stressor. In my house we quite literally never get a break. Little J is either testing his boundaries, embroiled in a disagreement because of his social issues or processing problems, screaming out of frustration, or getting into something he's not allowed to be into. He is so impulsive and so unresponsive to consequences that we really have to have an eye on him all the time. And when he's out of eyesight and is quiet an invisible alarm goes off in my head: *what's he doing?* Most of the time when I discover the answer I find out there was reason for the alarm.

Other sources of stress are worry about the future, worry about the child's social issues, disagreement between parents about the best way to deal with the child, and pressure, misunderstanding, and judgment by family members, teachers, and friends.

I worry about my son's future life constantly. With my older son, Big J, who is neurologically typical, I get excited when I think about his future. Girlfriends, school success, driving, college—these are all things I feel confident he'll navigate with a few bumps and bruises, but hopefully largely with ease. With Little J, my younger son, I spend a lot of time worrying about all of those things—not just how he'll manage those rites of passage, but if he'll experience them at all.

Co-parenting disagreements are, thankfully, not that big of an issue in my house, but I understand that in many marriages or partnerships, either with people who are living together or living apart, handling their child's behavior issues can be a serious source of conflict. The divorce rate for parents of children with ADHD is twice the rate of that of the general population. Twice! Never getting a quiet moment, disagreeing on the best way to handle discipline and behavior management, as well as the serious financial issues connected with children who see multiple doctors and therapists—these all take a toll on a relationship.

And the judgment thing—this is a constant for almost every parent who contributed to this anthology. Even when I'm around my friends and family I feel constantly judged. When we decided to put our son on medication I got a certain amount of flack, which was hurtful. I felt like others thought we were looking for a quick fix, or maybe that we were bad parents. I felt that they weren't taking what we'd been saying about our son's issues very seriously. I felt like they didn't trust that we were doing the best thing for our child. This feeling of judgment over our parenting has come up time and time again. We have to be stricter with our younger son than with our older son, and set more and stricter boundaries than our friends have to give to their children of the same age. For a long time I was certain that people thought my husband and I were control freaks. Now that our son is older, however, his differences are more apparent, which is obviously a double-edged sword. The gap between neurotypical kids and him is bigger, which is sad, but I think it seems more obvious that he's different, so we're judged less.

Q. What does the research say about parent stress levels when a child with behavioral issues is in a family? Is it just us, or do we really have a higher stress level?

A. The research shows that yes, it's a fact that people parenting children with behavioral issues have a much higher stress level than those parenting neurotypical kids or even kids who have other special needs that don't manifest themselves in behavior problems. In an article by Eve G. Spratt et al. in a journal called *Parents, Systems, and Health*, the researchers report that parents of children with reported behavior problems have a much higher level of stress than those with no problems, or those parenting children with cognitive impairment but no behavioral issues. There are countless articles that say the same thing. Cortisol (the hormone released when a person is under stress) levels are higher among parents of children with ADHD or oppositional behaviors. I already mentioned that the divorce rate of people with ADHD is twice the general population. And there are also reports that say that all this stress manifests itself in physical health problems as well. So we have a bunch of people in challenging parenting situations, on the edge of divorce, and with impending poor health. So yes, I'd say that it's not all just in our heads.

Q. Why do you think that the parents of our kids—those with behavioral challenges—feel such high stress levels?

A. I think a lot of this comes down to the fact that many of our children have "invisible" disabilities. These are children who look "normal," for lack of a better word, but don't act that way. I'm sure that parenting a child with Down's syndrome is challenging, but those kids look different and their parents are treated with kindness and empathy, for example. You can't look at our kids and know that their brains are wired differently or their brain chemistry is off. It's very misleading to assume that just because a kid doesn't "look" disabled that he or she isn't.

Many of our kids need additional coaching in public or social situations. As well, parents may have to choose their battles and let certain behaviors slide, which opens them up to all sorts of criticism. The other side of the coin is that they may need to be stricter than other parents, which is exhausting, and again, opens them up to more criticism. Many of our children also act one way in public and another way in private. They can pull it together when they need to, as long as it's a short period of time. So people who don't know them very well think they're fine, lovely, even-keeled children, when the reality is they behave quite differently when they're with their family.

Personally, I can't tell you how many ridiculous conversations I've had with my son in the grocery store, of all places. He spends the entire time badgering me for treats and snacks and food I never buy. Last week he called me a bitch because I wouldn't buy frozen pizza. I just pretended I didn't hear it. I've learned that giving attention to him when he says inappropriate things leads to more and more inappropriate talk, so the best thing is not to engage. But I'm sure every single one of the five people who heard him say it thought I should have spanked him or yelled at him or grounded him or something. The fact is that my child is slow to process, has memory problems, is highly impulsive and disinhibited— combine this with food issues that date back to his malnourished beginnings (he was adopted) and it's practically impossible for him to behave himself in the store. I've accepted that now, but it took a very long time. Even though I usually stay calm while this is going on I often wonder what other people think when they witness it.

Wherever I go with him, I feel judged. I know that people think it's my fault he acts that way. I know it because that's what I used to think about people who couldn't control their kids. Heck, I actually still think that about some people, although I'm really good at spotting neurodiverse kids now. I have ADHD radar. I can see executive functioning deficits from a mile away. When I run into those kids and their parents I turn all my judgment off. I just think, *bless your heart*, and wonder how I can lend them a hand.

Finally, I also see very little support for people parenting children with behavioral issues. Parents spend a lot of time battling with the powers-that-be, like the schools, or educating people, like their family or friends, or in some cases, even doctors and therapists, not to mention the time they spend coaching and negotiating with and dealing with their actual child, and what's left? Not a lot. That's why online support groups have been a lifesaver for me. What little bit of *me* that's left I can share with other people in my same boat.

Here, in brief, are some other research findings:

Studies have shown that parents of children with ADHD and other "invisible" disabilities report:

- greater parenting stress levels

- less social support

- a lower quality of life

- lower levels of parenting satisfaction

- greater levels of family dysfunction

Parenting a child with behavioral issues, in comparison to parenting a child without behavioral issues, is more stressful because of the severity of our kids' behavior problems, and the frequency of those problems.

Research suggests that parents of preschool and school-aged children with ADHD feel less competent as parents than parents of non-problem children, and the more severe the ADHD behavior, the worse parents rate their feeling of competence.

On a positive note, there is preliminary evidence that parents can decrease their stress levels and raise their feelings of competence and satisfaction as parents through programs aimed at educating parents about ADHD and other behavior challenges, helping parents learn to recognize when they are under stress and manage that stress, and address problem solving, negative thinking, communication, and self-care.

Summary of relevant research provided by Brigette Gorman, Ph.D

Up From the Depths
by Inez Holger

I wanted to blame Shamu, but I couldn't. I had not wanted to sit so close to begin with—the seats were suspiciously wet—but on that balmy April day at Sea World our insistent son would not settle down anywhere else. So we sat up front and center, the Plexiglas tank of frigid ocean water shimmering in the sun before us. Nine-year-old Gabriel popped up and down from his seat, yelling endless whale facts to his younger brother while my husband patted my knee.

"Calm down, Hon," Karl said, "Gabe will be fine."

I had my doubts.

Gabriel stopped bobbing and his eyes widened when the black and white orca raced into the tank and twirled through the water mere yards away from us. He held his breath as he watched the four ton killer whale barrel upward into the air and then smack its thick fluke on the water's surface as it dove back in. Sure enough, the "fun" moment Gabriel had been waiting for came—a deluge of freezing water splashed over the rim of the tank and drenched us all. Gabriel screeched and then whirled around and headed for the aisle.

"I want to go home!" he said. I grabbed his shoulder to stop him. He clamped his arms across his thin chest as water dripped from his blonde curls.

"Uh, I don't think so," I said, shivering beneath my clinging shirt. "We paid a lot of money to come here and *this* is what you wanted to do, sit on the front row and *get wet*." The last words came out through gritted teeth. Karl attempted to settle Gabriel down, but no line of reasoning or threatened loss of privileges could convince him to stay. I lowered my head for fear that the rage I felt would show on my face.

He makes me so angry, I thought. *I don't care that he has problems; that he can't help it.* We left the show abruptly, defeated one more time by our "difficult" child.

A year earlier Gabriel's third grade teacher noted his impulsiveness and inability to sit still.

"I have to spoon feed him his work because he has such poor focus," she said. "Frankly, he'll never make it when he hits fourth grade."

She urged us to talk to our pediatrician about Gabriel's behavior and the possibility that he needed medication, something I had avoided for years.

> *He makes me so angry, I thought. I don't care that he has problems; that he can't help it.*

I had struggled with manic depression since age 16 and felt the stigma, the shame of having a mental illness diagnosis. In no way did I want my son to be stigmatized by a label of attention deficit disorder (ADD), or *any* diagnosis in the mental health category. Still, I could not deny the problems that had been obvious since his birth, or my mounting ugliness about his dogged resistance.

Curly-haired Gabriel was my first child, and I fully expected him to be a heart-warming, placid Gerber baby. I was a quiet, orderly mom who liked to start a task and see it through to the end, and I had the notion I could tackle the usual parenting hurdles and succeed. But before long Gabriel had me stumped and I began to resent the weight his needs piled on top of my depression. I could not figure out why my restless blue-eyed child could not be consoled. From severe colic as an infant, to screaming sleeplessness as a toddler, to tantrums whenever we shifted tasks, nothing I did soothed him.

Each morning of those early years began with a battle that left me smoldering.

"My pants are hard," Gabriel said, nearing tears.

"Pants aren't hard, honey. They're…"

"These are hard."

"…made of soft fabric. I touched them myself before buying them. See?" I rubbed the brushed denim britches and smiled. He'd already torn off his shirt because he could feel the tag, the one I neglected to cut out, the one that sent him into a writhing fit.

"I can feel them on my legs." He gulped in air as if he was suffocating.

"Well," I said, pausing to take a deep breath, "you can't wear any pants without them touching your legs a little bit. You know that, right?" My smile was fake.

Gabriel flopped the offending pants off with a series of hard kicks. Three pairs of pants later he settled on corduroy. I popped up, ready to go. But he started shrugging off his shoes.

"I can feel my socks."

I closed my eyes and pictured dollar signs and the Kmart clerk asking how many children I have because I bought socks so often. A box in the closet held 23 pairs that did not pass the test.

By the time Gabriel and I left home—40 minutes late—I had hurled a drawerful of pants across the room and screamed at him all the way from the house to the car.

At his teacher's urging I finally spoke to Gabriel's pediatrician, who diagnosed ADD and prescribed medication. Another specialist diagnosed significant processing deficiencies, visual motor integration problems, low sensory threshold (the pants!), and an "innate difficult temperament" caused in part by "ineffective frontal lobe skills." What my son needed from his parents and teachers, he wrote in his report, was for them to be firm yet benevolent, highly engaging, active, and structured.

He got me instead—highly structured, yes, but also exhausted, depressed, and exasperated. I felt sorry for Gabriel for having to live with a mother who struggles with depression, but his behavior made me so mad!

Or did it?

A few years later at a marriage seminar, in a reading entitled "Watch Your Language," the author explained that we normally respond to our struggles by blaming our situation for our irritability or anger. Consider instead that behavior is based on what already lies deep in our hearts, not on what is currently going on around us. To illustrate his point he said that when you squeeze a sponge, whatever it holds comes out, whether clean or dirty. The same holds true for us. Stress squeezes something out of us too, something either good or bad.

> **What my son needed from his parents and teachers was for them to be firm yet benevolent, highly engaging, active, and structured. He got me instead.**

"You mean," I said to Karl, "instead of thinking 'this kid is making me so mad,' I have to recognize I'm an angry person, no matter what's going on?"

"Uh, well," he said, "you had a bit of a temper before he came along, don't you think?"

I felt nauseated for a moment, afraid of the truth I had to accept. The thought of facing my own selfish anger on top of depression seemed insurmountable. How much easier it was to blame someone else rather than myself.

But for the first time in my life I could see my anger differently. Gabriel did not cause anger to develop in me and I did not have the right to blame him for my poor behavior. He was not the problem—I was. I had long ago chosen anger as a way to respond to life's obstacles; my son's challenges simply stirred up the worst that already lurked in me, pushed it into full gear. Along with this revelation came a new choice: I could not alter Gabriel's processing difficulties or low sensory threshold, but I could choose better ways to respond to him, and ultimately, address the demanding and hopeless attitudes of my own heart which struck out at the world around me.

Molding hearts takes a while, a long while, and progress first comes in spurts, like water from the blowhole of a whale. I had a lot of anger to work on—a lot of dirty water in my sponge—and in the same way that my son required many "exposures to the information" before he could "encode it into long term memory" (those pesky processing issues), so would I. Counseling and praying helped me along the way. A good dose of my son's trait of dogged persistence helped too.

There would be no quick dive to the bottom of the heart, with a sudden triumphant leap out of the frigid depths. The journey upward would be slow. On that slow journey I often reminded my son that we were both growing.

"My anger and depression," I told him, "are *my* issues. You didn't cause them. But the same rules apply to us both—fits of anger aren't right for me or for you."

So together my son and I thrashed through the waters of his teen years, encoding and growing. I wish my point of view had changed when he was much younger, yet I can proudly say that my "difficult" son helped diagnose my difficult heart.

Gabriel turned 26 this year and will marry soon. As soon as he has children I plan to take them to Sea World to see Shamu. We'll sit front and center.

The author says:

My son, Gabriel, 26, who inspired "Up From the Depths" works in the office of a housing industry business and will be married this year. I am pleased to report that his socks don't bother him anymore.

Eve Speaks:

Dear Self,

You've known your son for more than 10 (long) years. In those years, you've learned every square inch of this child. You know you'll have to hold his hand and hug him against you before he enters any new situation for the first time. You know to hang back, but stay within view, until he flashes you the thumbs up that is the unspoken signal that you are allowed to leave.

You know him through and through. So why didn't you know he'd have a meltdown at the orthodontist's office? Why didn't you plan for it as painstakingly and thoroughly as you usually do? Why did you ask him to do his homework in the waiting room, push him to focus on the pages rather than the children playing around him? Why did you nudge for him to go back alone with the assistant when his name was called?

You knew better. At each and every step, you felt him spiraling further out of control. The tooth sucking and lip smacking, the eye rolling, the jerking away, the sudden flare of frustration disguised as anger. You saw it all and yet you tried to take the easy way out. You wanted to sit quietly and read your book. You wanted to take a mental break, and in doing so, you pushed your son off the figurative cliff.

And melt down he did. Full-on storming off into the parking lot, stomping and jerking when you forced him back into the building, talking back and arguing, anger anger anger. So much anger that the orthodontist asked if perhaps you should come back another day—alone. So much negative emotion that it stained the entire evening and left him crying and disappointed until bedtime.

You knew all along what would happen, and yet you kept making the wrong choices. Let's don't do that again, okay? It wasn't worth it, and you both suffered. But today's a new day. Grab onto it and make it count for both of you. But before you do anything else, tell that boy you're sorry and that you'll try harder next time.

Always,
Your hindsight

Kelly Quiñones Miller, mom of Javier (ADHD)

Part 6: The Struggle for Independence

An ADHD Horror Story
by Frank South

As an ADHD alcoholic adult, I spent years self-medicating with alcohol. And though it turned down the noise in my head, it just about destroyed me and my life in the process. I can never forget the damage cocktails and I did together, so alarm bells ring all over when it looks like my ADHD son, Harry, might head down the same road.

When Harry turned 21 he decided to try out drinking—piña coladas, schnapps, and other sweet vodka and rum drinks. He and his friends partied for the whole week of his birthday, and he spent all the birthday money he got from relatives on booze. We did everything we could to make sure he was safe and that nobody was drinking and driving. My wife, despite the work she's swamped with, even put the whole gang up at our house one of the nights. Par-tee! Woo-hoo! Though I want to be a supportive husband, I am glad I was in L.A. doing my one-man ADHD show and not home for that.

The weird thing is this: I've talked to my son and daughter about alcohol and drugs openly. We've talked about ADHD and substance abuse. Plus, Harry especially remembers when I got sober, and he's proud that I am. He brings it up to friends and parents of his friends. But here he is walking to 7-Eleven to spend the last of his birthday cash on peppermint schnapps, then coming home and throwing up.

Part of me wants to see this as how he'll learn. Part of me wants to laugh and shake my head at his youthful excess. But the largest part of me looks at my son and the challenges he's facing in life and I'm terrified for him. To his credit, he says that now that he's tried it, he's done with getting drunk. I hope that's true. But I remember how many thousands of times I said that before I stopped blowing apart my life and finally got sober. So I'm still terrified. And no matter how confused and stressed I get in my life, if he thinks I'm going to back off and keep my nose out of his life, he's crazy.

But after talking with my wife, Margaret, I decided that my son, Harry, was not me, and that overreacting to my fears with restrictions and lectures wouldn't help him make the right decisions. Maybe I won't be able to keep my son and daughter from repeating my mistakes, but I'll lighten up, keep talking and listening to them and maybe they'll at least have an idea what's coming.

So, when Margaret flew to L.A. for the closing week of my show last June, we left Harry at home alone to take care of the dog and look after the house while we were out of town and his sister stayed with friends.

> No matter how confused and stressed I get in my life, if he thinks I'm going to back off and keep my nose out of his life, he's crazy.

It was the honor system. He knew the rules: no parties and no drugs (which he promised us he hadn't even tried and had no interest in). We called to check in and he seemed fine. Then three days later we got a phone call from Harry. He had some things he wanted to tell us before we heard it from the neighbors. Apparently, as soon as Margaret got on the plane our house turned into Animal House. Only in real life it wasn't funny.

It was a nightmare of loud parties, drinking, pot smoking, and Harry's drunken friends arguing with furious neighbors at three a.m.—one of whom is a cop—as the dog gets out and runs down the street.

Now, Harry told us most of it, but not all. Margaret got the complete scoop when she got home. So my task was to handle Harry over the phone from Delaware where I'm visiting my parents, while Margaret's heading back to Hawaii to deal with him and the neighbors face to face.

Okay, I'm freaking out. My head's exploding with the biggest "I told you so" in human history—or my human history, anyway—on top of full-tilt fury slamming up against deep love and concern for my kid. And hey, what about our poor dog—he had to have been scared silly by all of that insanity. And the other kids' parents. Legal issues. And damn it, he *promised*.

But I knew—I did—I knew he wouldn't be able to resist temptation. I was a 21-year-old kid once. But this isn't about being a kid, this is about trust, ADHD, and alcohol, and the damage my boy can do to himself. This could have been even worse. What if someone had gotten seriously hurt? The more I think about it the more freaked and seriously pissed off I get.

God, I'm going tan that kid's hide.

I pick up the phone, start punching in Harry's number, and then snap it closed. I have to do some breathing. A panic attack could undermine the righteously indignant avenging angel rant I'm planning to bring down on his head. But as I breathe, I remember the nightmares I poured into my parents' lives when I was in my teens and twenties, and I realize that nothing I've been thinking about saying will help any of us. The truth is I don't really know what to say to Harry at all. But I'm his dad. I have to figure out something. Harry's sitting in Hawaii waiting for my call.

I'm angry and disappointed in my son, but I don't know what to say to him besides that. So since it's five o'clock here in Delaware, I avoid calling Harry by making martinis for my parents. I bring the drinks to my mom and dad in their matching wingback chairs along with some crackers and sliced cheese. I like waiting on them. Cripes, they should get something after everything I put them through over the years. I tell my mom and dad what's going on as I get them refills, and my dad, especially, has strong opinions about Harry's misdeeds.

As I close the door to the guest room and punch Harry's number on my cell, I'm hit by the weird irony of a recovering alcoholic son serving drinks to his mother and father, before calling up his own son to give him hell about getting drunk and screwing up. I stop the call. I dread the draconian restrictions and restitutions I must and will bring down on him, but I still don't know how to get Harry to really learn from this.

Then I remember when I dropped out of college. It was the morning after I'd shown up on my parents' front porch in the middle of the night screaming drunk, waving an empty scotch bottle and blaming them for everything before I threw up in the bushes. And I still remember what my father said to me.

So I punch in Harry's number again, and when he picks up I say, "First, I love you."

When I got back to Hawaii, Margaret and my daughter, Coco, had already left on a trip to see other relatives. So Harry and I spent a couple of weeks getting the house cleaned up for their return and talking. I was, as I've said, on edge and wanted to get some things talked out with my son. Things like responsibility, honesty, alcohol abuse, and the hard reality of living as an adult with ADHD and learning disabilities. But I couldn't find a way to bring any of that up that didn't fray my nerves worse than they were, and make Harry pull away and shut down.

Then, finally, we found something else to talk about instead of talking directly about his growing up, our relationship, his friends, his life goals, and the like. The conversational duck-blind we used was "Dexter," a TV show he's passionate about. During our two weeks alone he showed me all the episodes he'd saved, and during this "Dexter" marathon I began to see what attracted my ADHD son so strongly to the show.

Harry had been on me for over a year to watch "Dexter" with him, but I'd resisted. My god, the hero of the show is a serial killer. Nearly every week someone gets butchered by this guy. He pointed out that I read tons of thrillers and murder mysteries. But I said they don't glorify violence like that, and besides they're books. Books are better than TV, any intellectual snob knows that, and I'm an intellectual snob that used to write TV, so who knows better than me? Well, in this case, he was right and I was wrong. Every once in a while being wrong happens to a parent, with increasing frequency as everyone in the mix gets older. Admitting it is the hardest part.

But like I said, I could see what drew Harry to this series about a guy who feels like he's wearing a disguise so he can pass as being normal in a world where he struggles to find real connections to others. Harry identified with him, and as we watched I identified too.

Yes, Dexter definitely is way out there, but the character is struggling constantly with questions of morality, right and wrong, and the responsibilities of love. So episode after episode, night after night, of this very bloody and frightening TV horror show, Harry and I found a way to communicate about him, his life—and the even more frightening horror of growing up.

> **Every once in a while being wrong happens to a parent, with increasing frequency as everyone in the mix gets older. Admitting it is the hardest part.**

A version of this essay first appeared on the blog: ADHD Dad: Better Late than Never (http://www. additudemag.com/adhdblogs/6).

The author says:

Despite all the different labels attached to the challenges we each face, those of us with mental or physical disabilities work hard to develop coping skills to help us get past our labels and be just people. And that's how we want to be seen by others—as just people.

Tell Us More: Expert Q & A with Geurt van de Glind

Director, International Collaboration on ADHD and Substance Abuse (ICASA) Foundation (http://www.adhdandsubstanceabuse.org/)

Q. What is the relationship between ADHD and substance abuse?

A. It is important to realize that, fortunately, most ADHD children and adolescents grow up without developing problems with substance abuse. However, having ADHD increases their risks dramatically (Lee et al., 2011).

Children with ADHD, compared to children without the disorder:

- have a twofold risk of ever using nicotine, and a threefold risk of developing nicotine dependence.

- have an increased risk (1.7 times) for developing alcohol abuse or dependence.

- are nearly three (2.8) times more at risk of ever using cannabis, and over two (2.3) times more at risk for cannabis use or dependence.

- are two times more at risk for cocaine abuse or dependence.

- are over two and a half times more at risk for general illicit drug abuse or dependence.

It is certain that Conduct Disorder plays an important role in many ADHD children and adolescents developing substance abuse problems (Lee et al., 2011).

Q. How do medications for ADHD fit into the picture?

A. Stimulant medications for children with ADHD do not lead to an increased risk for development of substance abuse or dependence. On the contrary, it seems to have a protective effect for substance abuse and dependence in adolescence. However, studies so far have not shown a protective effect for development of substance abuse problems in adulthood (Faraone & Wilens, 2007). The latter does not mean there is not a protective effect; we do not know yet. Studies so far lack the necessary scientific methods for adequately addressing this issue.

References:

Faroane, SV & TE Wilens (2007). Effect of Stimulant Medication for Attention-deficit/Hyperactivity Disorder on later Substance Use and the Potential for later Stimulant Misuse, Abuse and Diversion. *Journal of Clinical Psychiatry* 68 (suppl 11) 15-22.

Lee, SS, KL Humpreys, K Flory, R Liu & K Glass, (2011). Prospective association of childhood attention-deficit/hyperactivity disorder (ADHD) and substance use and abuse/dependence: A meta-analytic review. *Clinical Psychology Review* 41 328-341.

Waiting for Independence Day
by Victoria M. Lees

My little girl is an adult now. At least that's what the world sees. When they first meet Marie people see a lovely, competent-looking 24-year-old woman. They don't see her learning disability, her impaired perceptions, her need for step-by-step instructions and repetition. The extra time she needs to complete a task; that is, if you can get her to listen, to connect to what you are saying. To calm down enough to have a chance to comprehend, to learn. The world sees an adult and adults don't require—aren't allowed, even—constant, step-by-step help from their mothers.

With the assistance of special education teachers at school and me on the home front, Marie succeeded in elementary and secondary school. She brought home mostly B's and C's on a modified program, and she earned a high school diploma. But then she left the protective womb of the public school's special education system after graduation and she embarked upon a new challenge: college as an adult.

Despite knowing how difficult college would be for her Marie wanted to go. In fact, she was adamant about it. She wanted to be a preschool teacher, and in order to do so she needed a degree in early childhood education. Extended family and friends encouraged her to go; the same family and friends who love Marie from a distance, the family and friends who saw only the modified report cards and "feel good" notes from Marie's many school assistants that I had displayed on the refrigerator over the years to keep up her self-esteem. They didn't understand the all-encompassing time, the bleary-eyed evenings, and the attention I couldn't give to Marie's four younger siblings that were behind Marie's success. I, who had labored much more since Marie's birth than during it, was one of a handful of people who realized how much work was performed on the home front, outside the warm womb of the public school system and the special education department. Marie's teachers and her core team of special education assistants realized it. In fact, they told me that my diligence at home had demonstrated to Marie how diligent she needed to be in the classroom.

I was terrified of what it would mean for me if Marie continued her education through a two-year Associate's Degree program, a program that I knew would take Marie much longer. Did I have the strength to continue to be Marie's mentor? To continue to give any down time I could possibly find to Marie? To center my world around her for the next five years? I am never one to tell my children they can't dream even if their dreams dissolve into my reality. Marie enrolled in community college with my blessing.

> **I am never one to tell my children they can't dream even if their dreams dissolve into my reality.**

Each year that Marie was in secondary school I would hope and pray that I could let go a little, that she could cope in the classroom and at home, with homework and projects, with less and less support. I believed that she could outgrow the distractibility, the social immaturity, that perhaps her memory could improve, and she'd be able to understand more of the subject material. But as Marie progressed from year to year these issues came up again and again. In order to succeed Marie continued to require high levels of direct support, both in class and at home.

I went over information again and again at home, her special education teachers reviewed the material numerous times at school. Repetition and time. So much time. Since Marie loved to sing I made up little jingles to help her remember facts and spelling words. More repetition, more time. Each year I prayed that the next year would be a little easier.

When I discovered that Marie could become part of the Program for the Academically Challenged Students (PACS) at the community college I felt a little better—until I realized one important thing: I was no longer Marie's guardian. She was 19 years old when she began college. I could only guide her. When she met with the counselors at college I wrote down key words or questions for her to ask, because they couldn't speak to me. I could not tell them how Marie has trouble taking notes from lectures, how she does better copying notes from the board or PowerPoint. And how note-taking takes time, much time, and that while taking notes Marie would miss what the professor was saying. My direct line of communication to people who could assist Marie with her education was severed. Gone were the study guides and CliffsNotes from Marie's public school teachers, my foundation for re-teaching Marie. I worried that without my direct involvement Marie would flounder, but I was floundering just as much as she was. I felt like a floating dock broken free in a storm, drifting, drifting free from any tether to the mainland of reality, unable to find anchor or support in my mission to help Marie with her education.

I felt like an expectant mother once again, waiting at the dawn of each semester to see whether Marie could grasp the concepts presented in class on her own, whether she'd matured enough to realize the necessity of reviewing the textbook and class notes, whether she could put questions for the professor into words. And, whether she was bold enough to advocate for herself with each new professor, to explain the modifications necessary for her to succeed in college. But as the semesters crawled along I was reminded that Marie's difficulties in academics were not something that she could outgrow. Despite experiencing some improvement in her ability to focus while taking Adderall, she still required repetition and time to learn.

Marie needed two semesters of basic skills courses in reading, writing, and math as she did not pass the basic skills test that would qualify her to enroll in college level courses. Family and friends convinced her that these classes would bring her "up to speed" for college. They encouraged Marie to enjoy the freedom that college brought. The second year of Marie's college career she was permitted to enroll in college level courses. She took three. I hid in the shadows praying. Tentatively, I asked how she was doing, reminding her about the PACS program and all its benefits.

"Fine," she answered.

And I held my breath. It wasn't until finals week that she revealed what her math professor told her. If she could only pass the final, he informed her, then he would pass her. She didn't. She failed concepts of math and received a D in English comp I.

Although I was in the throes of earning my own bachelor's degree, the realist in me came to the surface. I once again began to painstakingly read Marie's textbooks aloud to her, highlighting the important facts, translating the text into simpler terms and writing that translation in the books' margins. I racked my brain to find short, easy ways to explain psychological concepts, history, and political science to Marie. We reviewed what the professor might be talking about in class and what she needed to remember for tests.

> She did it. Or perhaps I should say *we* did it together, as we have her whole life long.

And then I'd pray, as I had done Marie's whole life. I prayed for understanding professors who would see a young person with perfect attendance, sitting right up front, wide-eyed, with consternation permanently etched upon her face, and a few cryptic notes in her notebook, a quiet young lady trying to make sense of it all. I prayed when Marie took tests at the testing center where she was permitted extra time to complete tests. The retesting that she had relied on throughout elementary and high school wasn't allowed in college. And I prayed for professors who would accept that Marie's essay answers would be short, much shorter than the average student's, and would contain spelling errors, but if the general idea was there, would count the answer as correct.

It took Marie five years to obtain her two year Associate Degree in Science for Early Childhood Development. She repeated a few classes with different professors, took only three courses per semester, and boosted by good grades in her electives (yoga, dance, music, and Tai Chi) finished strong with a 2.7 grade point average.

She did it. Or perhaps I should say *we* did it together, as we have her whole life long. We, it seems, must remain a team; Marie in the spotlight, while I support her from the wings.

Now I'm helping Marie apply for work. I help her focus and guide her as she answers questions on job applications. I still pray that each year will bring my adult child a little closer to independence, but even as I pray, I ready myself emotionally to be her coach—for life.

The author says:

Allowing a child with a disability the opportunity to dream creates a newfound struggle that takes planning, structure, and patience. Independence Day will have to wait.

Tell Us More: Expert Q & A with Patricia Quinn, M.D.

Developmental Pediatrician, Director, National Center for Girls and Women with ADHD, Washington, DC

Q. What are some things that parents of college-bound kids with ADHD should begin to consider as their children enter high school?

A. The hard truth is that half of all teens who enter college may not graduate on time or at all, and the statistics for teens with ADHD and/ or LD are even worse. And often it isn't academics and classwork that trip these students up. Instead, transitioning to independent living can be too much for teens and this sometimes gets the best of even the most gifted students. To ensure success, parents must realize that they are not going off to college with their teens, so they need to start moving out of the cockpit during high school. Parents need to look at their parenting style and switch to a coaching model that empowers their teens and allows them to learn how to prepare for life on their own, even if that means allowing them to make mistakes. While teens are still in high school, they can prepare for college life by assessing their "living-on-your-own" skills such as getting up in the morning and to bed at night on their own, and other important skills such as problem solving, decision making, communication, and self-awareness, and identifying what needs improving. Parents can work with their teens to make a plan to meet these challenges head-on and get ready for college.

I've written two books to help parents and teens assess and develop these skills: *Ready for Take-Off: Preparing Your Teen with ADHD or LD for College*, and *On Your Own: A College Readiness Guide for Teens with ADHD/LD*.

"Mom, You're an Asshole"
by Barbara Claypole White

When Zach was nine I cajoled him into calling me an asshole. As the word escaped his mouth, my son cowered in the bathtub and buried his face in his hands. I whooped with joy. Zach's obsessive-compulsive disorder (OCD) had convinced him, in an endless loop of anxiety, that I would die if he called me a bad name. By coaxing out one "asshole," and then two more, we broke the cycle.

Often described as a debilitating allergy to life itself, OCD generates irrational terror that can pop up anytime, anyplace. That night in the bath Zach found the courage to fight back and I have never been more proud of him. I was proud of myself too. After years of watching my child retreat into fear—and wondering if bad parenting was the cause—I glimpsed a brighter future, one I believed I could help sculpt.

Zach was just five years old the first time he collapsed into my lap sobbing, "Make it stop, Mommy! Make it stop!"

I watched him suffer and felt powerless to help. I didn't understand what had triggered his despair, but I knew Zach's monster wasn't hiding under the bed; it was deep inside his psyche, a place I couldn't reach with nightlights or a simple "There's nothing there, Silly Billy." Defeated, I started crying too.

A year earlier Zach had developed stomach problems and headaches and stopped sleeping through the night. He also became a worrywart, although this didn't concern me at the time. *So he's anal retentive*, I thought. *Big deal.*

When his sleep patterns deteriorated and his stomach complaints increased, I sought help in typical and non-typical ways: I turned to our trusted pediatrician, who ruled out any physical ailments, and took Zach to a homeopathic doctor who diagnosed anxiety. Eventually I found a respected child psychologist. She referred to OCD in passing, and over the course of two years taught Zach one element of Cognitive-Behavioral Therapy (CBT)—how to boss back an unwanted thought—and the rules of UNO.

Meanwhile Zach became increasingly fearful. He craved the comfort of repetitive rituals, or compulsions, and the safety of the predictable. The suggestion of a spontaneous play date threw his day off balance and caused him to huddle in tears; mention of a trip to his grandmother's compelled him to stomp on every other dandelion in the yard—"So the plane doesn't crash, Mom."

> Our biggest mistake in raising an obsessive-compulsive child was thinking as parents.

I learned that Zach inhabited a different dimension from the one I lived in, one in which every smudge of dirt concealed a fatal disease and every cumulus cloud contained a tornado. Every red traffic light signaled a delay, the worst of the worst, since delays strip you of control.

In the minefield of our OCD-riddled lives, my husband, Larry, and I fought over how to handle Zach's behavior. Larry's parenting tactics were the polar opposite of mine. He opted for punishment, but I followed my coddling instincts and reassured Zach constantly. Years later we learned that both approaches were equally harmful. My path fed the OCD beast; Larry's forced it underground. Our biggest mistake in raising an obsessive-compulsive child was thinking as parents.

While Larry offered tough love, I embarked on a doomed mission to edit fear from our child's life. Zach, for example, was terrified when I drove on highways. My solution? Plot alternative routes, even if they were three times longer.

Sleep deprived and emotionally beaten, I gave up trying to rationalize what was happening around me. I just needed to make it through each day. Part of me, a part I hated, missed the happy-go-lucky toddler with the killer smile and wanted him back.

Finally, on a family vacation to the Bahamas, my world imploded as we lurched from one OCD crisis to the next. Even the amount of time the cabin crew took to secure the airplane door triggered illogical, paralyzing panic. As Zach's obsessions and compulsions escalated, Larry's temper became brittle, and I worked tirelessly to conceal our unraveling family life. Two weeks in paradise ended in tears—mine—and Zach's psychologist declared our only option was to start him on antidepressants. I listened—and said, "No." Despite the fog of exhaustion I knew we hadn't scratched the surface of Zach's diagnosis. He was eight years old and I was not prepared to feed him adult drugs without more information. I scoured the Internet and discovered that medication was not, in fact, a cure-all for OCD.

My research led me to a form of treatment called exposure therapy and to the International OCD Foundation (IOCDF). Through the IOCDF I discovered that the country's leading pediatric OCD and exposure therapy expert, Dr. John March, had a clinic down the road at Duke University. I dumped the UNO-playing psychologist, made an appointment with a member of Dr. March's team, and dreamed of miracles—huge and instant.

I knew that for this treatment to succeed, Larry and I had to present a united front. We agreed that I would handle Zach's exposure therapy and Larry would defer to me on all things OCD.

From the second Zach entered the boxing ring to pound his OCD fears into submission, I became his coach. It was my new job—relentless, exhausting, and full-on.

Every day after school we tackled an exposure. Sometimes we went to a building with an elevator and rode up one floor but took the stairs back down. Sometimes we made up crazy songs about thieves breaking into our house. Sometimes we didn't wash our hands (hey, a few germs are good for you!). Encouraging Zach to bad-mouth me was our first big breakthrough. The night he called me an asshole I realized that with hard work and determination we could, indeed, find miracles. They didn't have to be huge, and they would never be instant, but each one deserved a celebration. And boy, did we reward ourselves for Zach's victories!

> **The night he called me an asshole I realized that with hard work and determination we could, indeed, find miracles. They didn't have to be huge, and they would never be instant, but each one deserved a celebration.**

In one year we made incredible progress, but it wasn't enough. New fears sprung up daily and psychologist number two, a woman we loved for her energy, humor, and encouragement, suggested a combination of exposure therapy and medication. Zach cried tears of failure all the way home from the session and I struggled not to join in.

Medication, however, softened the edges of Zach's anxiety, enabling us to intensify the exposures and tackle his biggest fears. When he was ready to get back on the highway we started one exit at a time. Two years into exposure therapy we could manage a 30 minute ride on the interstate with ease.

Then came the ultimate test. We were driving Larry to the airport when a dusting of snow propelled the entire area into chaos. Every school and business across eight counties closed at the same time. Roads filled with school buses, private cars, and emergency vehicles trying to deal with a string of fender-benders, and we were stuck in the middle of what was about to become the worst traffic jam in the region's history. The second we hit gridlock I knew this was the exposure to end all exposures. Imagine your worst fear. Now imagine someone forcing you to confront that fear in a confined space. That's what we were asking of Zach.

We had been stationary for over an hour and I had exhausted my entire repertoire as an OCD coach when Zach hit full OCD meltdown: hysteria, tears, and a desperate need to exit the car. His fight-or-flight response was screaming, "Danger! Danger! Run!" Larry, already stressed at missing his plane, snapped and reverted to threatening all manner of punishment.

One hour crawled into two before I remembered a staple of exposure therapy: use humor. As I looked around I realized our fellow travelers provided all the material I needed. Giving them nicknames based on their mannerisms I turned them into characters in a whacky story about the never-ending traffic jam. Gradually, Larry and Zach fell into silence and started to listen. When I got to Mr. Nose Picker in the Subaru, whose finger was permanently jammed up his left nostril and might have to be surgically removed, the unimaginable happened: Zach laughed. Moments later he announced he was no longer scared. He had faced his fear and won!

Larry declared me to be a genius, but I was simply applying the exposure therapy techniques I had learned. I did deserve some credit though. I was no longer the enabler, helping Zach avoid his OCD fears. I was the enforcer, helping him pick them apart bit by bit.

Zach experienced many setbacks after that day, such as the time I pushed too hard and dragged him into a crowded elevator while he begged me to let go. But with each baby step my confidence in Zach's ability to diffuse his OCD grew and so did my competence as his guide. Eventually we stopped concealing the hiccups of obsessive-compulsive behavior and learned to be open with family, friends, and teachers, who became our allies in the war on OCD.

At 15 Zach is both exposure and medication free. An award winning poet and an honor roll student with a gaggle of close friends and a wicked sense of humor, he navigates OCD blips and celebrates his quirkiness with t-shirts that read, "Normal people scare me," or "Some days it's not worth chewing through the restraints."

OCD no longer dictates Zach's life, but it is part of him, and I am convinced it has helped him become the person he is today. Compassionate and empathic, he knows when someone needs a hug or a smile, or a reminder to laugh at the nose-pickers in the traffic jam.

Recently I was retelling the story of that long ago day when Zach called me an asshole. He flashed his heartbreaking smile, the one I could never resist when he was a toddler.

"What's so funny?" I asked.

"Mom," he said, "you're still an asshole." Then we both cracked up.

The author says:

I dedicate this essay to Rev. Douglas Eric Claypole White and Miriam Grossberg, who would be so proud of the young man their grandson has become.

Tell Us More: Expert Q & A with John S. March, M.D., MPH

Director, Division of Neurosciences Medicine, Duke Clinical Research Institute

Q. The author of this essay describes her son "hitting full OCD meltdown." What's happening with her son at that time?

A. Kids with OCD get panicky when OCD is in full force. When OCD is on the rampage, avoidance behaviors are one option, rituals are the other. Exposure, which ends avoidance, and response prevention, which blocks rituals, are the solutions.

Q. Many of the children described in the book have several diagnoses. Is it common for kids with OCD to have comorbid conditions?

A. Half or more of kids with OCD will have comorbid diagnoses. The best way to think about this is that the neurological processes that are awry in OCD are held in common with other illnesses, such as ADHD (impaired allocation of attention) and Tourette (response inhibition for automatic behaviors). In the future, we will directly address these processes as the primary targets of treatment and as a result comorbidity won't be such an issue.

Q. What is the most effective treatment for OCD known today?

A. One of the clear findings in the OCD literature in patients of all ages is that cognitive-behavior therapy (CBT) alone or in combination with medication management is the best treatment for OCD. In our clinic, no one gets medications alone. Typically, we start with CBT alone in uncomplicated OCD and only add medication when other disorders like depression complicate the clinical picture. Unfortunately, good CBT is still hard to find. Figuring how to make it more available is the central challenge facing the field in the near term.

Against All Odds
by Janet Schraw Solie, P.A., M.S.

As soon my daughter, Kristyn, got in the car after school, I knew something had gone terribly wrong.

Kristyn had gotten up early that morning, packed a lunch, and planned to arrive in the lunchroom early to get a good seat. For Kristyn to be this excited about a school event it had to be a big deal, and to her this was: a lunch talk that featured the college admission counselor from her "dream" school, a highly competitive California university.

When I dropped her off at school that morning she was elated, and so was I. We had made a couple of trips touring both state and private colleges during the past summer, trips that were insightful and provoking. Attending this talk moved Kristyn one step closer to her goal of attending one of those colleges. I waited for her after school that day, anxious to hear about the talk.

And then, I saw her face.

"How did it go?" I asked, feeling nervous.

Kristyn paused for a moment, looked away, and then said, "That meeting wasn't for kids like me. Don't ask me anymore questions. I don't want to talk about it."

The words broke my heart.

Kristin reached the door to the classroom where the presentation was being held just as the meeting was starting. From the doorway, she heard the college admission officer begin reviewing the university's criteria for acceptance. "Last year's incoming freshman had an average GPA of 4.25," she said.

Diagnosed with attention deficit disorder (ADD) at age eight, Kristyn had worked hard to achieve a respectable 3.0 GPA, a solid accomplishment given the pressures of her private high school's challenging college prep curriculum. But at that moment, her success appeared hollow. Intimidated and embarrassed, Kristyn did a 180 degree turn and walked away from the classroom, wondering how many of her non-ADHD classmates had seen her. She knew what those who did would be thinking: *You're not good enough for this university. You don't belong here, but we do.*

Getting Kristyn to her senior year had been a challenging task, requiring me to alternate roles between mom, coach, and ADD advocate. Kristyn's number one concern was not to appear different from her peers at school, so she was often conflicted about accepting the help I arranged for. But the simple fact was that she required many specialists in order to maintain a B average at school. As her coach I interviewed, hired, and scheduled the best academic tutors, SAT tutors, psychiatrist, and educational psychologist I could find. As the ADD advocate I found myself patiently explaining to those tutors, and to school personnel, what Kristyn and others like her needed from them in order to succeed. Over the years my husband, David, and I both had frequent conversations with teachers, and regular appearances at "academic concerns night." Kristyn performed inconsistently from semester to semester throughout high school, despite all of the special services she received.

> **Getting Kristyn to her senior year had been a challenging task, requiring me to alternate roles between mom, coach, and ADD advocate.**

Many of her Kristyn's friends with ADD were no longer enrolled in her school by senior year. Most had transferred to schools with an easier curriculum and a more accommodating environment. Some of her peers with untreated ADD had disappeared from her school only to resurface in drug, alcohol, or behavior treatment programs in "the state with no beaches," California parent code for the many residential treatment programs in Utah.

Kristyn sometimes complained about taking her daily medication. David and I kept up an ongoing dialog with her about the importance of continuing to take it, citing the kids who'd disappeared as examples of what can happen to teens who opt out of taking ADD medication and start to self-treat with street drugs and alcohol. We worked with Kristyn's doctor to gradually reduce the dose of her medication, and she continued to succeed, a compromise that satisfied all of us.

Now Kristyn stood alone, the only one in her dwindling social network who faced the onerous task of applying to colleges. I was worried about her chances of success, but Kristyn assured me that when the time came she would have a plan.

> She was determined to prove the admissions counselor and the other students wrong. Despite her ADD, she *would* attend her dream college.

"Don't worry, Mom. I got it."

As Kristyn moved through the fall semester of her senior year I feared she wouldn't be able to pull everything together that was required to complete the arduous college application process. I worried about the multiple deadlines that approached. Kristyn needed to finish her SAT tutoring, take the test, and write her college essay, all by about the first of January. But being asked to leave the college admissions meeting in front of her peers—*you're not good enough*—had set Kristyn on a mission. She was determined to prove the admissions counselor and the other students wrong. Despite her ADD, she *would* attend her dream college.

When Kristyn said she had a plan, she meant it. Kristyn would author her own path to success by way of her college essay. Her story wouldn't be about GPA's, advanced placement (AP) classes and school-based extracurricular activities. The traditional milestones of high school success couldn't define or measure her personal worth. She would create a broader narrative for success. Over the years, Kristyn's teachers had made it clear that she always "marched to her own beat." That insight would become her ticket to college. It would gain her admission to the school of her dreams.

Since elementary school, Kristyn had demonstrated a passion for art, computers, and photography that drove her to create unique and compelling forms of digital art. Over the years she spent countless hours in her room late at night, working on her digital creations. I remember asking her—so many times—to *please* stop letting her computer art distract her, and *please* just finish her homework! But David thought we should encourage Kristyn's passion for digital media, and on her fourteenth birthday he presented her with a digital camera, a more powerful computer, and specialized software programs. With these new tools she flew off to pursue her passion.

And pursue it she did. Kristyn spent many late nights teaching herself how to use various software programs, like Photoshop, for digital creations. Previously she had avoided school related events, but now the camera strapped to her side became her VIP pass to school events. Her peers knew that she would add cool artistic elements to her photos, and then post them online at photography sites like Flickr.

Even though her school didn't offer a formal venue to express her talent, she found ways to incorporate her art into the school community. She designed t-shirts for fundraising, school posters, and even the cover of the yearbook during her senior year. At the end of her senior year she was awarded the title "Best Artist" at her school.

When it was time for Kristyn to complete the community service hours that the school required from students in ninth through twelfth grades, I enrolled her in our local Volunteen program. Volunteen is a community based summer program that mimics a workplace setting in various small businesses or city offices. The idea is to provide service to the community as well as prepare teens for the responsibilities of the real jobs they would someday perform. The program matches teens with available volunteer placements based on their interests. Kristyn offered up her art and computer skills, and was placed in a fledging advertising agency the first summer. The following summer she designed flyers and brochures for the city's parks department. The skills she developed during those first two summers caught the city media director's eye. At the end of the second summer Kristyn became the youngest paid intern the city-owned TV station had ever employed. For the two final years of high school she continued to work for the city, developing graphic design layouts for community related announcements and commercials.

As Kristyn's mom, it was redeeming to see her happy in her work environment. Kristyn felt proud of who she was at work. I was used to smoothing the way for Kristyn, but because this was a "real" job, having a parent play that role was no longer appropriate. Although I continued to worry that her ADD symptoms would affect her work performance, I saw a new confidence and maturity emerging in Kristyn. As hard as it was for me to believe, work was a space where Kristyn didn't require a mother-slash-ADD advocate in order to succeed!

Kristyn took a closer look at her dream university through the lens of her interest in photography and digital art. She went to the university's website and reviewed the various art programs and majors being offered. Within the professional school of art she identified design media studies as an ideal match for her unique talents, and she discovered that some students currently enrolled in the program were doing the kinds of Photoshop art she had been developing for years. Armed with her personal and commercial portfolios she was ready to complete her application.

Despite her artistic success, middle and high school had been academically challenging for Kristyn. How could she present her less than stellar academic record to her dream school, a school with such intimidating academic criteria? Kristyn decided to challenge the bias that grades are everything. She believed her success in the face of ADD was the real story, and was determined to prove that grades alone did not reflect her intelligence, true talents, or potential.

She opened her college essay outlining why she, a student with ADD, didn't fit the school's standard student profile. Writing with a compelling and authentic voice, she pointed out why the school's admissions criteria had major loopholes for applicants like her. Cases in point were her ACT and SAT scores. They were high enough to demonstrate that she possessed the intelligence and capabilities to handle college level studies. Her grade point, on the other hand, though respectable, didn't accurately reflect her true potential. To further her point, Kristyn cited the low grade she received in an AP psychology class, and then compared that to her remarkable score of five on the AP exam covering the same subject area. That score earned her two college credits. She concluded her essay by saying that ADD was indeed a burden,

> ADD was indeed a burden, but it was also an energy force that equipped her with creativity, passion and determination. Overcoming this adversity had given her practical life skills that, combined with her native talents, set her apart from the traditional high performing student.

but it was also an energy force that equipped her with creativity, passion, and determination. Overcoming this adversity had given her practical life skills that, combined with her native talents, set her apart from the traditional high performing student.

By the middle of January of her senior year Kristyn had submitted her applications, test scores, transcripts, essays, and portfolios to her "safe," "stretch," and "dream" schools. David and I had helped her track deadlines, but she completed all the details herself. Whether she got into her top schools or not, we were proud of her efforts.

At the end of each day Kristyn checked the mailbox and her email account for news. Finally, the first replies came rolling in. Kristyn was accepted to all of her safe schools, and surprisingly, most of her reach schools too. Now we were down to waiting to hear from her dream school.

On a Friday night in late March, while heading home with her dad after a school event, Kristyn received the long-awaited email from her dream school: a letter from the admissions office congratulating her for being accepted into the school of art, with a declared major of design media studies. Kristyn reacted first with disbelief and then pure joy. Later she told me, "Mom, getting that email made that the best day of my life. I will always remember that moment. The school everyone said didn't want me, picked me. I am so happy!"

Once Kristyn had completed the admission process I set up an appointment for the two of us to meet with the office of student disability services. I brought a thick file of records that included a document from her psychiatrist requesting accommodations, as well as all of the test results from her educational psychologist. After a brief meeting the university psychologist ruled that Kristyn was eligible for priority registration, extended test taking, tutoring, third party note taking and use of a computer for taking exams. Best of all, after years of paying for educational therapists, tutors, and expensive psychological testing, the university's accommodation services would be provided without additional fees.

Had I known the acceptance, recognition, and support that awaited Kristyn in a university setting, I would have carried myself with more faith and grace and with less anxiety during her high school years. Year after year, while her non-ADD peers won accolades and awards for superior scholastic and athletic achievements, Kristyn forged her own solitary path to success. Though my confidence in her sometimes waivered, she had enough belief in herself to carry us both through those trying years. I had discounted her eternal optimism as another manifestation of ADD, when in reality it was her optimism that gave her the courage, determination, and creativity to approach a situation in which the overwhelming odds had been against her.

I have come to believe ADD is like nuclear energy. You can use it to blow yourself up, or to light a city. Kristyn is living her dream now, learning how to light up her city. Although I am certain she will encounter roadblocks along the way, and I still worry, I know the odds against her have changed. I couldn't be more happy or proud of my daughter, Kristyn.

The author says

In pursuit of her dream, Kristyn, age 18, is a design/digital studies major at UCLA. In addition to working part time on campus in the area of visual marketing, she earned a place on UCLA's dean's honor list during her first year of studies.

To See What It's Like
by Sarah Conover

It was Thursday, garbage pick-up day. From our bedroom we heard the metallic groans of the truck's pincers swing to lift, one by one, the cans that lined Thirteenth Street like a row of obedient soldiers. Moaning plaintively and then crashing loudly, the cans emptied into the truck's maw. The men were a little behind schedule, but that was in our favor because we'd just realized that we'd forgotten to put out the recyclables. My husband, Doug, ran to the curb with our bottles only to find our five-year-old daughter, Jamey, ski-helmeted and goggled, strapped with duct tape to the garbage can.

"What in the world are you doing?" Doug asked.

"I want to see what it's like to take a ride in the air!"

Be careful what you name a child. Jamey, a diminutive of the name James, means *the conqueror* or *supplanter*. How to describe the rugged, ever-changing terrain of our years with her? I compare them to the mountaineering exploits that framed my courtship with Doug. When a map no longer helped, when a squall obscured all but the cliff in front of us, the only way out was to climb straight up. We began parenting Jamey equally blind, not knowing we faced such a challenging journey, one that would test our endurance, our ability to pilot our lives, our marriage, and our estimation of ourselves both morally and spiritually.

Had we raised only our firstborn, Nate, we would be oh-so smug, with little sympathy for or understanding of parents of high-maintenance children. Nate was the kind of child to whom you could calmly state, as you maneuvered the car onto a busy freeway, "You're in a time out," and he would immediately silence. He didn't argue with us until he was 15.

Jamey was different. She stood her ground right from the start. Her first word was "More!" Arms outstretched toward us, palms rotating like greedy little animals, she was hungry for more of *everything* life offered.

She was—and still is—perfectly clear on those wants. The first time that she could articulate her wishes to Santa she asked to be a boy. When Santa didn't come through she cut her hair and acted the part for the next seven years. Another year she requested a tuxedo. She paraded it like a natural-born movie star. The Christmas after that she wanted crutches. They turned out to be the neighborhood's most popular play item ever.

Nothing, however, seemed to entertain Jamey more than rocking her brother Nate's world. Her earliest memory, she tells us, is of setting up a booby-trap of diapers that would fling in his face when he walked in the door of their shared room. When asked why she felt it necessary to annoy her brother at every opportunity she squeezed her eyes shut, balled her small fists, and shivered with ecstasy.

> Had we raised only our firstborn, Nate, we would be oh-so smug, with little sympathy for or understanding of parents of high-maintenance children.

"I just *love* it!" she said.

We were living with a force of nature. We could neither control, nor manage, nor parent this child as we had our first. The heretofore-unremarkable parent-child interactions of a day now went awry. Our home became a battleground. For Jamey, choosing her own outfit was a non-negotiable. We couldn't dissuade her from wearing a cotton t-shirt to face sub-zero temperatures. Getting Jamey to swallow medicine of any kind was nearly impossible. A year battling giardia guaranteed a twice-a-day skirmish. We went from vegetarians to every-night carnivores in a quest to find something Jamey might eat without a fray. Even when we catered to her culinary desires, she'd wander off after a single bite of food, drawn to something far more interesting.

Who was in charge? Neither Doug nor I it seemed. Each night we collapsed into bed shattered by the day's innumerable meltdowns and the obvious failure of our best efforts to be the calm and loving parents we had hoped to be.

My friend, author Jean Ashbe, believes that it's the child that makes the parent, that a child's temperament shapes the tenor of the relationship more than we parents want to admit. We found ourselves needing to be wholly different parents for Jamey, a role for which she trained us and became our no-nonsense coach.

> **We could neither control, nor manage, nor parent this child as we had our first.**

Who first mentioned the idea that we might have a child with attention deficit hyperactivity disorder (ADHD) on our hands? I can't remember. I do recall my father-in-law, a surgeon, handing us a pamphlet from the manufacturer of Ritalin that, in my memory, claimed a third of America's children needed their product. Who could believe those numbers? We tossed it. Our child didn't have ADHD. She was simply "spirited."

Yet at home we continued to see difficulties—tantrums, the inability to sit still, a lack of impulse control—so much of the time that we couldn't completely dismiss the possibility that Jamey would end up with an ADHD diagnosis. Surprisingly, Jamey was able to mask these behaviors at school. The ADHD symptom surveys from our HMO, one filled out by Jamey's third grade teacher and one by us, showed starkly conflicting data. When we compared results her teacher said, "The child you describe in your survey could not be the same child I see each day at school!"

We were relieved, of course, that her school persona contrasted with the tumultuous Jamey we saw at home. However, soon we began to notice an alarming trend that bridged school and home: her impulsivity was quickly losing Jamey every friend. Watching this development we began to envision an incredibly lonely trajectory for her. That realization tipped us into the medication camp. We allowed the doctor to prescribe a trial of Ritalin despite the differing surveys from school and home.

The effectiveness of Ritalin on her ability to exert some impulse control in social situations was instantaneous. Jamey's teacher contacted us and said Jamey had indeed transformed in class. She no longer shouted guesses to answer questions, but actually paused to process information before responding.

We gained an unexpected ally during this time, Jamey's pediatrician, an ADHD specialist named Deb Harper. Petite and energetic, Dr. Harper referred to herself as "an outdoor pet needing lots of walks." She has ADD. She viewed ADD/ADHD not as problematic, but as various, unexpected, and wonderful ways of being in the world. She helped us see it that way, too.

To say Dr. Harper is a child-centered doctor understates the term. When we'd visit she'd laser in on Jamey addressing any and all questions to her.

"Are your grades homogenous or heterogeneous?" she asked Jamey during our first office visit. Jamey looked stumped.

Dr. Harper elaborated. "Are they all one grade, like all B's, or are some A's, some B's and some C's?"

"Oh!" Jamey replied with delight and pride, "Heterogeneous!"

Dr. Harper told it to Jamey straight. "School will likely always be hard for you. It's just going to be a bear."

Doug and I cringed. Jamey listened intently.

"But," Dr. Harper added with obvious mischievousness, "ADHD adults have more fun than anybody." She grinned. "We're never bored. We're the most creative grownups you'll ever meet. Just have some patience. You'll get there."

On parting Dr. Harper always asked, "How many ADD kids does it take to screw in a light bulb?"

Jamey knew the answer. "Want to go for a bike ride?"

"Want to go for a bike ride?" became our family's code for gently pointing out ADHD antics.

Dr. Harper helped us all reframe how we thought about ADHD. Doug and I felt like we needed Dr. Harper's pep talks more than our daughter, but perhaps we were wrong. Jamey must have hungered for the doctor's validation and beams of hope. Sadly, it took only a few days after an appointment for Doug and me to slide back into viewing ADHD as a bundle of vexations to quash.

Jamey doggedly forged a path through elementary and middle school while taking Ritalin. In public school Jamey hadn't qualified for special assistance, and with no one to help her focus she languished in the large classrooms. We moved her to a private school for a number of years where she worked at least twice as hard as other students to doggedly keep up. In retrospect, her perseverance through hours and hours of homework astonishes me. I don't know how she found the focus—night after night—to face the unpleasant tasks in front of her.

With medication, Jamey seemed better able to make—and keep—good friends, one of whom took charge in seventh grade and helped her change from a tomboy to a girly girl with a single trip to Old Navy. Jamey claimed new ground as an individual too. During a dinner conversation she pointed out that unlike her mother, who wrote poetry, and unlike her philosophical father and brother she was *not* deep, and furthermore, she was *not* boring Buddhists like the rest of us.

But is there ever stasis in family life? Hormones kicked in and reignited fiery habits we thought we'd left far behind. Jamey's emotional tantrums, bottomless narcissism, and implacable truculence re-emerged like a firestorm as she hit adolescence. Once again, life at home became a battlefield.

Jamey announced that she wanted to stop taking medication, and since she was tiny and we were worried about Ritalin's alleged effect of stunting growth, we took her off of it in eighth grade. We went through trials of a number of other ADHD medications, none of which Jamey liked, complaining that they left her with no personality.

Big brother Nate moved on to college. Left with just our daughter now, Doug and I tried to stare down our fears that high school would be an eternity of trials. Although Jamey's grades remained

> **Doug and I felt constantly on guard, as if some looming catastrophe lay right over the horizon, just out of view. Was this feeling simply a byproduct of our constant vigilance; of our many-years habit of running interference between Jamey and her world?**

"heterogeneous," her inclination "To see what it's like!" steered her towards risky experimentation. Alcohol binging became our ever-present worry. Two of Jamey's friends—good kids—nearly died from alcohol poisoning on Halloween night of their freshman year. Jamey called in the adults just before it was too late.

After that we looked for opportunities to remind Jamey of the scary statistics linking ADHD to high alcohol and drug use.

"You do know that you're more at risk for addiction and alcoholism than a non-ADHD kid?"

"Yes, Mom."

"You do know alcoholism and addiction run in the family?"

"Yes, Dad."

Those talks often took place in front of the family photo gallery. It makes an impression when there are more alcoholics than not in a family tree.

Jamey didn't roll her eyes at these sermons like she did with others. Alcohol abuse was one topic Jamey seemed willing to communicate with us about. We offered zero punishment in exchange for full disclosure. We wanted Jamey to tell us—honestly—all about her experimentation. She agreed. We heard plenty.

Despite this strategy something felt amiss. Doug and I felt constantly on guard, as if some looming catastrophe lay right over the horizon, just out of view. Was this feeling simply a byproduct of our constant vigilance; of our many-years habit of running interference between Jamey and her world?

Sure enough, the catastrophe we anticipated materialized directly under our noses. After we went to bed Jamey had been taking a laptop to her basement room to watch TV through the Internet. I found dozens of iTunes movie purchases on my account and Jamey confessed to being the person responsible. We learned, too late, and with no warnings from her teachers, that because of the hours she'd spent online she was so far behind in her schoolwork that she was failing all of her classes. The spring semester of her junior year was impossible to salvage.

Jamey realized that she had an addiction to the Internet, an addiction that science does not yet understand fully. Research shows that navigating to a single page on the Internet releases little bursts of dopamine in the human brain. Jamey had been self-medicating every night—heavily—through hours of computer-streamed TV. Learning this scared her to the bone. She asked to see a counselor. She asked us to remove all media, including the Internet, from our home. She asked for help.

Doug and I sought out a therapist for guidance in handling the situation. Over the years of parenting Jamey we'd worked with several. Despairing, with little reserve of goodwill left between our daughter and us to face the present calamity, we reviewed with the therapist, list-like, every behavior modification strategy we'd ever tried. They were all bankrupt. None had prevented the present situation, nor could any promise to control the future. What was left for us to try? What else was there?

Then, it was as if the room lightened, and Doug and I stepped out of a miasma. We looked at each other, struck

> Over the years we'd tried every natural consequence, every behavioral strategy we could think of. All we had left was unconditional love.

simultaneously by the same insight. Over the years we'd tried every natural consequence, every behavioral strategy we could think of. All we had left was unconditional love. We had one short year in which to repair our relationship with our daughter, before she left home forever.

Doug and I both grew up with angry, abusive fathers, so our belief that parenting meant dominance made some sense. Public schools, with their one-size-fits-all system of discipline, compounded the view that obedience is paramount. But seeing Jamey as a problem needing a solution had been a terrible mistake, one that we still feel remorse over.

Love, not control, would be our parenting mantra. We couldn't get out of the therapist's office fast enough. We wanted to be with our daughter in a wholly new way.

But who changed first—Jamey or us? Hadn't Jamey showed maturity, self-control, and responsibility when she faced her Internet addiction?

The fall semester of her senior year Jamey brought home a 3.9 grade point average, the best of her entire school career. She made up her missing credits while successfully juggling two Advanced Placement courses. She found, and was accepted by, a college in Arizona where the idea of a classroom stretches to the entire southwest.

She competed with me for best chef in the house. I never could match her garlicky Alfredo sauce or her balsamic reduction. She sought out our company, even for public outings at the mall. She showed up at our community sing-alongs with a guitar strapped on her back. She apologized for misunderstandings before I did. Somehow, as we replaced consequences with unconditional love, Jamey grew into a joyful, vivacious, charismatic young woman.

For the first time, a year seemed like a very, very short time together.

The author says:

Jamey Robnett-Conover, the star of my essay, "To See What It's Like," is presently thriving as a freshman at Prescott College, in Prescott, Arizona. It's a small, learning-by-doing college that treats the great southwest as its classroom. Jamey's horizons now include becoming an aquatic biologist.

Resources

This section includes books, websites, organizations, and blogs connected to the contributors of *Easy to Love but Hard to Raise*. We included specifics on resources that were pertinent to the subject of the book; all other websites, blogs, organizations, books and resources that are connected to the contributors are listed in the People section.

Books

American Psychiatric Association. *Diagnostic and Statistical Manual of Mental Disorders: DSM-IV-TR.* 4th edition. American Psychiatric Publishing, 2000.

Aron, Elaine. *The Highly Sensitive Child: Helping Our Children Thrive When the World Overwhelms Them.* 1st edition. Three Rivers, 2002.

Cohen, Cathi. *Raise Your Child's Social IQ: Stepping Stones to People Skills for Kids.* Advantage Books, 2000.

————. *Stepping Stones to Building Friendships: A Guide for Camp Counselors.* Advantage Books, 2000.

Eide, Brock and Fernette Eide. *The Mislabeled Child: Looking Beyond Behavior to Find the True Sources and Solutions for Children's Learning Challenges.* Hyperion, 2007.

Elkind, David. *The Hurried Child.* 25th anniversary edition. Da Capo Press, 2006.

————. *The Power of Play: Learning What Comes Naturally.* Da Capo Press, 2007.

Forehand, Rex, Ph.D and Nicholas Long, Ph.D *Parenting the Strong-Willed Child: The Clinically Proven Five-Week Program for Parents of Two-to Six-Year-Olds.* 3rd edition. McGraw-Hill, 2010.

Gatto, John Taylor. *Dumbing Us Down: The Hidden Curriculum of Compulsory Schooling.* 2nd edition. New Society Publishers, 2002.

Gillen, Lynea and James Gillen. *Yoga Calm for Children: Educating Heart, Mind, and Body.* Three Pebble Press, 2008.

Glasser, Howard and Jennifer Easley. *Transforming the Difficult Child: The Nurtured Heart Approach.* Nurtured Heart Publications, 1999.

Gordon, Thomas. *Parent Effectiveness Training: The Proven Program for Raising Responsible Children*. 30th edition. Three Rivers Press, 2000.

Hallowell, Edward M., M.D. and John J. Ratey, M.D. *Answers to Distraction*. Original edition. Anchor, 2010.

————-. *Delivered from Distraction: Getting the Most out of Life with Attention Deficit Disorder*. Ballantine Books, 2005.

————-. *Driven to Distraction: Recognizing and Coping with Attention Deficit Disorder from Childhood through Adulthood*. 1st edition. Touchstone, 1995.

Hallowell, Edward M., M.D. and Peter S. Jensen, M.D. *Superparenting for ADD: An Innovative Approach to Raising Your Distracted Child*. Ballantine Books, 2010.

Kraus, Jeanne R. *Annie's Plan: Taking Charge of Schoolwork and Homework*. Illus. Charles Beyl. 1st edition. Magination Press, 2006.

————-. *Cory Stories: A Kid's Book about Living with ADHD*. Illus. Whitney Martin. 1st edition. Magination Press, 2004.

Kurcinka, Mary Sheedy. *Raising Your Spirited Child: A Guide for Parents Whose Child Is More Intense, Sensitive, Perceptive, Persistent, and Energetic*. Revised edition. Harper Paperbacks, 2006.

Maitland, Theresa L., Ph.D and Patricia O. Quinn, M.D. *Ready for Take-Off: Preparing Your Teen with ADHD or LD for College*. 1st edition. Magination Press, 2010.

Mesibov, Gary B., Victoria Shea, and Eric Schopler. *The TEACCH Approach to Autism Spectrum Disorders*. 1st edition. Springer, 2004.

Meyer, Donald J., ed. *Thicker than Water: Essays by Adult Siblings of People with Disabilities*. Woodbine House, 2009.

———-. *Uncommon Fathers: Reflections on Raising a Child with a Disability.* Woodbine House, 1995.

———-. *Views from Our Shoes: Growing up with a Brother or Sister with Special Needs.* Illus. Cary Pillo. 1ˢᵗ edition. Woodbine House, 1997.

Meyer, Donald J. and David Gallagher. *The Sibling Slam Book: What It's Really Like to Have a Brother or Sister with Special Needs.* 1ˢᵗ edition. Woodbine House, 2005.

Meyer, Donald J. and Patricia Vadasy. *Living with a Brother or Sister with Special Needs: A Book for Sibs.* 2ⁿᵈ revised edition. University of Washington Press, 1996.

———-. *Sibshops: Workshops for Siblings of Children with Special Needs.* Revised edition. Paul H. Brookes Publishing Company, 2007.

Miller, Lucy Jane, Ph.D., OTR, and Doris A. Fuller. *Sensational Kids: Hope and Help for Children with Sensory Processing Disorder.* Perigee Trade, 2007.

Nadeau, Kathleen G., Ph.D., Ellen B. Littman, Ph.D., and Patricia O. Quinn, M.D. *Understanding Girls with AD/HD.* 1ˢᵗ edition. Advantage Books, 2000.

Nelson, Jane, Ed. D. *Positive Discipline.* Revised updated edition. Ballantine Books, 2006.

Papalos, Demetri, M.D. and Janice Papalos. *The Bipolar Child: The Definitive and Reassuring Guide to Childhood's Most Misunderstood Disorder.* 3ʳᵈ edition. Three Rivers Press, 2007.

Pearce, Joseph Chilton. *Magical Child.* Plume, 1992.

Phelan, Thomas W., Ph.D. *1-2-3 Magic: Effective Discipline for Children 2-12.* 4ᵗʰ edition. Parentmagic, Inc., 2010.

Lawton, Suzanne C. *Asperger Syndrome: Natural Steps Toward a Better Life for You or Your Child.* 1st edition. Praeger, 2007.

Quinn, Patricia O., M.D. *Attention, Girls!: A Guide to Learn All About Your AD/HD.* Illus. Carl Pearce. 1st edition. Magination Press, 2009.

————. *100 Questions & Answers About Attention Deficit Hyperactivity Disorder (ADHD) in Women and Girls.* 1st edition. Jones & Bartlett Learning, 2010.

Quinn, Patricia O., M.D., and Judith M. Stern, M.A. *50 Activities and Games for Kids with ADHD.* Illus. Kate Sternberg. 1st edition. Magination Press, 2000.

————. *Putting on the Brakes: Understanding and Taking Control of Your ADD or ADHD.* Illus. Joe Lee. 2nd edition. Magination Press, 2008.

————. *Putting on the Brakes Activity Book for Kids with ADD or ADHD.* Illus. Joe Lee. 2nd edition. Magination Press, 2009.

Sears, William, M.D. and Martha Sears. *The Fussy Baby Book: Parenting Your High-Need Child From Birth to Age Five.* 1st edition. Little, Brown and Company, 1996.

Shumaker, Laura. *A Regular Guy: Growing Up With Autism.* Landscape Press, 2008.

Siegel, Daniel J. *The Mindful Brain: Reflection and Attunement in the Cultivation of Well-Being.* 1st edition. W.W. Norton & Company, 2007.

Warner, Judith. *We've Got Issues: Children and Parents in the Age of Medication.* 1st edition. Riverhead Books, 2010.

Weldon, Laura Grace. *Free Range Learning: How Homeschooling Changes Everything.* Hohm Press, 2010.

Winter, Judy. *Breakthrough Parenting for Children With Special Needs: Raising the Bar of Expectations.* Jossey-Bass, 2006.

Organizations, Websites, Blogs and other Resources

Association for Behavior Analysis International (ABAI). http://www.abainternational.org/.

Bashista, Adrienne. *A Square Peg, A Round Hole :FASD. Gifted. Homeschooling. Us. Homeschooling, education, and parenting a gifted child as well as one with FASD.* http://asquarepegaroundhole.com/.

Bashista, Adrienne and Kay Marner, et al. *Easy to Love but Hard to Raise.* http://www.easytolovebut.com/.

Bipolar Parents: Support for all who deal with BP. http://health.groups.yahoo.com/group/BipolarParents/.

Celebrate Calm: Transform Your Family. http://www.celebratecalm.com/.

Early Intervention Program for Infants and Toddlers with Disabilities. http://www2.ed.gov/programs/osepeip/index.html/.

Federici, Dr. Ronald S., Psy.D. & Associates. http://www.drfederici.com/.

Flaminio, Kathy. 1000 Petals LLC: a transformative yoga and cycling experience. http://1000-petals.com/.

Gray, Peter. *Freedom to Learn: The roles of play and curiosity as foundations for learning.* http://www.psychologytoday.com/blog/freedom-learn/.

Greene, Mary. *When Rain Hurts: Parenting a child with FASD.* http://whenrainhurts.wordpress.com/.

Hallowell, Dr. Edward. *Live a Better Life.* http://www.drhallowell.com/.

Hopeful Parents. http://www.hopefulparents.org/.

Hutchins, Pamela. *Road to Joy: Hang on for the ride as I screw up my kids, drive my husband insane, embarrass myself in triathlon, and write utter nonsense.* http://www.pamelahutchins.com/.

InStep: Restore Your Family's Well-Being. Clinical information and multiple articles and other resources. http://insteppc.com/.

International Collaboration on ADHD and Substance Abuse (ICASA). http://www.adhdandsubstanceabuse.org/.

International OCD Foundation (IOCDF). http://www.ocfoundation.org/.

Marner, Kay. *My Picture-Perfect Family: a blog about raising a loveable, exhausting child with ADHD.* http://www.additudemag.com/adhdblogs/4/.

McClure, Kristin. http://www.how-to-be-happy-right-now.com/.

————. http://www.kristen-mcclure-therapist.com/.

————. http://www.charlotte-anxiety-and-depression-treatment.com/.

Miller, Kelly Quiñones. *The Miller Mix.* http://themillermix.blogspot.com/.

Murphy, Tammy. *Tammy Time: From parenting ADHD to navigating my own journey, Tammy Time is where I try to connect the dots.* http://www.tammytimeblog.blogspot.com/.

National Center for Girls and Women with ADHD. http://www.ncgiadd.org/.

National Tourette Syndrome Association (TSA). http://www.tsa-usa.org/.

Park Nicollet, Melrose Institute. http://www.parknicollet.com/eatingdisorders/.

Program in Child Affective and Anxiety Disorders, Duke Child and Family Study Center. http://www2.mc.duke.edu/pcaad/.

Quinn, Patricia O., M.D. and Kathleen Nadeau, Ph.D. *ADDvance: Answers to your Questions about ADD (ADHD).* http://www.addvance.com/.

Rhodes, Robin. *Bipolarperil.* http://bipolarperil.blogspot.com/.

Sensory Processing Disorder Foundation. http://www.spdfoundation.net/.

Shumaker, Laura. http://www.laurashumaker.com/.

Sibling Support Project. http://www.siblingsupport.org/.

South, Frank. *ADHD Dad: Better Late than Never.* http://www.additudemag.com/ahdhdblogs/6/.

STAR (Sensory Therapies And Research) Center. http://www.starcenter.us/.

Weldon, Laura Grace. *Free Range Learning.* http://www.lauragraceweldon.com/.

Williams, Penny, et al. *a mom's view of ADHD {everyday life with our ADHD kids}.* http://adhdmomma.blogspot.com/.

Winegardner, Jean. *Stimeyland: Get Your Quirk On.* http://www.stimeyland.com/.

————. *Austism Unexpected.* http://www.bit.ly/autun/.

People

Adrienne Ehlert Bashista is the co-editor of *Easy to Love but Hard to Raise*, and is also the author of two picture books about Russian adoption. She's had stories, essays, and articles published in a variety of journals, both print and online. She was a school librarian for many years before giving it up to devote more time to the rest of her life. She recently started homeschooling her eight-year-old son, and she's chronicling their adventures in the blog, *A Square Peg, a Round Hole.* She also writes for the blog, *a mom's view of ADHD* and has a personal blog, adriennebashista. net, as well. She lives in central North Carolina with her husband, two sons (one NT, leaning towards the gifted, the other not NT at all, although they're working on it), two dogs, thirty chickens, two parakeets, and a lot of bees.

Laura Duncan Boss Laura Duncan Boss lives in Seattle with her husband Al, son Nathan, and their cats, Saki and Arturo.

Laura, a recovering school-volunteer-aholic, has recently returned to writing after a long absence. After embracing the idea that creativity needs both structure and community to flourish, she has uncharacteristically joined a weekly writing group, taken classes, and developed a daily writing habit. The result has been amazing progress on a long-planned memoir about a life-changing year in France, as well as several essays, the first of which is published in this book.

Barbara Claypole White is an English-born writer living in Orange County, North Carolina with her professor husband, Larry, and their award-winning poet son, 16-year-old Zachariah. Following a career in publicity, marketing, and journalism, Barbara is chasing her childhood dream of becoming a novelist. Inspired by events in this essay, her hopefully soon-to-be-published manuscript, *Dogwood Days,* introduces the first obsessive-compulsive romantic hero in women's fiction. *Dogwood*

Days has been a winner in the SARA Merritt Contest and the Carrie McCray Memorial Literary Awards.

Cathi Cohen, a Licensed Clinical Social Worker and Certified Group Psychotherapist, is the founder and director of InStep, a mental health clinic in Virginia. She has worked with children, adolescents, and adults in a clinical setting since 1984. Early in her career as a social worker, Cathi recognized the power of treating relationship problems through group therapy. It was this interest and expertise that led her to create the Stepping Stones Social Skills Group Therapy Program in 1990. The success of this program led to the formation in 1995 of InStep, a comprehensive mental health practice. Cathi is the author of *Raise Your Child's Social IQ: Stepping Stones to People Skills for Kids*, and has become a leading expert in the field of social skills training with children. She has since completed two more books, *Stepping Stones to Building Friendships: A Guide for Camp Counselors*, and *Outnumbered, Not Outsmarted: An A to Z Guide for Working with Kids and Teens in Groups*. In addition to writing numerous articles and conducting regular workshops for parents, educators, and mental health professionals, Cathi has appeared on radio and television programs about the mental health needs of children and their families. Cathi graduated summa cum laude from Tufts University before receiving her M.S. degree from Columbia University School of Social Work.

Sarah Conover is a writer and teacher living in Spokane, Washington with her husband, Doug Robnett. Their children, Nate, age 22 and Jamey, age 20, have fledged the nest to attend college. Sarah's poetry has been published in numerous literary anthologies, and she is the author and co-author of five books addressing world wisdom traditions and the spiritual education of families. Sarah Conover's books, now published by Skinner House Books, include *Kindness: a Treasury of Buddhist Wisdom for Children and Parents* (2001); *Ayat Jamilah, Beautiful Signs: a Treasury of Islamic Wisdom for Children and Parents* (2004); *Chaos, Wonder and the Spiritual Adventure of Parenting: An Anthology* (2011); and *Harmony:*

Chinese Wisdom for Children and Parents (2008). She also co-authored *Daughters of the Desert: Remarkable Women from the Christian, Jewish and Muslim Traditions* (2003) published by SkylightPaths Press. *Kindness* was recommended by *Booklist* as one of the five best spiritual books for children in 2001. *Ayat Jamilah, Beautiful Signs* was cited by *Newsweek* as one of the best multi-cultural books of 2004.

Inez Holger is a writer and tutor living in Jacksonville, Florida with her husband, Karl. They have two sons, ages 21 and 26. Her non-fiction stories and essays have appeared in *Relief, Belleview Literary Review, Utne Reader, Greenprints, The Family,* and *Everyday Education.* She is currently working on a book for individuals struggling with depression and a novel about an adolescent girl coming to terms with the needs of her autistic brother. You can reach Inez at ifholger@comcast.net.

Kathy Flaminio, M.S.W, RYT, has 17 years of experience as a social worker in the Minneapolis Public Schools in general and special education settings. She is the founder of 1000 Petals LLC, a total wellness company that trains educators on how to integrate yoga-based activities, mindfulness techniques, and social/emotional skills into classroom and therapeutic settings. She currently works at Minnesota Amplatz Children's Hospital providing yoga therapy for patients on the Child/Adolescent Mental Health Unit and Chemical Dependency/Dual Diagnosis Unit. Kathy has presented at several conferences including Minnesota Association for Children's Mental Health (MACMH), Educate Minnesota, Minnesota's Occupational Therapy Association (MOTA), Professionals in Practice, and was the keynote speaker for Minnesota School Social Workers Association (MSSWA). She holds a Master's degree in social work. She is ACE (American Council on Exercise), Yoga Alliance and Yoga Calm™ certified.

Brigette Gorman completed her Ph.D. and post-graduate diploma in clinical psychology at the University of Otago in Dunedin, New Zealand in 2010. Her Ph.D. thesis involved examining the efficacy of a parent stress management program for parents of children with

ADHD. Currently, Brigette is working part-time as a clinical researcher at the University of Canterbury on a project examining the efficacy of micronutrients in the treatment of adults with ADHD and mood dysregulation. Brigette also works part-time as a clinical psychologist working mainly with adults and adolescents with a range of mental health difficulties, including ADHD.

Peter Gray, Ph.D., is a research professor of psychology at Boston College, and author of the *Freedom to Learn* blog, *Psychology Today*. He has conducted and published research in comparative, evolutionary, developmental, and educational psychology; published articles on innovative teaching methods and alternative approaches to education; and is author of *Psychology* (Worth Publishers), an introductory college textbook now in its sixth edition. He did his undergraduate study at Columbia University and earned a Ph.D. in biological sciences at Rockefeller University. His current writing focuses primarily on the life-long value of play.

Mary Greene is an attorney and environmental law professor living in Red Hook, New York with her husband, Patrick, eight-year-old daughter, Sophie, and nine-year-old son, Peter. She has written articles on adoptive and special needs parenting for *Adoptive Families* and *Adoption Today*, and is currently writing a book, *When Rain Hurts*, about her journey to reach her son Peter. Excerpts of the book and other writings can be found at http://whenrainhurts.wordpress.com/. Greene is represented by literary agent Alanna Ramirez of Trident Media Group.

Bestselling author **Edward Hallowell, M.D.** is a graduate of Harvard College and Tulane School of Medicine. Dr. Hallowell is a child and adult psychiatrist and the founder of The Hallowell Center for Cognitive and Emotional Health in Sudbury, Massachusetts. He was a member of the faculty of Harvard Medical School from 1983 to 2004.

Dr. Hallowell is one of the foremost experts on the topic of attention deficit hyperactivity disorder (ADHD). He is the co-author, with Dr.

John Ratey, of *Driven to Distraction*, and *Answers to Distraction*, which have sold more than a million copies. In 2005, Drs. Hallowell and Ratey released their much-awaited third book on ADHD, *Delivered from Distraction*. Hallowell's other titles include *Shine: Using Brain Science to Get the Best from Your People*, *Married to Distraction: Restoring Intimacy and Strengthening Your Marriage in an Age of Interruption* (with his wife, Sue Hallowell), *Superparenting for ADD: An Innovative Approach to Raising Your Distracted Child* (with Peter S. Jensen), and *CrazyBusy: Overstretched, Overbooked, and About to Snap!: Strategies for Handling Your Fast-Paced Life*, among others.

Rachel Penn Hannah, Psy.D. is a clinical psychologist living in the San Francisco Bay area with her wonderful husband and three kids, ages 10, 14, and 16. When not mothering, working, driving, cleaning, or losing her mind, Rachel tries desperately to find time to write and do yoga.

Pamela Fagan Hutchins writes award-winning suspenseful women's fiction. She also writes essays on her experience parenting her ADHD son, her midlife efforts at triathlon, and couples who make you want to puke. She is the co-author of the textbook *Preventing Workplace Harassment*. In her non-writing life, she is a recovering employment attorney, business owner, human resources consultant, and harassment/discrimination investigator. She and her husband live in Houston, Texas—transplanted from St. Croix in the U.S. Virgin Islands—and between them have a "Brady Bunch" family of five offspring, two dogs, a cat, and countless fish. Visit her website, http://www.pamelahutchins.com/, where she manages to share a little too much about practically nothing.

Cyn Kitchen is a writer and English professor living in Galesburg, Illinois where she makes her home with her four children: Robb, 23; Bailey, 21; Joe, 20; and Jacob, 17. Cyn's first book, a collection of short fiction called *Ten Tongues*, was published by MotesBooks of Louisville, Kentucky in October 2010. More information on Cyn is available at http://www.cynkitchen.com/.

Jeanne Kraus is an elementary reading specialist living in Tamarac, Florida with her husband, George, and assorted pets. Her two sons, Jeff and Cory, are both grown up and work in the computer industry. Jeanne is a children's author and frequent speaker. Her two books, *Cory Stories: A Kid's Book About Living With ADHD* (2005), and *Annie's Plan: Taking Charge of Schoolwork and Homework* (2007) were published by Magination Press. Information about Jeanne's books can be found on her website at http://www.jeannekraus.com/ or on her blog, http://www.jeannekraus.blogspot.com/.

Victoria M. Lees is a substitute teacher and freelance writer living in Stratford, New Jersey with her husband, Bill, and their five children, of which Marie is the oldest. Victoria graduated from the University of Pennsylvania in 2009 with a B.A. in English with a creative writing concentration. She has published nonfiction in *Listen* magazine, fiction in her university's literary magazine, and has placed in poetry contests. She was the editor of her college newspaper when it won a "General Excellence" award, and she won an individual award for college news writing. She currently maintains two blogs: *Substitute Teaching* (http://subbinginschools.blogspot.com/) and *Camping with Kids* (http://campingwithfivekids.blogspot.com/).

Ann M. is an educator of children with autism and lives on the east coast with her husband, Michael, daughters Lia, age 12, and Sarah, age seven, and son Jax, age five. Lia attends a private religious school that accommodates her learning differences. With accommodations and a battery of tutors and therapists, she is doing well academically and socially. She is a typical tween who adores dogs and horses, loves to shop, and talks endlessly on the phone with her friends.

John March, M.D is Professor of Psychiatry and Chief of Child and Adolescent Psychiatry at Duke University Medical Center, and also holds faculty appointments at the Duke Clinical Research Institute and in the Department of Psychology: Social and Health Sciences.

Dr. March is an elected member of the American College of Neuropsychopharmacology (ACNP), the Collegium Internationale Neuro-Psychopharmacologicum (CINP), and of the Council of Academy of Child and Adolescent Psychiatry (AACAP). He is an appointed member of the AACAP Workgroup on Research, the Tourette's Syndrome Medical Advisory Board, the Depression/Bipolar Support Alliance Scientific Advisory Board and, until recently, the Anxiety Disorders Association of America Scientific Advisory and the Obsessive-Compulsive Foundation Scientific Advisory Boards. Widely published in the areas of OCD, PTSD, anxiety, depression, ADHD, and pediatric psychopharmacology, his most recent books, *OCD in Children and Adolescents: A Cognitive-Behavioral Treatment Manual* and *Phobic and Anxiety Disorders: A Clinician's Guide to Effective Psychosocial and Pharmacological Interventions* define the state of the art in the care of anxious youth. In addition to published and ongoing research, Dr. March is active in teaching and training in the treatment of child and adolescent mental disorders locally, nation-wide, and internationally.

Kay Marner is a freelance writer and editor living in Ames, Iowa with her husband, Don, 14-year-old neurotypical son, Aaron, and 10-year-old daughter, Natalie, adopted from Russia, who has ADHD and other challenges. Marner specializes in writing about special needs parenting, attention deficit hyperactivity disorder (ADHD) and its common comorbid conditions, learning disabilities, and adoption. She's the co-editor of this book, *Easy to Love but Hard to Raise: Real Parents, Challenging Kids, True Stories*. She also contributes regularly to *ADDitude* magazine, the top publication about ADHD and learning disabilities, and *Adoptive Families* magazine, the award-winning national magazine for parents before, during, and after adoption. Marner writes ADDitudeMag.com's ADHD parenting blog, *My Picture-Perfect Family: a blog about parenting a loveable, exhausting child with ADHD* (http:/ www.additudemag.com/adhdblogs/4) and contributes to other blogs, including: *a mom's view of ADHD {everyday life with our ADHD kids}* (http://www.amomsviewofadhd.com/), *Easy to Love but Hard to Raise* (http://www.easytolovebut.com/), and *Spruce Kids {Blog}* (http://www.spucekidsblog.com/). You can reach Marner at kay@kaymarner.com.

Kirk Martin is a behavioral therapist, author, and founder of CelebrateCalm.com. Together with his teenage son, he has trained over 100,000 parents and teachers how to help the most challenging children be wildly successful. His family has invited 1,500 intense children into their own home. He is a fierce advocate for children who don't fit the mold. 45,000 people read his free weekly newsletter and listen to his radio show. He is based in Nashville, Tennessee and can be reached at Kirk@CelebrateCalm.com.

Kristen McClure, M.S.W. attended undergraduate school at the State University of New York at Albany where she received a B.A. in psychology, and the State Univeristy of New York at Buffalo, where she received a Master's degree in social work. Kristin has worked as a therapist with children and adults with anxiety, depression, and bipolar disorder for 16 years. Learn more at http://www.how-to-be-happy-right-now.com/, http://www.kristen-mcclure-therapist.com/, and http://www.charlotte-anxiety-and-depression-treatment.com/.

Don Meyer is the director of the Sibling Support Project, and the creator of Sibshops, lively programs for young brothers and sisters of kids with special needs. Currently, there are over 200 Sibshops in eight countries. Don also created SibKids and SibNet, no-cost listservs for siblings which allow hundreds of siblings from around the world to connect with their peers. Don has conducted hundreds of workshops for siblings, fathers, and grandparents of children with special needs and trainings on the Sibshop model throughout the United States, Canada, Ireland, Iceland, England, Italy, New Zealand, and Japan. Don is the senior author or editor of six books.

Kelly Quiñones Miller is the mother of an adopted son with ADHD, inattentive type. She works from home as a freelance writer and designer while trying to teach her son the strategies and skills he'll need to succeed.

Kelly blogs about family issues, casual environmentalism, backyard chickens, and more at *The Miller Mix* (http://themillermix.blogspot.com/).

Lucy Jane Miller, M.D. founded the Sensory Processing Disorder Foundation in 1979, serving as its executive director since then. She was an associate professor at UC Denver Medical School with a double appointment in Pediatrics and Rehabilitation Medicine for 11 years. In 2005 Dr. Miller founded the STAR (Sensory Therapies And Research) Center, co-located with the Foundation in Denver. For 35 years Dr. Miller has devoted herself to the study and treatment of Sensory Processing Disorder and is spearheading the effort to get SPD recognized as a diagnostic entity separate from other disorders. She is a prolific author, with over 50 articles in peer-reviewed journals. Her book, *Sensational Kids: Hope and Help for Children with Sensory Processing Disorder* (SPD) has become the definitive source of information on SPD. She has developed the STAR treatment model, which has been demonstrated through research to be effective. Dr. Miller also develops norm-referenced standardized assessments that are in use worldwide, including the Miller Assessment for Preschoolers, the Leiter International Performance Scale–Revised and the new Miller Function and Participation Scale or M-Fun. She talks about learning family-centered care during her three terms, totaling nine years, on the Governor's Interagency Coordinating Council for IDEA in Colorado. In 2005, she received the Martin Luther King, Jr. award from the State of Colorado.

Elizabeth Moore is a stay-at-home mom living in Burlington, Ontario with her husband, Greg, and her daughter, Kate, 16. She enjoys gardening, painting, reading, and cooking. Kate has struggled throughout her teenage years as so many young people with Asperger's do, but as she becomes more aware of her unique strengths and abilities, her confidence is growing. Greg and Elizabeth are working hard to loosen the tight bond that parents of special needs kids often have with their children and encouraging Kate to become more independent.

Tammy Murphy is a journalist on hiatus. She's the mother of two—Nathalie, a strong-willed and usually level-headed 14-year-old, and Joe, a funny and sensitive 11-year-old who was diagnosed with ADHD in kindergarten. Tammy is a native of Maryland who loves being on or around the water, and a recent Georgia transplant. She's working as a public relations consultant and blogging about her up and down experiences with Joe—and life in general—as much-needed therapy. You can read her honest attempts at connecting the dots on *Tammy Time* at http://www.tammytimeblog.blogspot.com/, recognized by WEGO Health as one of the six Best Blogs by Parents of Children with ADHD. Tammy is also a contributing "adhd momma" on *a mom's view of ADHD* at http://www.amomsviewofadhd.com/.

Robbi Nester is a professor of writing living in Irvine, California with her husband, Richard, who is also a writer and college educator. Her son Jeremy, age 20, lives nearby and attends the college where she teaches. Robbi writes the blog: *Shadow Knows* (http://robbi-shadowknows. blogspot.com). She is looking for publishers for her collection of poetry: *A Likely Story,* and *Balance*, a chapbook of yoga poems. Her poems have recently appeared in the online journal *Qarrtsiluni, Caesura* and the literary and arts magazine *Floyd County Moonshine*. Her essay "Confessions of a Book Addict" appears in the anthology *Flashlight Memories* (Silver Boomer Books, 2011).

Marsha Partington Marsha Partington is a freelance writer and School-Age Care Coordinator in Minneapolis, Minnesota. Her daughter, Cara, is attending the University of Utah in Salt Lake City, Utah, studying criminal justice.

Marsha's essay, "Susie's Story," about her hospital work following the death of her infant daughter, was featured in *Today's Health and Wellness magazine (May 2007)*. She contributes frequently to area newspapers and professional journals. Marsha is working on her memoir, *Real Women Drive a Stick Shift*. A certified therapy team with her golden retriever Tessa, they routinely visit the Eating Disorder Clinic where Cara was a patient.

Renee Perrone is a teacher living in North Carolina with her husband of 22 years and their son, Jimmy, 17. Their daughter, Ashley, 21, is a junior at the University of North Carolina Wilmington where she is studying Exercise Science and Psychology.

Renee encourages other parents of difficult children through a monthly support group, the online support group bpkidsparents@yahoogroups. com, and a Facebook page, "Parents of Children with Bipolar and Mood Disorder," which focuses on teaching parents to advocate for their kids.

Warren H. Phillips, Ph.D. is a licensed psychologist. He is the owner and director of Central Iowa Psychological Services, with offices in Ames and West Des Moines, Iowa, and a Senior Lecturer, Department of Psychology, Iowa State University. Dr. Phillips received his Bachelor of Arts degree at the University of Maryland, College Park, Maryland and his M.A. and Ph.D. in Clinical and Developmental Psychology at the University of Illinois at Chicago. He has worked as a Clinical Child Psychologist in private practice with Central Iowa Psychological Services and taught undergraduate and graduate classes in Psychology at Iowa State University since 1996. Dr. Phillips specializes in working with children, adolescents, and adults with neurodevelopmental issues including ADHD, depression and bipolar disorder, obsessive compulsive disorders, and autism spectrum disorders. Dr. Phillips enjoys conducting psychological evaluations and psychotherapy with individuals and families with a wide variety of presenting issues.

Patricia Quinn, M.D., a developmental pediatrician, is a well-known international expert and speaker on the topic of ADHD. In addition, she has authored several bestselling and groundbreaking books on the topic, including *Understanding Girls with ADHD* and *100 Questions and Answers about ADHD in Women and Girls*. For the last decade, she has devoted her attention professionally to the issues confronting girls and women with ADHD, as well as high school and college students with the disorder. She is currently the director of the National Center for Girls and

Women with ADHD. Dr. Quinn received the CHADD Hall of Fame Award for her work in these areas.

Lisa Randazzo is a full-time mom living in Norfolk, Virginia with her husband and their two boys, ages eight and 10. She is a member of Hampton Roads Writers and enjoys writing juvenile and adult fiction. Lisa is currently working on a children's novel whose main character is inspired by her older son and his experience with hearing loss. She hopes one day her craft will earn enough money to support her 10-year-old's book-a-day reading habit, and keep her eight-year-old well stocked in Sweetarts and Legos.

Robin Rhodes is a stay-at-home mom, author, entrepreneur, and much more living in Salem, Wisconsin with her husband, Michael, 12-year-old daughter, Katrina, nine-year-old son, Lucais, and six-year-old son, Spencer. Writing has been an outlet for her thoughts and dreams since she was a child, and she has been published in several magazines and e-zines. Robin writes two blogs: http://awritersperil.blogspot.com/ follows her writing journey, and http://bipolarperil.blogspot.com/ documents her journey as a parent and a woman living with bipolar disorder.

J. Delayne Ryms is a poet living in Tyrone, Georgia with her husband, Jaymz, and 12-year-old son, Avery-Jorin. She has received numerous awards for her poetry, including two Academy of American Poets awards, a grant from the California Arts Council, and a Pushcart Prize nomination. Her poetry has been published in many arts journals (print and online) as well. She earned a Master's degree in English/Creative Writing from the University of California-Davis.

Rachel Zients Schinderman is a writer living in Los Angeles, California with her husband, Jay, five-year-old son, Benjamin, and his new baby brother, Eli. Her writing has appeared in *The Los Angeles Jewish Journal*, *The Los Angeles Times Magazine,* and *Lifestyle Magazine* to name a few. She wrote a parenting column called "Mommie Brain" for The Santa Monica Daily Press until the new baby came along and also runs writing groups for moms, to document their experience of parenting, under the same name. To learn more, go to http://www.mommiebrain.com/.

Michael Shay is individual artists' program specialist at the Wyoming Arts Council. He lives in Cheyenne, Wyoming, with his wife, Chris, and daughter, Annie, 17. His son Kevin, 25, lives in Tucson. Michael has served on the Governor's Mental Health Advisory Council and as board chair for UPLIFT, the Wyoming affiliate of Federation of Families for Children's Mental Health.

His fiction and essays have been published in *Northern Lights*, *High Plains Literary Review*, *Colorado Review*, *Owen Wister Review*, *Visions*, *High Plains Register*, and *In Short*, a Norton anthology of brief creative nonfiction. His book of short fiction, *The Weight of a Body*, was published in 2006 by Ghost Road Press. One of those stories appears in the 2010 anthology from Coffee House Press, *Working Words: Punching the Clock and Kicking out the Jams*. He was co-editor of *Deep West: A Literary Tour of Wyoming*, published in 2003 by Wyoming's Pronghorn Press.

Maureen Sherbondy is a writer and graduate student living in Raleigh, North Carolina with her husband, Anthony, and their three sons: Jacob, 20, Ethan, 18, and Zachary, 17. Maureen has written three books of poetry: *After the Fairy Tale* (Main Street Rag, 2007), *Praying at Coffee Shops* (Main Street Rag, 2008), and *Weary Blues* (Big Table Publishing, 2010). Her short story collection, *The Slow Vanishing* (Mint Hill Books/ Main Street Rag) was published in 2009. Visit Maureen's website at http://www.maureensherbondy.com/.

Laura Shumaker is the author of *A Regular Guy: Growing up with Autism*. She writes a nationally recognized autism blog for the *San Francisco Chronicle*. Her websites and publications can be found at: http://www.laurashumaker.com.

Janet Schraw Solie, P.A., M.S. is a pediatric physician assistant, integrated health coach, ADD advocate and sometime health writer, who lives in Calabasas, California with her husband, David, and 16-year-old daughter, Gretta. She also co-leads a parent support group for parents of special needs kids in middle school in the San Fernando Valley. You can reach her at: janet@risktutor.com.

Frank South is a writer and performer living in Warner Robins, Georgia with his wife, Margaret, and 15-year-old daughter, Coco. He was diagnosed with ADHD and other comorbid conditions when he was 49.

Frank has spent years in New York and Hollywood as a playwright, screenwriter, TV writer, producer, and director. In 2009 Frank performed his one-man show about ADHD and Hollywood, *Pay Attention,* in Honolulu and Los Angeles. He also writes a blog, *ADHD Dad: Better Late than Never* (http://www.additudemag.com/adhdblogs/6), about his adventures as an ADHD adult, husband, and father of two ADHD children for *ADDitudeMag.com.*

Frank's son, Harry *("ADHD Horror Story"),* now 22 years old, has recently moved out on his own and is doing well. Frank's daughter, Coco *("ADHD Supergirl," "Report Card Blues"),* is getting A's and B's in her first year of high school and has taken up electric guitar.

Kathy Stump is an occasional writer who lives in Kansas City, Missouri with her husband, Phil, and their two children, Erica, 14, and Mason, 11. Kathy squeezes in some writing time while being a stay-at-home mom, albeit one who spends more of her time in her car than at home. She writes for *Kansas City Parent* magazine on a variety of family-related topics. Lately, she's been venturing out onto the World Wide Web, contributing to the *Easy to Love but Hard to Raise* blog (http://www. easytolovebut.com/). When she's not writing or shuttling kids, Kathy volunteers at a food pantry and teaches English to Hispanic women in Kansas City's urban core.

Judith Warner has been a freelance writer for over two decades, and is best known for her New York Times column, "Domestic Disturbances" and her 2005 best-seller, *Perfect Madness: Motherhood in the Age of Anxiety.* Her book, *We've Got Issues: Children and Parents in the Age of*

Medication, followed in 2010. A former XM radio host and special correspondent for *Newsweek* in Paris, Warner is currently a Contributing Writer for the *New York Times Magazine*.

Laura Grace Weldon is a writer, editor, and conflict resolution trainer. She lives on Bit of Earth Farm in Ohio with her husband and their four children. She teaches communication and conflict resolution skills to school systems. Her articles appear in international publications on topics that include learning, parenting, and community building. She is the author of *Free Range Learning: How Homeschooling Changes Everything.* Find out more at http://www.lauragraceweldon.com/.

Erica Wells is a special education teacher living in Phelps, New York with her husband, Brian, son Ken, daughter Gabrielle, grandchild Lexi, her mom, four dogs, two cats, and two bunnies. It's a very full house! Another of Erica's essays is included in the anthology *You Look Too Young to be a Mom.* Always providing inspiration, Ken fed the creative process for Erica's children's picture book, *Diamonds in the Snow.*

Lorraine Wilde is a freelance journalist and scientist living in northwest Washington state with her husband, Mike, and twin seven-year-old sons, Tristan and Will. She is a regular contributor to the parenting web site Neighborhood-Kids.com and has recently published in *Entertainment News NW* and the *Whatcom Watch.* Lorraine is writing a memoir, *Egg Mama*, and posts regularly on her blog at http://www.lorrainewilde.com/.

Penny Williams is a freelance writer and real estate broker living in Asheville, North Carolina with her husband, Tim, tween daughter, Emma, and Luke, age eight. Penny is the creator and editor of the website, *a mom's view of ADHD {everyday life with our ADHD kids}* (http://www.amomsviewofadhd.com/) where she writes candidly about the everyday experiences of parenting her young ADHD/SPD/LD son. She has published several articles in *ADDitude* magazine, the number one national publication dedicated to living well with ADHD.

Jean Winegardner claims to be many things, most of which are more or less true. Among those things are writer, mom, autism mom, wife, work-at-homer, and person. She also likes little animals a lot. Known in the blogosphere primarily as Stimey, Jean's main blog is *Stimeyland* (http:// www.stimeyland.com/), where she writes about her life, her three kids, her son Jack's autism, and the occasional guest gerbil. (Yes, really.)

Passionate about creating a positive view of special needs children and adults, Jean writes "Autism Unexpected" (http://communities. washingtontimes.com/neighborhood/autism-unexpected/), a column located in the Washington Times Communities. She is also a contributor at http://www.hopefulparents.org/, a collaborative blog by parents of children with many types of special needs. Through her writing, Jean hopes to help change the perception of autism as a devastating life sentence and to improve the lives of individuals with autism. She runs an autism information and events website for Montgomery County, Maryland at http://www.autmont.com/. Find her on Twitter as @Stimey.

Jean currently lives in the Maryland part of the DC metro area. She is married to Alex and mother to three little dudes, Sam, Jack and Quinn. Her driving philosophy is that when you have a choice between laughing and crying, you should always try to laugh—although sometimes you may have to do both.

Judy Winter is an award-winning writer and speaker and the author of *Breakthrough Parenting for Children with Special Needs: Raising the Bar of Expectations*. Winter is also co-founder of the Eric 'RicStar' Winter Music Therapy Camp at Michigan State University named in honor of her son, Eric, who had cerebral palsy and passed away in 2003 at age 12. Judy Winter is passionate about honoring her son's legacy by changing the lives of other children with special needs and their families. To learn more, visit http://www.judywinter.com/, http://winterramblings.blogspot.com/, or e-mail jappwinter@aol.com.